Peninsula Press

Edited by John Wilson & Stephen Ede-Borrett

Gosling Press

www.goslingpress.co.uk

Contents

i

Introduction

Some time ago whilst searching through some war diaries for the Gallipoli Campaign I came across a single issue of *Peninsula Press*, I was intrigued. I tried to find more issues and was unable to discover the full set of 96 issues in any archive. There are a number of places that hold between 50 and 70 issues but none seemed to hold the full run. Hence this volume which brings together all 96 issues for the first time.

This journey would not have been possible without the help of a range of people including The Hocken Collection at the University of Otago, The Australian War Memorial, Archives New Zealand, and special mention must go to Andrew Connolly in New Zealand who managed to turn up the final missing issue no. 93.

The *Peninsula Press* was a news sheet produced throughout the Gallipoli campaign, from May 1915 to January 1916. Initially it was produced daily but as the campaign continued it reduced in frequency to weekly. It was, apart from the first issue, always a single sheet in two columns with an amazingly wide range of information covering military information from all other theatres as well as political stories from around the world. It also on occasion included information on actions that had taken place on the Gallipoli Peninsula.

According to Compton Mackenzie in *Gallipoli Memories* the *Peninsula Press* was run by Captain William Maxwell: 'Maxwell, in addition to acting as official censor and running the OI mess, was editing a daily sheet called The Peninsula Press which was served out to the troops as a tonic and even translated into French. This was the apple of Maxwell's eye.'[1] Maxwell had served as a war correspondent for the *London Evening Standard* covering the Sudan and the Boer war and he later covered the Russo-Japanese War for the *Daily Mail*. 1914 saw Maxwell working for the *Daily Telegraph* attached to the Belgian Army. In April 1915, he received a commission as Captain on the Special List attached to the Imperial General Staff, and embarked for the Dardanelles to join the Headquarters Staff of Sir Ian Hamilton as Chief Field Censor. Under regulations drawn up and enforced by the British Army, press correspondents at Gallipoli were required to submit all their writings to Captain Maxwell, whose approval was required prior to their transmission. Again according to Compton Mackenzie, Maxwell came in for some criticism after his reports about the Battle of Gully Ravine in June 1915 when the 'Peninsula Press which had come out with a

---

[1] Compton Mackenzie, *Gallipoli Memories*, (New York: Doubleday, Doran & Company Inc. 1930).

rosified account of our "success," though of course it was recognized that a daily sheet of unmitigated gloom would hardly be worth printing and circulating.'[2]

Regimental Sergeant Major John Thomson of the New Zealand Field Engineers commented in a letter to the Hocken Collection in 1965

> Radio not then being in use at Anzac and no newspapers being available the sojourners on Gallipoli had no current news whatever about the outside world, for all they knew theirs was the only war then operating.

> To overcome this, the "Brass Heads" on the "Posh" ship at the Expedition's base in one of the harbours of the neighbouring Greek Islands, probably Imbros, had the brain-wave to issue a newspaper.

> This paper was then delivered at Anzac and other places on Gallipoli at (very) irregular intervals. Usually it was stuck to a biscuit box at a ration dump where most congregated and where all could read.[3]

So was *Peninsula Press* just propaganda? Probably not although it did attempt to put a positive spin on events. It provided a regular flow of mainly positive news stories to help pass the time of the troops. What is fascinating is the wide range of stories that were considered 'important' to be communicated to the troops. From a modern perspective it is interesting to contrast this wide range of political information, such as the issues in the Greek Parliament, to what is considered 'news' in today's newspapers. Its real value is in the eclectic mix of stories published which include a number of gems for the historian.

NB. Spelling, grammar, style, et cetera have been left largely in the same format as the original although obvious spelling and typeset errors have, on occasion, been corrected.

---

[2] Compton Mackenzie, *Gallipoli Memories*, (New York: Doubleday, Doran & Company Inc. 1930).
[3] Hocken Collection, University of Otago

Peninsula Press

The Cunard liner "Lusitania," homeward bound from New York, was torpedoed and sunk on May 5th near Queenstown. Of 2,160 passengers, many of whom, doubtless, were Americans, only about 800 were saved. 22 died after landing at Queenstown. Most of the officers perished. Passengers who were on deck saw a submarine half-a-mile away fire two torpedoes.

The Admiralty deny emphatically the report that the "Lusitania" was armed. In American official circles the situation is regarded as extremely grave. Neutral countries are horrified, and declare that it will cost Germany dear. World-wide telegrams brand this outrage as a lasting infamy. France is overcome with anger at such a colossal murder.

The "Lusitania" had a gross tonnage of 30,396, and a length of 762 feet. She was built in 1907, and made one of the record trips between England and New York:- West, 4 days, 11 hours, 42 minutes; East, 4 days, 15 hours, 50 minutes.

Athens reports two prolonged Cabinet meetings, owing, it is believed, to a rupture between Austria and Italy.

Rome reports say that the Kaiser has telegraphed to the King of Italy urging him to support the Kaiser's efforts to bring about a settlement between Austria and Italy. This is believed to be a last desperate effort.

The personnel of the Austrian Embassy at the Vatican left on May 9th.

The dispute between China and Japan is ended, China having accepted Japanese Final Note.

The French have made considerable progress in the neighbourhood of Arras. At some points they have advanced 2 and half miles, 2000 German prisoners, and 6 guns were taken.

A great battle is being fought between the Vistula and the Carpathians. The German attacks have failed, and the enemy have had enormous losses and shows signs of fatigue. The Russians are following up their successes.

Our Australian troops, who are firmly established on the Peninsula, will be interested to learn that, according to Turkish reports, they have been "driven into the sea"

It may also surprise our troops to know that the beach near Sedd el Bahr "has been purged of their presence."

The Turkish newspapers appear to be better informed than the Turkish official communiques. The "Tanin" contains the following:-
30th April. "The obstinate British have not admitted their defeat in spite of the blows they have received. They have come on again. In this, we recognise some peculiarities which have been noted by the Germans in Flanders. The British, when fighting, show an astonishing persistence and obstinacy which is peculiar to them. In the most desperate situations, they will not allow that they are beaten, and persist to the end. This useless obstinacy has usually caused them such terrible losses in Flanders that the English newspapers from time to time utter complaints. As for the present useless persistence, it is not for us to complain of it. The more obstinate they are, the worse blows they will receive, and that will assure the final result."

Peninsula Press

No. 2.   Wednesday, May 12, 1915.   Official News.

The Sinking of the Lusitania.

Never has such a wave of wrath surged throughout Great Britain as at this moment. The sinking of the Lusitania. and the savage murder of several hundred innocent men, women and children has roused the whole civilised world. Its consequences are seen in the action of Public bodies, like the Stock Exchange which hitherto has shown good humoured tolerance of members of enemy blood. Anti German riots have taken place at Birmingham and Liverpool.

Feeling in the United States, whose citizens are among the victims, is so bitter that President Wilson was evidently saving to allay it when he spoke at Philadelphia last night. The President is supposed to have been referring to the crime when be used these amazing words :-
"There is such a thing as being too proud to fight. A nation may be so right that it does not need to convince others by force that it is right."

Germany has "explained" in a message to the United States Administration, saying it is "really sorry" for the loss of American lives, but blame Great Britain for the disaster "which through its plan of starving the civilian population of Germany has forced Germany to adopt measures of retaliation."
[When the Germans were besieging Paris in 1870, did they feed the civilian population?]

The Cunard Liner was torpedoed and sunk off the Old Head of Kinsale outside Queenstown harbour. Her passengers were 290 first class, 662 second and 365 third, making with the crew nearly 1900 people. She was in difficulties at 2·12 p.m. on May 5th and disappeared at 2·33. Twenty of the Lusitania's boats were seen on the spot and 16 other boats. The liner sent out the call "Come immediately: big list." The Admiral at Queenstown instantly despatched to the resene [sic] four vessels, five trawlers, a lift boat and a tug.

Will Italy Fight?

The prospect of Italian intervention is causing acute anxiety in Germany. The newspapers are very downhearted. The "Vossiche Zeitung," the "Berliner Tageblatt" and the "Lokal Anzeiger" admit that the situation has become extremely grave in the last few days, even during the last few hours.

The Italian Parliament meets to-day.

The Milan Correspondent of the "Petit Parisien" reveals the fact that negotiations have been taking place between Italy and the Entente Powers (Great Britain, France and Russia) with regard to the future of the Adriatic, where Italian and Austrian interests are in conflict. These negotiations, it is understood, have been concluded and a convention is about to be signed.

The Italian Government, says the "Temps," has decided to suspend the sailings of Trans-Atlantic ships, which will be requisitioned as transports and auxiliary cruisers.

Roumania's Attitude.

Under the Agreement by which Italy undertook to protect Roumanian interests, Roumania will, according to a Greek news agency, follow Italy's example and the two countries will cooperate in military matters.

Roumania is ambitious to secure possession of Transylvania where there are about 4,000,000 Roumanians under Austro-Hungarian rule.

German Attacks Fail.

For these political reasons and in the hope of impressing neutrals, the Germans have been attempting during the past fifteen days a big offensive in France and Flanders. They have completely failed.

The French official accounts state that the Germans were checked everywhere, lost thirty five thousand men, did not pierce the Allies line anywhere and did not take any important point even in Belgium, where they have violated the laws of war by employing asphyxiating gases. The experiment which they have attempted has been turned against themselves.

Sir John French reports that the Germans delivered five unsuccessful attacks yesterday east of Ypres. The enemy's losses were very heavy.

What the Turks Think of Us!

We quoted yesterday from the Constantinople newspaper, the "Tanine," which on April 30th complained of British obstinacy. Two day before, the "Tanine" was apparently of quite another opinion. Here is the evidence:- "The enemy having suffered a complete defeat cannot make any fresh attempt. He can neither bring up fresh troops nor try to accomplish anything with his demoralised soldiers. In a word, another similar decisive defeat will close the question of the Straits for good."

4

"The Greeks will congratulate themselves at having escaped this disaster."

"Information is still lacking as to the composition of the enemies forces. But it appears from indications received from Europe that they must consist chiefly of black men from Africa and Australia. Thus the Straits for the first time in history have had to endure an attack by cannibals."

PENINSULA PRESS.

No. 2.	Wednesday, May 12, 1915.	Official News.

The Sinking of the Lusitania.

Never has such a wave of wrath surged throughout Great Britain as at this moment. The sinking of the Lusitania and the savage murder of several hundred innocent men, women and children has roused the whole civilised world. Its consequences are seen in the action of Public bodies, like the Stock Exchange which hitherto has shown good humoured tolerance of members of enemy blood. Anti-German riots have taken place at Birmingham and Liverpool.

Feeling in the United States, whose citizens are among the victims, is so bitter that President Wilson was evidently saving to allay it when he spoke at Philadelphia last night. The President is supposed to have been referring to the crime when he used these amazing words :—

"There is such a thing as being two proud to fight. A nation may be so "right that it does not need to convince others by force that it is right."

Germany has "explained" in a message to the United States Administration, saying it is "really sorry" for the loss of American lives, but blames Great Britain for the disaster "which through its plan of starving the civilian population of Germany has forced Germany to adopt measures of retaliation."

[When the Germans were beseiging Paris in 1870, did they feed the civilian population?]

The Cunard Liner was torpedoed and sunk off the Old Head of Kinsale outside Queenstown harbour. Her passengers were 290 first class, 662 second and 365 third, making with the crew nearly 1900 people. She was in difficulties at 2·12 p.m. on May 5th and disappeared at 2·33. Twenty of the Lusitania's boats were seen on the spot and 16 other boats. The liner sent out the call "Come immediately : big list." The Admiral at Queenstown instantly despatched to the rescue four vessels, five trawlers, a lift boat and a tug.

Will Italy Fight?

The prospect of Italian intervention is causing acute anxiety in Germany. The newspapers are very downhearted. The "Vossiche Zeitung," the "Berliner Tageblatt" and the "Lokal Anzeiger" admit that the situation has become extremely grave in the last few days, even during the last few hours.

The Italian Parliament meets to-day.

The Milan Correspondent of the "Petit Parisien" reveals the fact that negotiations have been taking place between Italy and the Entente Powers (Great Britain, France and Russia) with regard to the future of the Adriatic, where Italian and Austrian interests are in conflict. These negotiations, it is understood, have been concluded and a convention is about to be signed.

The Italian Government, says the "Temps," has decided to suspend the sailings of Trans-Atlantic ships, which will be requisitioned as transports and auxiliary cruisers.

5

Peninsula Press

No. 3   Friday, May 14, 1915   Official News.

The Earl of Crewe informed the House of Lords yesterday that on the night of May 2nd the Turks made a violent general attack in the Gallipoli Peninsula and were repulsed with heavy loss. The enemy attacked on each succeeding night until the 6th but were easily repulsed. We made some advance and consolidated our positions. The Turkish dead before the 29th Division were very numerous. The French gained an important position on the right, inflicting heavy losses with the bayonet. The Australasian troops have been engaged in most valuable work in the narrow neck of the Peninsula. The warships rendered valuable assistance.

Sir John French reports that the Germans yesterday heavily bombarded our trenches East of Ypres and made an infantry attack under cover of asphyxiating gas. Their attack failed, our shrapnel inflicting heavy casualties on the enemy who were in massed formation and were literally mown down.

Marked progress has been made by our troops in the neighbourhood of Arras and La Bassee. In the last week of October the German line had succeeded in making, north of Arras and south of La Bassee, a salient which drove the French line to the West and was marked by the spur of Notre Dame de Lorette, Ablain Saint Nazaire, Carency, Sonchez, la Targette. The spur of Notre Dame de Lorette, long and hotly disputed, rested finally in the hands of the French last month. Some days ago La Targette in its turn also fell into the French possession. The operations have been continued with brilliant success by the conquest of almost all the positions at Neuville Saint - Vaast and the complete occupation of Carency. The defences of the village of Carency had been very strongly organised by the enemy and its garrison was composed of one battalion of the 209th Infantry, one battalion of the 136th, a battalion of Bavarian riflemen, and six companies of pioneers, each 300 strong. In the night (May 12-13) the French succeeded in occupying Carency and the wood north of the village.

They killed with the bayonet several hundred Germans and made 1050 prisoners of whom thirty were officers, among them a colonel and the officer commanding the Bavarian riflemen.

Mr Lloyd George told the House of Commons the other day that the war had cost L307,000,000 in eight months, or Ll,370,000 a day. If the war ends in September next, said the Chancellor of the Exchequer, the total expenditure will be L786,000,000, of which the Army takes L400,000,000, the Navy L100,000,000 and advances to Allies L100,000,000. If the war last another year the total cost will be Ll,136,000,000. Mr Lloyd George declared that the duration of the war depends on the events of the next two or three months.

The Armenians have risen against the Turks. Twenty thousand well armed mountaineers are defending Zeitoum which the Turkish soldiers have been ordered to raze to the ground. The city which lies near the Turco-Russian frontier is almost impregnable and can be approached only by two narrow paths. The Armenians are provisioned for four months. In Sultan Abdul Hamid's time 100,000 Turks besieged this mountain fastness for seven months.

The German newspaper "Der Tag" complains bitterly of the miscalculations of German politicians:- "We expected that British India would rise when the first shot was fired against us, but in reality thousands of Indians came to fight against us and the Colonies seem to be closer than ever to the Mother Country even Ireland has sent her best soldiers against us."

(Sister, writing letter to brother at the Front) "And hae ye onything else tae say, father?

Father: "Ay! Tell Donal' that if he comes ower yon German waiter that gaed us a bad saxpence for chinge when we had a bit dinner in London a while syne, tell him tae-tak-steady aim.' - (Punch.)

Peninsula Press

The Hand of the German.

Those of our soldiers who have received a shower bath of proclamations inviting them to surrender to the mercy of the Turk will easily recognise both the grammar and the handwriting. Not content with describing us as "black men" and "cannibals," the German masters of Turkey must need imagine that we are as ignorant of the real facts of the war in France and Poland as are their own Ottoman dupes.

Italy and the War.

The decision of the Italian Government is awaited with intense interest. 'Wireless messages to-day tell of great excitement in Rome. Huge crowds gathered in Milan to demonstrate in favor of war. Processions, being forbidden, were stopped by the soldiers who received a popular ovation. Cheers were given for "Trieste and the Trentino," which Italy demands from Austria and have been the subject of unsuccessful negotiations.

The Attitude of Greece.

The Greeks, like the Italians, are still trying to make up their minds. The situation in Athens is reported to be grave. Popular feeling is in favour of co-operation with the Allies, while the Government seeks guarantees that will assure Greece in her present possessions and will avoid any sacrifice of territory in order to placate Bulgaria.

Another Threatened Incursion.

The Daily Telegraph Correspondent in Egypt foreshadows an other effort of the Turks to reach the Suez Canal and points out the interest which Italy has in any such attempt. We are ready to receive the Turks and to repeat more effectively the lesson we gave them some weeks ago. Even should there be any interruption of traffic through the Canal, we have still two routes open to the East, whereas Italy would be forced to circumnavigate Africa before she could come to the aid of her colonies in Somaliland and Erythria.

Russians Naval Activity.

While we are hammering at the gates of the Dardanelles, the Russians are knocking at the door of the Bosphorus which is the other entrance to Constantinople. Last week a Russian fleet of five battleships, two cruisers, twelve torpedo boats and several transports approached the

Bosphorus and renewed its bombardment. A detachment of the Russian Baltic Fleet cruising in the neighbourhood of Windau exchanged long distance shots with several German cruisers and torpedo boats. The enemy showed no disposition to come to close quarters, but after their customary manner took to their heels.

Operations in France.

Heavy rains have impeded operations north of Arras. The French have, however, continued their offensive with success. During the past week nearly 4000 German prisoners, of whom one hundred are officers, have been taken; twenty guns, including eight heavy pieces, and one hundred machine guns and trench mortars have been captured. A German colonel in command of a brigade committed suicide because be was unable to rally his decimated regiments. German prisoners admit that very heavy losses have been inflicted and that all their counter attacks failed. The French are clearing the enemy out of the slopes south-east of Notre Dame de Lorette and are firmly established in this important position which has been so long and hotly contested.

Peninsula Press

No. 5   Monday, May 17, 1915 Official News.

Weapons of Despair.

It is surely a proof of despair when men who claim a monopoly of "Kultur" resort to the wholesale murder of unarmed civilians at sea and the use of poisonous gases on the battlefield. The legitimate weapons of courage and civilization having failed them, the Germans are employing poisonous gases in France and Flanders.

The gases have been ejected from pipes laid into the trenches, and also produced by the explosion of shells especially made for the purpose. The German troops who attacked under cover of these gases were provided with specially designed respirators, which were issued in sealed pattern covers. This, as Field Marshal Sir John French says in his report, all points to long and methodical preparation on a large scale. Mr. Tennant, Under Secretary for War, stated in the House of Commons that at first it was not believed that any Power signing the Hague Convention would have committed so heinous a breach of their solemn obligations. The question of using similar expedients against the enemy is under consideration.

The Art of Lying.

In the concoction of official reports the Turks have taken lessons from the Germans, yet they have not mastered the art. Only clumsy amateurs or "drivellers" could write with the same pen:
(1)   That they have driven us into the sea and
(2)   That they are slaying us in battalions on land.
We have only to contrast the German with the Austrian reports of alleged victories over the Russians, in order to realise how anxious the Germans are to impress neutrals, like Italy, Roumania and Greece, at this critical moment. Where the Germans report 30,000 prisoners, the modest Austrians are content to put the figure at 3,000.

Where are the Austrians?

The Emperor Francis Joseph will soon have more soldiers in Russia than in Austria. According to the Russian War Minister there are already in the depots of Siberia over 600,000 prisoners of war, the majority of whom are Austrians. Russia has armed and put into the field several million soldiers and can still considerably increase that figure.

Moslem Support of the Allies

The Arab is not so credulous as the Turk and is not likely to be deceived by fanciful tales of the conversion to Islam of eminent Germans, such as that of Hajji Wilhelm and his harem, with an escort of captured British Dreadnoughts, arriving at Constantinople. The efforts of the German Emperor to excite the Moslem world to a Holy War against Christian Powers have failed ignominiously. Many Moslem communities have sent contributions to the Allies' War Fund, accompanied by regrets at the action of the Sultan in making common cause with the Germans. The latest messages come from Moslem Chiefs in West Africa who pray the Allies not to cease their efforts until the Germans are driven out of Africa, where their methods of Government have made them universally hated.

Men as Trees Walking

We have heard of soldiers whose equipment made them look like Christmas trees. But the Turks have gone one better. A Correspondent with the Australians reports the capture of a sniper who was got up to look like a tree. He had tufts of scrub stuck all over him. It is even said that his rifle and his face were painted green. The men who "got" him were passing down a gully when two or three shots whizzed past. They looked and saw that what they had taken to be a small shrub had moved. The man-tree had on him some Australian money and Australian identity discs. The idea is that the sniper is paid so much per head and has to produce these discs before he is rewarded.

Step by Step.

Fierce fighting continues in the neighbourbood of Arras. On the heights East and South of Notre Dame de Lorette hand grenades were used and the French made some progress. In Neuville the enemy tried in vain to retake the houses captured by the French and the trenches outside the village. North of Bassee, on Sunday night, the British won several trenches.

Another Miscalculation.

The Turks are brave enemies but have never been judges of character. They evidently imagine that by another display of "liveliness" on the Suez Canal they will be able to weaken our assault on the Gallipoli Peninsula. Turkish cavalry have again been seen at various points on the Sinai Peninsula and strong forces are reported to be encamped on the El-Arish-Nakhil line. To the surprise of experts they seem to have water in plenty, which shows that the Sinai's capacity in this respect was underestimated or that the Turks have organised an elaborate camel transport to carry water from the wells. Their object, of course, is to

11

upset our plans in Gallipoli, which proves how little they know of our character and our resources.

PENINSULA PRESS.

No. 6.   Tuesday, May 18, 1915.   Official News.

Report on German Atrocities.

The Commission appointed last December to investigate German methods of war in Belgium has just made its report. Lord Bryce presided over the inquiry and no fewer than 1,200 witnesses were examined. The conclusions at which this judicial body arrived are:—

(1) In many parts of Belgium there were massacres of civilians, deliberately and systematically organised, and accompanied by numerous isolated murders and assaults.

(2) Women have been violated and the throats of children have been cut.

(3) German officers have sanctioned and ordered, without cause or justification, the pillage, burning and destruction of houses.

(4) From the beginning of the war preparations were made for systematic incendiarism. Acts of incendiarism and destruction of private property were undoubtedly part of the German plan with the object of spreading terror.

(5) The rules and usages of war have been violated, notably by using civilians, even women and children, as shields to protect German troops against rifle fire, by the massacre of prisoners and wounded and by the abuse of the Red Cross and the white flag.

The Commission declares that these conclusions have been established by evidence which cannot be refuted. Murder, rape and pillage have been committed in many parts of Belgium to a degree that has never been known for three centuries in any war between civilized nations.

The March Bombardment.

Mr. Kellaway inquired, in the House of Commons, whether Lord Fisher was consulted with regard to the March attack on the Dardanelles by the Fleet; and whether Lord Fisher expressed the opinion that the attack ought not to be made in the circumstances in which it was made.

Mr. Churchill said the answer to the first part of the question was "Yes," and to the second part "No."

Is this Victory.

The alleged victories over the Russian army seem to have had an amazing effect in Vienna. According to the report of a Dutch correspondent in the Austrian capital, "when the people wanted, on Sunday, to go for their usual walk in the woods, they found themselves confronted with notices that entrance was forbidden. The reason is that trenches have been dug, and barbed wire entanglements erected, and even gun positions have been prepared to protect the city against attack by the enemy."

The Operations in France.

Wireless messages received this morning announce that the French have repulsed another German counter attack at Steenstraet. In the regions of Het-Sas, the French have occupied the first line of German trenches bordering the river and canal and have taken 145 prisoners and four machine guns.

British troops have taken nearly half a mile of German trenches south-west of Ritchebourg l'Avoué and 1600 yards of trenches north-west of Festubert. This second attack was afterwards pressed in the direction of Quinquerne where we have advanced nearly 1600 yards along a front of 650 yards. The enemy's losses were very heavy.

Our troops continue to advance to the north of Arras where they and the French have consolidated their positions.

[Steenstraet and Het-Sas are situated on the Yser Canal, a little more than four miles north of Ypres. Rickebourg l'Avoué, Festubert and La Quinquerue are three adjoining villages between Neuve-Chapelle and the canal of La Bassée, about four miles north of the Canal.]

The Sinking of the Lusitania.

Lord Mersey has been appointed President of the Commission of Inquiry into the sinking of the Cunard liner Lusitania which was torpedoed by a German submarine near Queenstown. Among the passengers who lost their lives was Mr Charles Frohman, well-known in England and the United States as the owner of many theatres.

Illness of the King of Greece.

The King of Greece is suffering from pleurisy. Prayers are being offered for his recovery in all the Greek Churches. The latest bulletins are favourable.

Another raid of "Frightfulness."

The Germans appear to have discovered that Southend, like Scarborough, is one of our strongly fortified cities. At 3 o'clock one morning last week a couple of Zeplins made a tour over this seaside resort and included in their itinerary Westcliff and Leigh. Eighty incendiary bombs were thrown, fifty of them falling on Southend where several houses were damaged and burned. The airships continued their progress to within 26 miles of London. As soon as the Thames forts opened fire the Zeplins made off toward the east.

G.H.Q. Printing Section,
Med. Exped. Force.

12

Peninsula Press

No. 6   Tuesday, May 18, 1915   Official News.

Report on German Atrocities.

The Commission appointed last December to investigate German methods of war in Belgium has just made its report. Lord Bryce presided over the inquiry and no fewer than 1,200 witnesses were examined. The conclusions at which this judicial body arrived are:-

(1) In many parts of Belgium there were massacres of civilians, deliberately and systematically organised, and accompanied by numerous isolated murders and assaults.

(2) Women have been violated and the throats of children have been cut.

(3) German officers have sanctioned and ordered, without cause or justification, the pillage, burning and destruction of houses,

(4) From the beginning of the war preparations were made for systematic incendiarism. Acts of incendiarism and destruction of private property were undoubtedly part of the German plan with the object of spreading terror.

(5) The rules and usages of war have been violated, notably by using civilians, even women and children, as shields to protect German troops against rifle fire, by the massacre of prisoners and wounded and by the abuse of the Red Cross and the white flag.

The Commission declares that these conclusions have been established by evidence which cannot be refuted. Murder, rape, and pillage have been committed in many parts of Belgium to a degree that has never been known for three centuries in any war between civilized nations.

The March Bombardment.

Mr. Kellaway inquired, in the House of Commons, whether Lord Fisher was consulted with regard to the March attack on the Dardanelles by the Fleet; and whether Lord Fisher expressed the opinion that the attack ought not to be made in the circumstances in which it was made.

Mr. Churchill said the answer to the first part of the question was "Yes," and to the second part "No."

Is this Victory.

The alleged victories over the Russian army seem to have had an amazing effect in Vienna. According to the report of a Dutch correspondent in the Austrian capital, "when the people wanted, on Sunday, to go for their usual walk in the woods, they found themselves confronted with notices that entrance was forbidden. The reason is that trenches have been dug and barbed wire entanglements erected, and even gun positions have been prepared to protect the city against attack by the enemy."

The Operations in France.

Wireless messages received this morning announce that the French have repulsed another German counter attack at Steenstraet. In the regions of Het-Sas, the French have occupied the first line of German trenches bordering the river and canal and have taken 145 prisoners and four machine guns.

British troops have taken nearly half a mile of German trenches south-west of Ritchebourg l'Avoue and 1600 yards of trenches north-west of Fest ubert. This second attack was afterwards pressed in the direction of Quinquerne where we have advanced nearly 1600 yards along a front of 650 yards. The enemy's losses were very heavy.

Our troops continue to advance to the north of Arras where they and the French have consolidated their positions.
[Steentraet and Het-Sas are situated on the Yser Canal, a little more than four miles north of Ypres. Rickebourg l'Avoue, Festubert and La Quinquerue are three adjoining villages between Neuve-Chatpelle and the canal of La Bassee, about four miles north of the Canal.]

The Sinking of the Lusitania.

Lord Mersey has been appointed President of the Commission of Inquiry into the sinking of the Cunard liner Lusitania which was torpedoed by a German submarine near Queenstown. Among the passengers who lost their lives was Mr Charles Frohman, well-known in England and the United States as the owner of many theatres.

Illness of the King of Greece.

The King of Greece is suffering from pleurisy. Prayers are being offered, for his recovery in all the Greek Churches. The latest bulletins are favourable.

Another Raid of "Frightfulness."

The Germans appear to have discovered that Southend, like Scarborough, is one of our strongly fortified cities. At 3 o'clock one morning last week a couple of Zeplins made a tour over this seaside resort and included in their itinerary Westcliff and Leigh. Eighty incendiary bombs were thrown, fifty of them falling on Southend where several houses were damaged and burned. The airships continued their progress to within 26 miles of London. As soon as the Thames forts opened fire the Zeplins made off toward the east.

Peninsula Press

No. 7   Wednesday, May 19, 1915   Official News.

Turkish Attack on the Australians

Last night and this morning two determined attacks were made on the Australian position. The first attack began at midnight and was easily repulsed the second started at three in the morning and continued until 10 a.m. and was strongly pressed with heavy rifle and machine gun fire, supported by guns of every calibre from 9·2 downwards.

General Liman von Sanders, the German leader, personally directed the operations for which two fresh divisions, numbering from 15,000 to 20,000 men, had been brought from Constantinople. These troops are dressed in light uniforms, which seems to indicate that the supply of khaki is exhausted.

Both attacks failed, though the Turks displayed great bravery and determination, advancing in masses to be mowed down by our fire. After the last assault had failed the enemy kept up an incessant musketry fire all day but did no damage.

Daylight showed the Turkish dead lying in heaps in front of our trenches. In one spot eight acres were covered with them and the dead alone can safely be put down at no fewer than 2000. Including wounded the enemy's losses must exceed 7000. Our men are very pleased with the nights work and only hope that the Turks may come on again and that General Liman von Sanders may direct their attack.

Raiding the Enemy's Beach.

A successful air raid was made on Tuesday over Maidos, an important depot and landing place for Turkish troops, on the Narrows in the Straits. The beach was crowded with men, horses and supplies, and made a fine animated target for our airship. Fifteen bombs were dropped one, weighing 100 Lbs, crashed into the middle of the pier which was piled up with cases of material. "The attacks on our beach are avenged" was the comment of the gallant airman.

Brilliant Victories in France.

French official report, Paris, Tuesday:-
Threatened by a complete enveloping movement, the Germans have evacuated the positions they still hold west of the Yser Canal, leaving on the field nearly 2,000 dead and a great number of rifles

North of La Bassee, British troops have captured several German trenches and inflicted heavy losses on the enemy. Seven hundred Germans, caught between the fire of British machine guns and that of their own artillery, were exterminated. The British took a thousand prisoners and some machine guns.

The number of prisoners taken by the French on Sunday, in the affair of Ville-sur-Tourbe, was 350, and 500 wounded. Today (the 18th) the French attacked Bois d'Ailly and captured several German works, three machine guns and 250 prisoners, several of whom are officers.

The Germans hoisted the green Ottoman flag at Bailly, doubtless hoping to impress French Moslem troops. The African soldiers promptly replied by fusillading and capturing the flag.

Zeppelins at British Resorts
Two abortive Zeppelin raids are reported. One of the great German airships dropped 20 bombs in a field near Deal and injured three people.

The Admiralty announce that a Zeppelin was chased by Eastchurch and Westgate aeroplanes and was afterwards attacked near Nieuport by eight naval aeroplanes from Dunkirk. Three of them attacked at close range. Flight Commander Bigsworth flew 200 feet above the Zeppelin and dropped four bombs. It is believed that she was severely damaged. All our pursuing aeroplanes were exposed to heavy fire but there were no casualties.

Italy and the War.
Italian newspapers announce that the departure of the German and Austrian Ambassadors is imminent. There is great rejoicing in Italy where popular feeling is in favour of intervention.

Neutrals and Crimes Against Humanity.
The wholesale murder of nearly one thousand passengers in the American liner "Lusitania" is described by the "Frankfurter Zeitung" as "an extraordinary success of the German Navy."

Seeing that many of these murdered men and women were citizen of the United States, the Attitude of President Wilson is watched with much concern. New York reports that since the tragedy he has refused to receive callers and has not seen even the Foreign Secretary, Mr Bryan, who issued a mesage to the nation, saying "Don't rock the Ship!"

The President's address to naturalised Americans at Philadelphia is construed as meaning:- "We will remain at peace and seek to convince Germany of the injustice to mankind." On the other hand the New York World" which is regarded as the exponent of the President's views, is of opinion that he will "make a last attempt to bring Germany to reason."

Mr Asquith, Prime Minister, speaking in the House of Commons said that Germany has carried on the war with progressive disregard for the accepted rules of warfare. But there is no object in approaching neutrals unless they are prepared to take some action (cheers). We trust that neutrals are growingly realizing the issues involved – issues that affect the whole civilized world and the future of humanity. (Loud cheers.)

Mr Churchill stated that the size and number of the German submarine which sank the Lusitania are known.

Peninsula Press

No. 8   Thursday, May 20th, 1915   Official News.

Lord Kitchener on the Peninsula Operations.

Lord Kitchener, speaking in the House of Lords, said that the news from the Gallipoli Peninsula was thoroughly satisfactory.

Rumoured Changes in the Government.

London, May 19th.

There are persistent reports in the Lobby of the House of Commons that a Coalition Government is to be formed. Three Unionist leaders conferred with Mr. Asquith, the Prime Minister, to-day. The exact allocation of offices is determined, but it is rumoured that Mr Balfour, Mr Bonner Law (Leader of the Opposition), Mr. Chamberlain, the Earl of Derby, and Mr F.E. Smith will enter the Cabinet, while Lord Haldane (Lord Chancellor), Earl Beauchamp (Lord President of the Council), Lord Lucas (President of the Board of Agriculture), Mr. Harcourt (Colonial Secretary)and Mr. Birrell (Irish Secretary) will retire.

Note:- The Second Parliament of King George was elected in December, 1910, and, under the Quinqunnial Act, would be dissolved at the end of this year. In the probable event of the war lasting beyond that date, measures may be adopted to prolong the life of the present Parliament without an appeal to the constituencies. The necessity of avoiding a general election while the war is in progress is doubtless one of the reasons for proposing a Coalition Government.

Mr. Balfour has been for some time a member of the Committee of Imperial Defence, and, as the Prime Minister stated in the House of Commons, he has been consulted by the Government in important matters.

Changes at the Admiralty.

It is understood that Lord Fisher, First Sea Lord, Admiral of the Fleet, has resigned, and that Mr. Churchill, First Lord of the Admiralty, will leave the Admiralty, but remain in the Cabinet.

Mr. Balfour is mentioned as the probable successor of Mr. Churchill at the Admiralty.

(Reuter's Agency).

New Methods and New Armies.

London, May 19th.

Lord Kitchener, Secretary for War, announced in the House of Lords that the British and French Governments felt that their troops must be protected from the poisonous gases used by the Germans, by employing similar methods against the enemy. Only in this way could the risk of an enormous and unjustifiable disaster be removed.

Lord Kitchner called for 800,000 more recruits to form new armies.

He emphasized the brilliant successes of the French in the neighborhood of Arras, and declared that the Russians are not only holding a strong line in West Galicia but have achieved a big counter offensive in Bukovina.

Lord Kitchener paid a glowing tribute to General Botha, Prime Minister and Commander- in-Chief of the Forces operating against the Germans in South Africa.

(Reuter Agency).

Austria Bids for Italian Neutrality.

The German Imperial Chancellor (Dr. Von Bethmann Hollweg) stated that Austria had made every effort to ensure the friendship of Italy having offered to Italy the sovereignty of Valona (one of the principal ports of Albania) the Italian portions of the Tyrol, and the country on the western bank of the river Isonzo which flows into the Gulf of Trieste.

Austria, moreover, proposed that Trieste (the chief port at the head of the Adriatic) should become a city of Italian character. Austria also declared her political disinterestedness in Albania and promised to respect the interests of Italian nationals in Austria and grant an amnesty to political prisoners.

The impression made by the Chancellor's speech on the majority of hearers was that war with Italy is inevitable.

(Reuter's Agency).

Note:- The territorial concessions demanded by Italy from Austria have not been stated. Unofficial programmes put forward the following claims:-
(1) The province of Istria with the port of Fiume, east of the Adriatic, and the islands of Quareno. (2) Dalmatia and the islands from Zara to the river Narenta. On the other hand, the Southern Slavs who form 95 per cent of the population of Dalmatia, contend that this province

should be ceded to them. For strategic reasons Italy would not be willing to see the whole of Dalmatia handed over to the Serbo-Croatians.

Mutinous Spirit in Gallipoli.

London, May, 1 915.
The following Cablegram has been received from Headquarters:-
"Reliable information from Constantinople is to the effect that mutinous spirit has appeared in Gallipoli; that some 50,000 Turks are hors de combat in the Peninsula, and that the "Goeben" was thrice hit during operations on May 11th."

Civilisation Against Barbarism.

"Eyewitness," the official correspondent, at Field-Marshal Sir John French's Headquarters, urges Britons to realise the German incredible savagery, and says:

"The British spared the life of a Prussian Officer even in the heat of a charge. The Prussian, on being escorted to the rear, saw two British in their death agony by gas. He stopped, laughed, pointed and said; "What do you think of that!" Captured Prussian Guardsmen also behaved with the ferocity of beasts. They are rude and ungrateful. Germany has opened a new phase of war, and her savagery must be crushed. It is now a struggle of civilization against barbarism."

Armenian Revolt.

Turkey has troubles within as well as without. There is a revolution at Zeitun and at Van. The Armenians are frankly on the side of the Entente, though it may be doubted whether they would have carried their convictions into action, had it not been for Turkish massacres at Bitlis, Erzerum, Varr, Mush and Sasun. Three Armenian bishops, many priests and some prominent political leaders have been arrested and sent into the interior.

Peninsula Press

No. 9　　　　Friday, MAY 21st, 1915　　　Official News.

Attack on Australian and New Zealand Positions.

A RUSE THAT FAILED.

The Turks have taken lessons from their German masters. Towards the close of Thursday a Turkish staff officer, accompanied by two medical officers, approached our lines with white flags and Red Crescents, the counterpart of the Red Cross. One of our Divisional Commanders went out to meet them and was told that they had come to ask for an armistice to　remove their dead and wounded. The hour and conditions were calculated to excite suspicion. Night was drawing near and it was seen that the enemy's trenches were lined with double rows of armed men. Glancing at the bristling trenches, the divisional commander gave his answer- Neither of them had power to arrange a suspension of arms, but if the Turkish officer would return at a reasonable hour in the morning, they might exchange letters on the subject. Meanwhile hostilities would be resumed after ten minute's grace.

Orders were instantly given and stretcher bearers (British as well as Turkish) withdrew from the death-strewn battlefield of Wednesday. We had not long to wait before justification came for the suspicions that, under the cloak of humanity, the enemy was seeking to gain the advantage of darkness in order to escape the fire of our guns which had caused them　so　many losses in their last assault. From the Turkish trenches advanced masses of armed men. They came on behind a screen of weaponless soldiers who held up their hands as though eager to surrender. But the ruse could not have deceived a child. Along the whole line rifle and gun spoke. The bombardment went on furiously till dark, after which rifle and machine gun continued the combat until four in the morning. One rush the enemy attempted, but it was not pressed with vigour and our artillery soon drove them back into their trenches. At 4 a.m. the rifle fire died down and half an hour's bombardment reduced the enemy to silence. The Turks paid dearly for their attempt to abuse the privileges of the Red Cross.

This morning (Friday) there came galloping over the sandy beach from Kaba Tepe a Turkish staff officer, smartly and beautifully arrayed. He came, it is reported, to arrange under less suspicious conditions an armistice for the burial of the dead. At the hour of going to press the pourparlers had not ended.

Note:- We regret that by an error the word New Zealand was omitted from our description of the previous attack on this position.

The Coalition Government.
The Labour Members of the House of Commons have accepted Mr. Asquith's invitation to be represented in the Coalition Government. It is understood that Mr. Henderson, member for Barnard Castle, will join the Cabinet.

The House of Commons has adjourned until June 6th when the new Coalition will assume office

Italy Preparing for Action
The Governments of Italy and Austria have asked the United States Government to represent their interest in Vienna and Rome respectively, in the event of a rupture.

The "Cologne Gazette" one of the best informed of German newspapers, says that the German and Austrian Consular Staffs have left Rome.

Note:- Military service in Italy is universal and compulsory. The war strength of the first and second line forces only is estimated at 750,000. Since the outbreak of the war the effective strength of the army has been greatly increased.

Naval rivalry between Italy and Austria has existed for many years, and, like that between Great Britain and Germany, was accentuated by the appearance of the Dreadnought. The fighting fleet of Italy in 1914 consisted of nine battleships, nine cruisers, fourteen light cruisers thirty destroyers, ninety-four torpedo boats and, eighteen submarines. The authorised strength of the naval personnel is 40,063. Spezia, the chief naval and military port, is strongly fortified.

Bulgaria Waiting
Mr. Tontcheff, the Bulgarian Minister of Finance, declared in an interview the other day that Bulgaria will maintain her neutrality as long as such a policy is compatible with the realization of national ideals. Bulgaria will intervene at the last moment, when most needed. At the present moment any action on the part of Bulgaria would be premature and not in the interests of the country.

Raising the Age Limit

The age limit of Lord Kitchener's Army has been raised to forty years.

Newmarket Only

The Government has requested the Jockey Club to suspend all racing after the present week, except Newmarket Races.

Methods of Barbarism

The Press Bureau publishes the declaration of Mr Martin, Editor of the "Rotterdamsche Nieuewsblad," and of Mr Vanditmar, a Rotterdam journalist, reproducing statements made to them on separate occasions by three German deserters whose names, regiments, company, etc., were fully given. They all said that the Bavarian regiments under Prince Ruprecht had received formal orders to take no British prisoners. The order existed exclusively in the Bavarian Army, and soldiers contravening it were severely punished. The prisoners thus taken were not sent to Germany but brought to the quarters with their hands bound at the back, their eyes bandaged and shot under the supervision of the officers. They were not told that they were going to be shot, and were mostly wounded men. The deserters gave full details of several such shootings and the names of the officers who were present. One of the deserters himself shot five British prisoners though he disapproved of the order.

Peninsula Press

No. 10   Saturday, MAY 22nd, 1915   Official News.

Italy enters the Arena.

Italy, as everyone foresaw, has ranged herself on the side of the Allies, in the war against barbarism.

Though no formal declaration has yet been made, the signs cannot be mistaken. The appeals of the Kaiser, the blandishments of Prince Von Bulow, the bribes of Austria, the false reports of crushing victories in Russia, and France, and Flanders, all have failed. If, for a time, the Italian Government seemed to hesitate, the people did not: from the outset they clamoured to take up arms.

Wireless messages from Rome this morning tell us that the inevitable step has been taken. By 407 votes to 74, the Italian Chamber of Deputies adopted the Extraordinary Powers Bill, amid cheers for Britain, France, and Russia.

The German and Austrian Ambassadors are still in Rome but a train is in readiness to carry them to the Frontier. Mindful of the insults and the indignities to which the Ambassadors of Great Britain, France and Russia were subjected by the populace of Berlin, the Italian Government has taken wise precautions. The German and Austrian Ambassadors will not be allowed to cross the Frontier until the Italian Ambassadors have returned safely from Berlin and Vienna.

The Italian Consulate in London is busy signing passports of Italians who are returning to their own Country to join the Army, which is mobilizing.

The Austrians, according to telegrams from Vienna have already begun to terrorise Italians in the territory on which the War of Liberation will be fought. 59,000 Italians in Austria have been sent to Concentration Camps. Austrian troops are taking their station on the frontier, and men are working day and night on trenches and field fortifications.

Our Advance has Begun.

Some months ago (so runs the story for which we do not vouch) when Lord Kitchener was asked when the war would end, his reply was: "I cannot tell you when the war will end, but I can tell you when it will begin. It will begin in May."

Read in the light of our recent activities in France and Flanders, the laconic telegram from Field-Marshal French's Headquarters is significant:- "On Tuesday night our advance commenced."

The weather continues to be unfavourable for operations. A telegram on May 21st states that the ground is "impracticable" between Nieuport and Arras, that is to say, on the British and Belgium front as well as in the region of the recent French successes to the North of Arras. On the other hand, we have made progress in Champagne near Beausejour and have captured several trenches in the wood of Ailly. Two German aeroplanes have been brought down.

On the Russian Front.

A Petrograd official telegram states that the battle on the whole Galician front continued on May 19th. The Russians made 4,000 prisoners. The enemy's aeroplanes dropped some bombs on Przemysl.

The Austro-German forces succeeded in capturing some trenches to the South of Przemysl.

Brilliant Attack by Indian Troops.

Three German Officers Killed.

The enemy made a determined attack this afternoon on the left of our Indian Brigade and succeeded in gaining a footing in an isolated part of our advanced trenches. This success was temporary and costly. A Counter-attack was at once organized and the enemy was driven out. Every Turk who had reached the trench was killed and among the dead were three German officers.

The War's Post Bag.

The Postmaster General states that every day 400,000 letters and 60,000 parcels (about 80 or 90 tons in weight) are sent from the United Kingdom to France. To Egypt and the Dardanelles are sent every week, about 250,000 letters and 5,000 parcels, while the weekly letters to the Fleet number 4,500,000, and the parcels 45,000. About 1,200 postal servants engaged in delivering postal correspondence at the front.

35,000 men from the Post Office are serving and seven or eight hundred have been killed and a large number wounded

As a proof of the sound condition of trade finance and industry, the Postmaster General drew attention to the interesting fact that for the quarter ending March 31st the deposits in the Post Office Savings Bank exceeded the withdrawals by £4,000,000 or £3,000,000 in excess of any previous record for any corresponding period.

Dutch Opinion of Germans.

Commenting on the German suggestion that a Dutch and a Greek trading vessel had been sunk by a British and not by a German submarine, the Amersterdam Journal "Nieuwss van den Dag" says:-
"We do not consider that Englishmen are capable of infamies, although the Germans do. There has not been a single occasion in the course of the war when British sailors have given any proof of being lacking in chivalry, much less of such contemptible baseness as the intentional destruction of a defence-less ship."

Fall in German Peace Stock.

An amazing change has come over the ambitious dreams of German Political Agents in the United States. A few months ago, Count Bernstorff, the German Ambassador, and Herr Dernurg, the former Colonial Minister, amused American citizens with peace terms that would make France a dependent and Great Britain a poor relation of Germany. To-day the terms are modest. Herr Dernburg hints that Morocco and Madagascar are countries which France does not need and that the price of German withdrawal from Belgium is the "Freedom of the Seas" and liberty for Germany to expand outside Europe. "If England refuses this," adds the ex-Minister, by way of threat, "Germany will establish a permanently fortified base on the English Channel." Herr Dernurg may have become more modest, but evidently be has not ceased to count his chickens before they are hatched.

Peninsula Press

No. 11   Sunday, MAY 23rd   Official News.

Berlin Mobs Italian Ambassador.

Communications Broken.

The Italian Ambassador in Berlin was mobbed when leaving the Embassy on Thursday evening. The Imperial Chancellor and the Foreign Secretary immediately apologised.

The Austrian Military authorities on the frontier have sent back the Italian mails, broken the telegraph lines and destroyed the railway communications.

The Italian Senate has passed by 262 votes to 2 the bill granting extraordinary powers to the Government. The Chamber of Deputies had already agreed to this measure by 407 votes to 74.

(Wireless message from Rome).

Note:- This display of German "Kultur" towards the diplomatic representatives of a foreign power recalls the disgraceful scenes that marked the departure of the British, French and Russian Embassies from Berlin last August. The repetition of these outrages on civilised usage was foreseen by the Italian Government when they determined that the German and Austrian Ambassadors shall not be allowed to cross the frontier until the Italian Ambassadors have returned safely from Berlin and Vienna.

Great Progress in France

Supplementary reports received by wireless emphasise the importance of the check sustained by the Germans on the night of the 20th, 21st, North of Ypres. The number of prisoners taken by the French was 1,400: several trench mortars were captured and more than 500 German dead were counted.

The weather having improved, the French have developed with brilliant results their attack on the slopes South of Notre Dame de Lorette. They have also taken possession of some German defensive works known as "Blanch Ferme," the only spur that remains in partial German occupation out of the five spurs of the mountain mass of Notre Dame de Lorette. From this point, the enemy's machine guns embarrassed our action on the plateau to the West of Sanchez.

The whole mountain mass of Notre Dame de Lorrette, with its defences, so stubbornly defended by the Germans for more than six months, is now at the mercy of the French. During the night of May 21-22, the enemy made several counter-attacks which were beaten off with great loss to the Germans. The French have won part of the line of Albain Sainte-Nazaire which unites the positions of Blanche Ferme with the North East of the village where the Germans still remain. In this engagement the French took more than 250 prisoners including several officers, and one gun. The Germans replied to this success of the French with a violent bombardment but did not attempt any counter-attack.

In the Black Sea.

An official telegram from Petrograd states that the Russian Black Sea Fleet has landed troops East of Eregli, 187 miles due East of the Bosphorus. The Russian soldiers broke through the enemy's resistance and destroyed the quays and stations.

On the Russian Frontier.

On the left bank of the Vistula, the Russians continue to press the enemy and dive them South of the Radom-Kielce railway. Our Allies have gained important successes on both flanks of the enemy on the left bank of the river San. The repeated attacks made by the enemy between Przemysl andl the marshes of the Dniester, with the object of piercing the Russian front, reached their culminating point and were attended with enormous German losses.

A desperate battle is in progress in the direction of Stryi where the Russians have retaken some trenches.

The Kaiser's Threat.

A Greek newspaper says the Paris "Journal," publishes the following telegram from the German Emperor to his sister the Queen of Greece:-
"Our offensive is advancing successfully on all fronts. On the Eastern front the Russians have lost, since the beginning of the war, more than 700,000 men, including 70,000 officers. On the Western front the French have had certain small successes at various spots, but with such great sacrifices that it would suit us perfectly if they had gained a large number of similar successes. Our final victory is certain. Woe to those who still dare to draw the sword against me!
     My Compliments to Tino
       "William."

Note:- "Tino" is King Constantine of Greece, the Emperor's brother-in-law.

Running Amok

Inspired by the sinking of the Lusitania, which the Berlin newspapers continue to describe "with joyful pride" as one of "the greatest achievements in this naval war," Herr Dernburg, has issued a statement in New York, foreshadowing an aggravation of brutality and lawlessness. The American flag declares the former German Colonial Secretary, will afford not the slightest protection for vessels carrying what Germans regard as contraband. "England," he adds, "cut off Germany from the outside world, and we intend to isolate her in like manner." Only if Americans travel in neutral vessels not carrying contraband can they expect to be safe.

It is manifest from their acts as well as their words that Germans do not care in the least what the United States may say or do. Mr. Roosevelt and his followers, who hold that President Wilson's "invertebrate diplomacy" is indirectly responsible for the present situation, insist that "not only our duty to humanity at large, but our duty to preserve our national self-respect, demands instant action on our part and forbids all delay."

In our account of the assault on our position yesterday, we ought to have given to the Indian Brigade, and not exclusively to our Indian troops, credit for having made the brilliant and successful counter-attack.

Peninsula Press

No. 12   Monday, MAY 24th, 1915   Official News.

Italy at War with Austria.

An official telegram, received this afternoon at the French Headquarters, from the Minister of War in Paris, announces that Italy has proclaimed "A State of War" between herself and Austria from to-day (May 24th).

According to a wireless message this morning, "A state of war, has been proclaimed from Sunday, the 23rd in the northern province of Italy."

"An encounter is reported between Italy Chasseurs and an Austrian patrol which entered Italian territory. The Chasseurs 'attacked and pursued the enemy's patrol."

Telegrams in Greek Journals just recieved describe the emotion with which Germans awaited the formal declaration of war by their late Ally. Immense crowds in front of Berlin newspaper offices reviled Italy and bandied sarcasms at the expense of Austria and the Emperor Francis-Joseph. The approaches to the Imperial Palace were thronged and the Empress, appearing on the balcony, saluted the multitude and spoke a few words, ending with these:-
"God alone is with us."

The popular emotion, recalled the memorable days immediately preceding the war. Despite official assurances that the action of Italy cannot affect the issue, it was manifest that the people do not share the confidence of their rulers.

Bearding the Turk.

A Large Turkish gun boat was sunk off Constantinople last night.

At the Front.

There was heavy fighting last night from the Turkish trenches all along our front. The enemy made no advance. Our line was strengthened and former gains were consolidated.

More Successes in France.

The French official report today states:- the French took some more houses in the district North of Albain and captured a number of prisoners. They also repulsed an attack to the North of Neuville. During the night of 22nd and 23rd the Germans delivered several counter attacks which were in all cases repulsed with very heavy loss to the enemy. Two counter-attacks were launched at the plateau de Lorette but failed to reach the French positions. Two others were aimed at the French positions at Neuville St. Vaore and at the cemetery in the village; two more further South near the Larbarifnette. At one point the Germans gained a footing in the French trenches but under the enfilading fire of the French lines they were all killed or taken prisoners. In Argonne the Germans exploded several mines and have endeavoured with large forces to occupy the excavations created by the explosions. The French threw the Germans back into their own trenches inflicting heavy loss. The German defeat was complete.

Pour Encourager les Autres.

Among Turkish orders for the attack on Maly 1st were the following:-
"The Battalion Chaplains (Imams), placed in the front line, will do their best to maintain the moral of the troops, and to encourage them at the critical moment."

"Let it be clearly understood that those who remain stationary at the moment of the attack, or who try to escape, will be shot. For this purpose, machine guns will be placed behind the troops to oblige these people to advance, and at the same time to fire on the enemy's reserves."

"Men who do not go forward into action and those who stop to pick up the wounded without any written authority, will be executed for cowardice."

A Mobile Monster.

A correspondent of the "Frankfurter Zeitung," describing the Austro-German 42-centimetre howitzer, says that the gun, which is usually hauled into position on its own special truck, can be anchored and "built in" ready for action within two days. The gun bed is over six feet deep. Particular care is taken to guard the gun against detection by enemy aircraft. On one occasion, when one of these pieces had evidently been spotted by a hostile airman, the gun was transferred during the night into a neighbouring wood. The next day sixty heavy shells were fired by the enemy into the abandoned position. The gun can he fired in two minutes. Its deep boom is "more agreeable" to the human ear than the report of the 30.5 howitzer. Its accuracy is likewise commended. The flash of the discharge is so blinding that the gun crew have orders not to look up when the gun is fired. The concussion affects the men at the gun a little: but on one occasion a truck containing ammunition had its sides shattered, although 60 yards away. One gun seen by this correspondent had fired over 800 shots since the beginning of this year.

Rioting in Trieste.

Trieste, which the Austrians proposed to make a free Port of the Adriatic, by way of concession to Italy, appears to be in a state of insurrection. Mobs, composed chiefly of women, parade the streets, shouting: "Death to the Emperor!" They burned the yellow and black flag and the effigy of the Emperor Francis-Joseph. Soldiers and police charged the mobs, wounding 800 and killing a considerable number·.

Turkey's Peace Terms.

Turkish newspapers which have just come to hand, while disclaiming any desire to make peace – unless urged by their enemies – lay down conditions that must alarm their German Allies. According to the "Ikdam," the terms are as follows:- (1) Neutralisation of the great ocean routes in time of war (2) the "open door" for trade with Colonies, especially British Colonies "which have erected barriers against imports from other countries!" (3) Restitution of German Colonies (4) Commercial freedom for Germany on the great continental railways. The Turks are better as soldiers than as merchants or diplomatists or they would not need to be told that in British Colonies all nations have equal commercial privileges. The curious and significant thing about these peace conditions is that Turkey asks nothing and is concerned for its Ally alone.

Peninsula Press

No. 13   Tuesday, MAY 25th, 1915   Official News.

20,000 Austrians Captured.

The latest newspapers to hand state that:- The Russians have retreated from the Carpathians in order to re-arrange and shorten their front. Their complete withdrawal from the mountain region was obviously involved in the rapid advance of the Germans in the last few days, since the enemy's possession of Sambor and an extensive district South-East of Przemysl threatened the Russian communications with the whole region in the Carpathians which they still held.

Further details are now available of the great Russian victory in East Galicia, in which they pushed the Austrians back from the Dniester to the Pruth. In this battle on a 100 mile front they took 20,000 prisoners in the course of five days.

Italy and the War.

German Chancellor's Threat.

The German Imperial Chancellor, Count von Bethmann-Holweg, stated in the Reichstag that Austria had gone to the extreme limit of possible concessions in order to ensure the neutrality of Italy. These concessions had been offered in vain, and the two allied Empires were therefore under the necessity of punishing their "faithless ally."

The "Messaggero" (Rome) commenting on these "concessions," says:- "Italy will ram down the throat of the sneaks of the house of Bulow our reply to the miserable offers made by Austria, the acceptance of which would have meant: the door always open to Austria in the Trentino: the final sacrifice of Italian interests in Trieste, Po Ia, Fiume and Dalmatia: the continued strategic inferiority of Italy in the Adriatic: the exclusion of Italy from all heritage from the dying Turk: the loss of our position in the Eastern Mediterranean : perpetual isolation in the future and the chance for Austria and Germany to take their revenge in order to chastise the "felons" and "robbers" of May, 1915."

On the Western Front.

Between Steenstraete and Ypres, the Germans have attacked, after making use of asphyxiating gas; they were driven back. The British have made some advance to the East of Festubert. North of Arras, the battle continued with extreme violence throughout the 23rd and the following night. The French took 120 prisoners. North-East of Notre Dame de Lorette, they have advanced several hundred yards.

The French have reached the cross roads of Neuville St. Vaast and have taken some new groups of fortified houses in the village itself. Several German counter-attacks were defeated. The struggle continues.

Latest information shows the extent of the check sustained in this region by the Germans on the 22nd-23rd May. Despite the considerable reinforcements hurried forward, and the vigour of their effort, the Germans have failed in all their attempts and have had considerable losses.

"Those Queer English."

The people of Gallipoli Town, says a Turkish correspondent, have seen only four British prisoners of war. The men "excited great admiration among the people, because it was seen that they were indeed soldiers. They wandered about freely and drank coffee, creating great excitement by their queer remarks and causing no ill-feeling."

3,000 Turkish Dead.

The burial of the dead on the Australian and New Zealand Front was completed yesterday under the armistice asked for by the Turks. The number of the enemy's dead lying between the trenches was estimated at 3,000, counting only those who have fallen since May 18th. Rifle fire broke out soon after the close of the armistice.

"Rounding up Aliens."

The work of apprehending all enemy aliens in London continues vigorously, and at the principal police stations there is a continuous stream of arrivals. Although by far the larger number are voluntary surrenders, some have recieved from the police a special warning that they must give themselves up within a limited time. Most of the prisoners seem to be more or less well-to-do. In West London the police have comparatively little trouble, but in the East End there are still many enemy aliens to be "rounded up." One of the difficulties is that since registration began, a certain proportion of less reputable Germans and Austrians have tried to pass themselves off as Russians, a trick which is hard to check in districts where mixed nationalities abound.

Awaiting the Verdict.

The Greek newspaper "Athinai" writes:- "The Triple Entente (Great Britain, France, and Russia) awaits the result of the Greek Elections.

Twenty-five days (June 13th) separate us from the popular verdict. If the people give the victory to the party of M. Venizelos, then the Entente powers will have no further anxiety concerning us. Greece will be ready for war in accordance with the programme of M. Venizelos, and with the engagements he has assumed."

The British navy has rescued 1,282 German seamen and marines from German warships sunk. Not one British seaman or marine has been saved by Germans in like circumstances.

Britain to America.

On the Sinking of the "Lusitania."
In silence you have looked on felon blows,
On butchers work of which the waste lands reek;
Now, in God's name, from Whom your greatness flows,
Sister, will you not speak?
[From "Punch", May 12th]

Peninsula Press

No. 14   Wednesday, MAY 26th, 1915   Official News.

Burying the Turkish Dead.

Amenities of the Armistice.

In accordance with the terms of the armistice, requested by the Turks for the burial of their dead, delimitation parties of two staff officers, two medical officers and 100 men with white flags met on Monday morning in front of line held by the Australian and New Zealand Forces. The delimitation was completed by noon and burying parties moved out as the delimitation parties moved up the lines. The lines come very close to each other in certain places, but the correct attitude of the Turkish staff officers made easy what might well have been a delicate operation. The Turkish arrangements were good; their burial parties worked quietly and quickly, and were supplied with cotton wool prepared with some solution to avoid the smell.

The enemy's dead were numerous. Counting only those killed since the attack of May, 18-19, 3,000 would be a fair estimate. In front of one section alone were 400 corpses within a space 80 yards by 100 yards.

There was no friction between the burial parties, though one incident is reported.

A Turkish soldier seized one of our hand grenades, and, despite shouts of protests, ran off with it to the trenches. He was promptly pursued by a Turkish officer who kicked him soundly, recovered the bomb, and with a bow and apologies presented it to one of our officers.

French Official Report.

Paris, May 26th

Lively artillery engagements have been provoked between Nieuport and Ypres by the effective fire of the French heavy batteries on the position at Raveiszette, South-West of Ostend. After a violent bombardment, the Germans attempted to deliver an attack deploying along the road from Langemarche to Ypres. This attack was easily checked.

To the North of Albain, the Germans twice attacked, and were repulsed each time.

To the North of Neuville St. Vast on the 24th, the Germans made an attack of some considerable importance, judging by the forces used. During the night of 24th and 25th, they delivered four attacks, but, being caught under the fire of the French guns, they were checked, and suffered very heavily.   Reports completely confirm the French successes in the North and at the Chapell of Notre Dame de Lorette on the 23rd. By means of a bayonet charge the French succeeded in carrying the positions.

Tortured Prisoners

Lord Grenfell laid before the House two remarkable letters from British prisoners in Germany. The writer of one of these communications - a trooper - stated that the prisoners food consisted of rice-water and beans, with one loaf of bread in six days, that several men bad been run through with the bayonets of the guards, that a large number were tied for six hours at a stretch to barbed wire posts with their toes just touching the ground, and that the guards knocked them about unmercifully with rifles and sticks. The other letter was from an officer, who declared that both officers and men were being abominably ill-used, and that their food was unfit to eat.

The Kaiser and "Unser Alt Gott."

The tone of the German Emperor's public utterances is very different now from what it was at the beginning of the war, when His Majesty missed no opportunity of informing his subjects that he would, "with God's help," soon impose his will on the presumptuous nations that had dared to withstand him. The citizens of Dusseldorf recently telegraphed to His Majesty offering their homage on the occasion of the hundredth anniversary of the day on which the Rhenish Province was added to Prussia. The Emperor in reply, expressed their homage, and made the following, for him, very temperate remark:-

"God the Lord has graciously directed the destinies of the German people in the past; He will also turn the present grievous affliction into a blessing for us, and for our descendants."

Methods of Barbarism.

A French officer, who has lately returned from the front in France, gives the following experience of the asphyxiating bombs used by the enemy:- We were traveling approximately two miles behind the English lines, when our eyes began to water and smart. We thought at first this was due to the raw North-Easterly wind, but soon we all began to cough, and the air was pervaded with a strange, pungent, suffocating odour. It is very difficult to give an accurate description of it, as it was entirely unlike anything I had ever smelt before, but I may say that it bore some resemblance to escaping acetylene gas, such as is used for lighting motor cars. We were obliged to stop, as our eyes were burning to such an extent that it was impossible for the chauffeur to see the road. In the distance could be seen clouds of dense yellow smoke, which was entirely different from that which exploding projectiles make, looking like a thick curtain of green-yellow fog.

Fighting in the Garden of Eden.

An officer serving in the Persian Gulf describes how a mixed force of 1,000 men was saved by 80 men of a British Regiment. They were attacked on three sides by 10,000 Arabs and Turks. The native troops fell back and these thirty, with two field guns, a doctor and a few British officers, saved the situation. Some of the Indian Contingent which have been doing duty near the Garden of Eden since the late summer has gone to a new camp at Makima Massa, which means "liquoric factory." The officer adds: "I had to take a convoy out to a place seven miles off the other day. The floods are terrific, and the first five miles of the road was through water up to the pony's belly. It was like wading through five miles of sea. The mobile Kurdish Cavalry appear to be quite a sporting crowd. They ride like billy O! and when operating are like the whirlwind. They resemble a scene from Buffalo Bill. One could imagine oneself looking over an arena and mounted men of the Buffalo Bill type suddenly making an appearance, dashing through, waving scimitars, letting off their rifles from horseback in any direction regardless of aim or range and yelling."

Peninsula Press

No. 15   Thursday, MAY 27th, 1915   Official News.

The Coalition Cabinet.

According to a German wireless message, the following is the constitution of the new Coalition Cabinet:-
Prime Ministers:- Mr. Asquith and Lord Lansdowne.
Lord Chancellor:- Sir S. Buckmaster.
Lord President of the Council:- Lord Crewe.
Lord Privy Seal:- Lord Curzon.
First Lord of the Admiralty:- Mr. Balfour.
Home Secretary:- Sir John Simon.
Foreign Secretary:- Sir Edward Grey.
Colonial Secretary:- Mr. Bonar Law.
Secretary for War:- Lord Kitchener.
Indian Secretary:- Mr. Chamberlain.
Chancellor of the Exchequer:- Mr. McKenna.
Secretary for Scotland:- Mr. McKinnon Wood.
President of the Board of Trade:- Mr. Runciman.
President of the Local Government Board:- Mr. Walter Long.
Chancellor of the Duchy of Lancaster:- Mr. Churchill.
Secretary for the supply of Munitions of War:- Mr. Lloyd George.
Mr. Lloyd George leaves the Treasury to assume a new office specially created.

German Anger Against Italy.

The "Frankfort Gazette" after accusing Italy of shameless breach of faith, predicts her speedy overthrow and her resurrection under the benign influence of German culture. "A few Bavarian Divisions," says the Gazette, "assisted by Tyrolean Imperial Rifles will suffice to make the sham army of Italy show us its back, to break open the door to Veona, to conduct all our expelled compatriots back to Milan and entrust to them the scientific and military re-organisation of this unhappy country."

The "Deutsche Tageszeitong" utters a shriek: "Germans! One enemy more – an army of vagabonds, pirates, and mandolin players is preparing to march against you!"

Tenacity of the French.

Paris, May 27th.
The official report states:- North of Arras, the French attacks of May

39

23rd have made important progress. North-West of Angres, we captured the salient of a great German defensive work. In the same region, we carried by assault another strongly fortified position. East of the road from Aix-Noulette to Souchez, the French troops have won, on a front of nearly half a mile, a trench which the enemy defended for a fortnight. West of the same road we have made considerable progress in a ravine where the German defences were strongly organised.

The French have gained some ground South West of Souchez.

The checks they have sustained have led to extremely violent action on the part of the Germans.

The French troops have given proof of magnificent courage and tenacity and have held fast to all they won.

Some ground has been gained also on the heights North east of Notre Dame de Lorette.

On May 25th French aeroplanes were very active along the whole front and made some successful bombardments.

A Queenly Retort.

The German Emperor recently wrote a letter to the Queen Mother of Italy insisting on the advantages that Italy would derive if she remained neutral and urging her Majesty to intervene in order to avoid war with Austria. The widow of King Hubert replied to the German Emperor; "In the House of Savoy one King reigns at a time."

Honouring Joan of Arc.

The "Cologne Gazette" announces that the Bishop of Metz, Mgr. Benzlon, has ordered his clergy to remove from all the churches in his see the statue of Joan of Arc.

By a remarkable coincidence a London newspaper of the same date announces that Mrs. Pankhurst, Leader of the Women's Suffrage Movement, laid a wreath on the shrine of the Heroic Maid of France.

Allies of "Kultur."

News has reached London of terrible massacres of Christians by Kurds in the North-West of Persia. The head of the American Mission at Oarrmia reports that thousands of Christians have been put to death and that 2,000 have died from disease. The Russian Vice-Consul sends accounts of the violation and murder of women and the burning of villages. At Salivras several hundred Christians were massacred three days before the arrival of the Russian Army. At Gulpashan, the Turkish Consul gave orders for the burning and pillaging of the town. Eighty-five notables were taken to the cemetery and garrotted before the eyes of their relatives. A priest has been crucified, another was burned alive, and a bishop was hanged. People who took refuge in the Catholic Mission were dragged before the Turkish Consul and sixty-four were beheaded.

Women Special War Service.

The number of women registered for special war service up to April 16 is approximately 47,000, and of these 8,089 are entered as willing to undertake work in armament factories. As to armament labour, the immediate demand for women is not in excess of the number that could be supplied in the ordinary way, but some of the principal factories have informed the Board of Trade that the number of women who will be wanted by these firms within the next few months will be 18,000.

Cleansing the Stock Exchange.

Since the sinking of the Lusitania,150 German members have been warned not to enter the London Stock Exchange. Those who disregarded the warning were threatened with personal violence by British members of the Exchange. All Germans and Austrians, even those who are naturalised, have been excluded from the Liverpool Cotton Exchange. At the Corn Exchange German members were ordered to quit in five seconds, if they did not want to be thrown out. The number of enemy aliens of military age who are still at liberty in the United Kingdom is estimated at from 15,000 to 25,000.

Peninsula Press

No. 16   Friday, MAY 28th, 1915   Official News.

Daring Submarine Exploits.

Our submarines have been busy in the Sea of Marmora, and have scored some notable successes. One of them captured and destroyed a ship containing a 6-in. gun, a number of gun mountings, and a large quantity of ammunition, including charges for large calibre howitzers. The submarine chased in to Rodosto a heavily laden supply ship, and torpedoed her alongside the pier. A small paddle storeship was also chased ashore.

The submarine then proceeded to Constantinople, and fired at a transport alongside the Arsenal, beyond the Golden Horn. The torpedo was seen running straight for its objective, and the explosion was heard but the result could not be observed, owing to certain obstacles.

Not less remarkable is the record of another submarine. In the Narrows, at Chanak, she attacked a Turkish gunboat, but could not wait to see the result, beyond observing a big explosion alongside the gunboat. Near Sharleui, in the Sea of Marmora almost midway between Redosto and the town of Gallipoli, another Turkish gunboat was sunk. Extending her patrol over the Sea of Marmora, the same submarine chased one ship into Rodosto and sunk a large transport carrying many Turkish troops, as well as a smaller transport.

After an adventurous career lasting twenty days, this submarine has returned safely, and was welcomed with cheers from our ships.

His Majesty has conferred, a V.C. on the gallant Commander   the D.S.C. on two of his Lieutenants and the D.S.M. on each member of the crew.

Grave Condition of the King of Greece

A wireless message yesterday says:- "The Condition of the king of Greece is causing grave anxiety." His Majesty is suffering from an acute attack of pleurisy, and must have had a relapse, as the bulletins issued some days ago were most favourable and clearly indicated that in the opinion of the doctors the crisis was then over.

The Greek elections are approaching. On June 18, the people will decide whether they will support King Constantine in his policy of non-intervention or will recall M Venezelos who is pledged to active intervention on the side of Great Britain, France and Russia.

Another Raid on Southend.

The Germans seem to have made up their minds that Southend is one of our fortified places. For the second time in less than a fortnight they have raided this seaside resort. On Thursday night a Zeppelin appeared over the town and dropped 23 bombs killing a woman and two girls.

The steamer Nebraska was torpedoed by a German submarine off the South of Ireland. No lives were lost. The vessel proceeded to Liverpool under her own steam with the forehold inundated.

On Our Front.

The British and French lines made some advance on Thursday night. The casualties were light.

On the front occupied by the Australian and New Zealand troops the enemy fired a good deal during the early part of Thursday night and in the early morning.

On the Western Front

Paris, Friday, 27th

The French official report states:- British troops have made further progress in the direction of la Bassee. North of Arras the Germans continue their desperate efforts to retake positions they lost on the 25th in the region of Angres, but were driven back to their defended positions. At the adjoining positions the Germans succeeded in recapturing part of the Northern Slopes. The French retain their position on the Western slope and have taken part of the Southern slopes. Between these positions, and on the road from Aix-Norlette to Souchez, the French have set foot in the German lines on the hills to the North-East of La Chapelle de Lorette and have advanced 125 yards in spite of a heavy bombardment. To the South-West of Souchez the French have taken a trench at Chateau-de-Carleud and captured a number of prisoners among them several officers. At Neuville-Saint Vaast the French captured a group of houses which, in view of their position, were assisting the enemy in his defence.

A German aeroplane flying towards Paris on the 26th was attacked by a French machine in the region of Soissons. Both the German pilot and observer were killed.

French aviators successfully dropped 30 bombs on the aerodrome at la Brazelle near Douai. The aeroplane sheds and works were destroyed. This morning a squadron of 18 French aeroplanes dropped bombs on Ludwigshafen where an important explosives factory is situated. Sheds and factory were set alight by incendiary bombs.

This expedition against a military establishment is in return for the German air attacks on Paris.

A Righteous Protest.

The Imperial Person beckoned to the General to approach.

"Have you blown up the Cathedral?"

"Yes Sire."

"And bayoneted the wounded."

"Yes Sire."

"And shot the women and old men and children?"

"Yes Sire."

"And made arrangements for tomorrow for the white flag ambush?"

"Yes Sire."

"And issued the dum-dum bullets?"

"Yes Sire"

"And the asphyxiating gases?"

"Yes Sire"

"Then you had better get on with the report to the Neutral Powers protesting against the breaches of the Hague Convention by the enemy."

(Extract from Punch.)

Peninsula Press

No. 17   Saturday, MAY 29th, 1915   Official News.

The New Sea Lord.

London, Friday.

(By Wireless).

Vice-Admiral Sir Henry Bradwardine Jackson, K.C.B., has been appointed First Sea Lord in succession to Lord Fisher.

Admiral of the Fleet Sir Arthur Wilson remains in an advisory capacity on the Board of Admiralty.

[Sir Henry Jackson has been Chief of the War Staff since 1912. He was born at Barnsley in Yorkshire in 1855, and entered the Navy in 1868. He was in command of the Royal Naval College from 1911 to 1913, and has served on numerous Technical Committees in connection with the equipment and design of warships. Admiral Jackson was the first in England to put to practical use the Hertzian Waves, and has done much towards introducing and organising wireless telegraphy, in its early stages, in British warships.]

King Victor Takes Command.

Rome Friday

(By Wireless)

King Victor Emmanuel has gone to the front in supreme command of the land and sea forces.

The Duke of Genoa, His Majesty's brother, has been appointed Lieut.-General, and, during the absence of the King from the Capital, will be entrusted with Royal Prerogatives.

[The approximate war strength of the Italian Army is something over a million men: 515,000 for the Standing Army, 245,000 for the Mobile Militia, and 340,000 for· the Territorial Militia.]

Austria Invaded.

On Tuesday Italian troops crossed the frontier of the Tyrol and occupied Altissimo, North of the Baldo Range, which runs East of Lake Garda. The Austrians were forced to retire, abandoning some war material.

From the Tonezza Plateau our Artillery bombarded the enemy's defensive works. Onr success in the valley of Gazona on the frontier of the Province of Carinthia is confirmed. We also occupied Prevala at the head of the Ruccolana Valley, and the approaches of the Dogna Valley, North-West of the Province of Carniola.

Our losses were slight.

French Successes

Paris, Friday.

The official report this evening states that there were several hot actions North of Arras, which resulted in fresh successes for the French. In the region of Angres two German counter-attacks were repulsed. The French in their attack captured some trenches, and advancing beyond the village of Oblain took 400 prisoners, including several officers.

It is feared that 200 people perished in the disaster to the "Princess Irene," besides a crew of 76. Dockyard workmen were on board re-fitting the vessel.

Attack on our Front.

Saturday.

In the section occupied by the Australian and New Zealand forces simultaneous attacks were made last night, on the Turkish trenches facing our right flank, a thousand yards North of Kaba Tepe, and also on the left flank on trenches opposite our most Northern post. In both cases the attacks were successful, and the trenches were taken, though the latter only were permanently held by us.

At 3.30 a.m. the enemy exploded a mine under Quinns Post, and then attacked and took that portion of the post which had been isolated by the explosion. It was however retaken by the bayonet and large number of Turks were killed and 20 prisoners taken. During this action, the Turks attempted a general attack but came under our Artillery fire, and are reported to have lost very heavily. Full details are not yet to hand.

In the Southern section the British Force made a further slight advance during the night, and the French at midnight captured a small but important redoubt on the extreme left of the Turkish line.

Russian Victories.

Petrograd, Friday.

The official report states that the Russians are fighting successfully in the Shalle regions, and have taken several hundred prisoners as well as some automobiles.

The enemy in a pressing attack at Jedwabuo was unsuccessful.

The enemy attacked our whole front in Galicia and on the Vistula and the River San but was everywhere repulsed

Berlin in Disgrace.

The following noteworthy instances are taken from an appeal for help issued by the Berlin City Mission:-

"Germany is invincible as long as it is united. Is the spirit of lying and of hate to raise its head again among our people? Is the whole country to be infected again from Berlin with lack of faith and immorality? Shall our soldiers who have fought heroically and have suffered for us on the field of battle obtain the impression during their stay in Berlin that the people here play, dance, laugh, and enjoy life as before? We fear that our people will fall from the heights of national and religious exaltation into the depths of the old life, of the old shame and vices. We fear that the blessing that God destined for us in this great time will pass by our people."

Peninsula Press

No. 18   Sunday, MAY 30th. 1915   Official News.

Notice

The issue of "The Peninsula Press" will be suspended for a day or two, owing to the re-arrangement of our printing establishment, and the enlargement of our premises.

THE ATTACK ON OUR FRONT

The action – reported in yesterday's "Peninsula Press" – in the section occupied by the Australian and new Zealand forces, was more serious and more successful than was at first realised. After blowing in "Quinn's Post," the Turks effected a lodgement not only in the crater, but also in the support trenches. When the firing line was retaken with the bayonet, the Turks in the support trenches surrendered. During this hand to hand fighting heavy columns of the enemy advanced to make good their local success. Visible in the bright moonlight to our gunners these were able to bring a cross fire at accurate and known ranges, the consequences being that the Turks got demoralised and fired into one another.

The enemy's casualties were between 1500 and 2000.

Last night the Turks twice attacked the new post gained on the previous night but without success.

The new redoubt captured by the French on the extreme left of the enemy's line is a valuable acquisition. The Turks fired heavily upon it during the night, but did not come on to attack, being held in check by artillery fire. The enemy attacked on the left of the 42nd Division, but were beaten back.

NAVAL ENGAGEMENT IN THE ADRIATIC

Rome

A Naval action took place at Porto Corsian and Barletta. An Austrian torpedo boat, three destroyers, and a scout were seriously damaged, and had many casualties. The Italians lost a destroyer, which was attacked by four ships, while chasing the enemy. His ammunition being exhausted the Commander ordered the seacocks to be opened in order that his ship might not fall into the enemy's hands. Nine of the crew were rescued. Thirty four Austrians also were picked up. (Wireless)

THE WAR IN FRANCE

Paris

The British have progressed in the direction of la Bassee. The enemy made seven very violent attacks in 24 hours in the direction of Angres. All these attacks were repulsed.

A very fierce artillery duel was proceeding all day along the whole front between Angres and XXX

IMPERIAL CHANCELLORS ANGER

Amsterdam

The German Imperial Chancellor, Baron Von Bethmann-Hollweg, made a violent attack on Italy in the Reichstag. In the bitterest terms he denounced their former ally, suggesting that Italy has been threatened and bribed by Great Britain, France and Russia. The Chancellor accused Italian statesmen of bad faith and disregard of heavy obligations.

The fury and fear excited in Germany by Italy's entry into the war on the side of the Allies were manifest from the frantic applause with which the Imperial Chancellor's abusive words were received by the Reichstag.

German messages assert that even as late as May 1st. four-fifths of the Italian Senate and two-thirds of the Italian Chamber of deputies were in favour of peace. "Germany stands faithfully by the side of her allies, Austria Hungary. Their united armies have withstood the Russian advance, and are now driving back the enemy, having broken the Russian line marching form Pelica and Bukovina. On the West Front – in France and Flanders – the enemy was unable to make the advance boastfully announced five months ago.

(Wireless)

A FALSE REPORT

Petrograd

An official denial is given to the story that a Turkish submarine sank a Russian Battleship. No Russian warships in the Black Sea has been sunk or damaged.

(Wireless)

POISONOUS GASES AND REPRISALS

According to the special correspondent of the "Morning Post", the French military authorities have found a means of replying to the German poisonous gases. If the enemy means to use poisonous gases in warfare, the French are ready to retaliate with a weapon which should prove very effective, though it in no way contravenes the regulations accepted by all civilised nations except Germany. This weapon consist of a hand grenade, filled with certain chemicals, which when released produce a gas that has no deadly effects, but is quite powerful enough to paralyse a man for several minutes. The smell of the fumes is not unpleasant: it is suggestive of pear-drops combined with very strong ammonia, and it produces such violent smarting of the eyes and nose that it would be hopeless to try to use a weapon while under its influence. These bombs have not yet been used, and will only be employed if the Germans make any further use of asphyxiating gas.

PENINSULA PRESS.

| No. 18. | SUNDAY, MAY 30th. 1915. | Official News. |

NOTICE.

The issue of "The Peninsula Press" will be suspended for a day or two, owing to the re-arrangement of our printing establishment, and the enlargement of our premises.

THE ATTACK ON OUR FRONT.

The action—reported in yesterday's "Peninsula Press"—in the section occupied by the Australian and New Zealand forces, was more serious and more successful than was at first realised. After blowing in "Quinn's Post", the Turks effected a lodgement not only in the crater, but also in the support trenches. When the firing line was retaken with the bayonet, the Turks in the support trenches surrendered. During this hand to hand fighting heavy columns of the enemy advanced to make good their local success. Visible in the bright moonlight to our gunners these were able to bring a cross fire at accurate and known ranges, the consequence being that the Turks got demoralised, and fired into one another.

The enemy's casualties were between 1500 and 2000.

Last night the Turks twice attacked the new post gained on the previous night, but without success.

The new redoubt, captured by the French on the extreme left of the enemy's line, is a valuable acquisition. The Turks fired heavily upon it during the night, but did not come on to attack, being held in check by artillery fire. The enemy attacked on the left of the 42nd Division, but were beaten back.

NAVAL ENGAGEMENT IN THE ADRIATIC.

Rome.

A Naval action took place at Porto Corsini and Barletta. An Austrian torpedo boat, three destroyers, and a scout were seriously damaged, and had many casualties. The Italians lost a destroyer, which was attacked by four ships, while chasing the enemy. His ammunition being exhausted, the Commander ordered the seacocks to be opened in order that his ship might not fall into the enemy's hands. Nine of the crew were rescued. Thirty-four Austrians also were picked up.

(Wireless.)

THE WAR IN FRANCE.

Paris.

The British have progressed in the direction of La Bassée. The enemy made seven very violent attacks in 24 hours in the direction of Angres. All these attacks were repulsed.

A very fierce artillery duel was proceeding all day along the whole front between Angres and xxx

IMPERIAL CHANCELLOR'S ANGER.

Amsterdam.

The German Imperial Chancellor, Baron von Bethmann-Hollweg, made a violent attack on Italy in the Reichstag. In the bitterest terms he denounced their former ally, suggesting that Italy has been threatened and bribed by Great Britain, France and Russia. The Chancellor accused Italian statesmen of bad faith and disregard of heavy obligations.

The fury and fear excited in Germany by Italy's entry into the war on the side of the Allies were manifest from the frantic applause with which the Imperial Chancellor's abusive words were received by members of the Reichstag.

German messages assert that even as late as May 1st, four-fifths of the Italian Senate and two-thirds of the Italian Chambers of Deputies were in favour of peace. "Germany stands faithfully by the side of her allies, Austria and Hungary. Their united armies have withstood the Russian advance, and are now driving back the enemy, having broken the Russian Line marching from Pelica and Bukovina. On the West Front—in France and Flanders—the enemy was unable to make the advance boastfully announced five months ago."

(Wireless)

A FALSE REPORT.

Petrograd.

An official denial is given to the story that a Turkish submarine sank a Russian Battleship. No Russian warship in the Black Sea has been sunk or damaged.

(Wireless)

POISONOUS GASES AND REPRISALS.

According to the special correspondent of the "Morning Post", the French military authorities have found a means of replying to the German poison gases. If the enemy means to use poisonous gases in warfare, the French are ready to retaliate with a weapon which should prove very effective, though it in no way contravenes the regulations accepted by all civilised nations except Germany. This weapon consists of a hand grenade, filled with certain chemicals, which when released produce a gas that has no deadly effects, but is quite powerful enough to paralyse a man for several minutes. The smell of the fumes is not unpleasant; it is suggestive of pear-drops combined with very strong ammonia, and it produces such violent smarting of the eyes and nose that it would be hopeless to try to use a weapon while under its influence. These bombs have not yet been used, and will only be employed if the Germans make any further use of asphyxiating gas.

Printing Section, G.H.Q., M.E.F.

Peninsula Press

No. 19   Tuesday, JUNE 8th. 1915   Official News.

Attack on Our Front.

On the night of the 3rd-4th June the Turks, having heavily bombarded the small fort - which the French had captured in front of their extreme right - and breached its N.E. angle, launched an infantry attack against it which was repulsed. About the same time they set fire to scrub in front of the left centre of the 29th Division and attacked but without success. On the morning of the 4th instant, we made a general attack on the Turkish trenches in the Southern area of the Peninsula, commencing with a heavy bombardment by all guns, including two battleships, two cruisers and several destroyers with four inch guns. On the cessation of the bombardment our troops rushed forward with the bayonet and were immediately successful all along the line, except in one spot near the left where a heavy entanglement had not been destroyed by gun fire.

The 6th Gurkhas on the extreme left made a fine advance and took two lines of trenches, but, owing to the regiment on their right being hung up by this wire, they were eventually obliged to retire again to their original trenches.

The 29th Division made good progress in the left centre, capturing a strong redoubt and two lines of trenches beyond it, about 500 yards in advance of their original line.

The Territorials in the centre did brilliantly, advancing 600 yards and capturing three lines of trenches, but, though the most advanced captured trench was held all day and half the night they had to be ordered back in the morning to the second captured line, as both their flanks were exposed.

The Naval Division on the right centre captured a large redoubt and a formidable line of trenches constructed in three tiers, some 500 yards to their front but were so heavily enfiladed when the French retired that they also had to come back to their original line.

The French 2nd Division advanced with gallantry and elan and retook for the fourth, time that deadly redoubt which they call "The Haricot." Unfortunately the Turks developed heavy counter-attacks through prepared communication trenches, and, undercover of accurate shell fire were able to recapture the redoubt. On the extreme right of the French line the French Division captured a line of trenches which, though counter-attacked twice during the night, they still hold.

We captured 400 prisoners including 10 officers. Amongst the prisoners were 5 Germans, the remains of a volunteer machine gun detachment from the Goeben, whose officer was killed and whose machine gun was destroyed.

During the progress of fight we received information from the Australian and New Zealand Headquarters that enemy reinforcements had been seen advancing from Maidos towards Krithia. Consequently General Birdwood arranged to attack the trenches in front of Qninn's Post at 10 p.m. which attack was successfully carried out and the trenches were held during the night. The Turkish casualties were heavy. At 6.30 a.m. however, the enemy heavily counterattacked and bombed our men out of the captured trench with a new heavy description of bomb, though we still hold the communication trenches which had been constructed during the night.

To sum up a good advance of at least 500 yards, including two lines of Turkish trenches, has been made along a front of nearly 8 miles in the centre of our Southern section but we are back to our original right and left.

Notice.

We regret the delay in the re-appearance of the "Peninsula Press." In the interval news has accumulated which we are compelled to hold over for want of space.

Turkish Defeat on the Tigris.

London, June 6th.

General Nixon wires from Amara, on June 4th, as follows:-

"General Townsend, accompanied by Captain Nunn, R.N., and Sir Percy Cox, in a small gunboat flotilla received the surrender of the Governor of Amarah with some 30 officers and about 700 soldiers on June 3rd. Amara is now occupied by us in force. The captured troops comprise the advance guard of the Turkish forces retiring before us. The main body which was following was seen to disperse into the marshes. Our total captures up to date, including the above, amount to about 80 officers, 2,000 men, 7 field guns, 6 naval guns on gunboats, 12 large steel barges one large river steamer, a considerable number of rifles and ammunition of all sorts. Further surrenders are expected. Of six Germans with the Turks three are prisoners, two were killed by Arabs in the marshes, and the fate of the six is doubtful."

52

From wireless messages which suffered in transmission, we learn that towards the end of last month a combined naval and military force marched North of Korna, the traditional site of the Garden of Eden, to Ezra's tomb, on the Tigris. Our troops, some wading, others in boats, captured the enemy's position. The heights held by the Turks were carried by assault at noon, the enemy leaving many dead and wounded beside 150 prisoners. A further advance was made on June 1st when the Turks hastily evacuated their camp and retreated up the Tigris in steamers and boats, pursued by the British flotilla.

Note:- Amara is a thriving town on the Tigris about 100 miles south-east of Bagdad. It is a military post and the seat of a Turkish Governor. The population consists of Moslems, Sabaeans, or Baptists, Jews and Roman Catholics. Below Amara are the great marshes of the Tigris, where, in Spring, little is visible but reeds and sedges. The Beni Lam Arabs who live near give much trouble.

Zeppelin Raid on London.

The long threatened Zeppelin raid on London was made on the night of June 1st when 20 airships reached certain out-lying districts of the capital. The wireless message announcing the raid gives no details beyond the facts that 90 bombs, mostly incendiary, were dropped, that one man, one woman, one boy and one infant were killed, and that there were three fires. Much amusement has been caused in England by the German report that extensive damage was done by the raid.

Bombarding the Crown Prince's Quarters

Twenty-nine French aeroplanes bombarded the General Headquarters of the German Crown Prince on June 3rd. They dropped 178 bombs and several thousand darts. The machines were subjected to heavy fire but all returned unhurt.

Another Submarine Raid.

Another of our Submarines is making a daring and successful raid in the Sea of Marmora where she has sunk up to date, one Turkish gun boat, three transports, one ammunition ship and three supply ships, one of which was probably an ammunition ship, for when she was torpedoed there was a very heavy explosion.

United States Firm Attitude.

The text of the United States Note to Germany on the sinking of the Lusitania reveals a firmness of tone that was not manifest in the short wireless messages we have already published. With relentless logic and in uncompromising words, President Wilson rejects the pretension of Germany to be a law unto herself.

If, as Germans say, the security of their submarines is endangered by the laws of humanity and of nations, then not these laws but the submarines must go. The Government refuses to admit any restriction on the rights of United States citizens to travel in merchant ships of belligerent nations and will hold the German Government strictly to account for any infraction of these rights, whether it be intentional or accidental.

"It is manifest" says the Note "that submarines cannot be employed against a merchant ship without inevitable violations of the sacred principles of justice and humanity." In conclusion, it is added that "expressions of regret and offers of compensation for the destruction of neutral vessels sunk in error, while they may satisfy international engagements in cases where there has been no loss of life, will not justify or excuse a practice the natural and unavoidable effects of which is to subject neutral nations to new and immense risks."

The Imperial German Government need not hope that the United States Government will neglect to resort to any action necessary for the execution of its sacred duty which is to maintain the rights of the United States and its citizens and to safeguard the free exercise and enjoyment of those rights."

It is stated that the German Government has received an American unofficial suggestion that Germany should abandon submarine warfare in consideration of concessions which Great Britain will be asked to make.

The German reply to this suggestion is reported to be as follows:-

Germany is willing to examine all ships before deciding their fate, provided Great Britain agrees to admit into Germany not only foodstuffs but also copper, cotton, rubber, petroleum and other raw material not designed for the use of the German Army and Navy. Great Britain must further agree to keep all merchant ships unarmed and to forbid the ramming of submarines and the use of false flags.

In a word Germany asks us to give her the freedom of the sea and immunity for her submarines.

The New War Ministry.

The Coalition Government appointed to carry on the war consists of 48 members, of whom 26 are Liberal, 18 Unionist, 8 labour and 1 non-party.

Lord Kitchener.

The Most Noble Order of the Garter has been conferred on Lord Kitchener.

Italian Victories.

Rome, June 3rd.

Our troops continue to advance on the Tyrol front. We have occupied the important heights North of Aloconiz and the only Austrian fortress at Rovereto, which is on the main railway line between Verona and Trent.

Artillery engagements on the plateau are proceeding. Our infantry are establishing themselves on the front of the Austrian Province Carniole, whence Trieste is their objective. The enemy made five violent attacks and were defeated by our Alpine troops.

Recapture of Przemysl.

German wireless messages report the retaking of Przemysl, an important manufacturing town in Galicia, which the Russians besieged and captured from the Austrians some weeks ago. The Germans who have "big eyes," claim that in the month of May, the Austro-German Army on the Eastern front took 300,000 Russian prisoners, including

1,000 officers, 251 field guns and 408 machine guns!

They also report successful engagements 80 miles north-east and 40 miles south-east of Libau, on the Baltic sea, as well as fighting 11 miles east of Przemysl where the Russians are holding the heights of Myslatylze.

These German reports are dated the 3rd and 4th June.

Russian reports of June 2nd state that after several days preparations, the enemy attacked furiously the forts on the West and North of Przemysl and succeeded at 8 p.m. on May 30th, in entering fort 7, round which a desperate battle raged till two in the following afternoon, when the Austro-Germans were repulsed with enormous loss. Five hundred and ninety three survivors of those who entered the fort were made prisoners.

The Russians continue to be victorious on the river Switeza where they took 10,660 prisoners between the 28th and 30th of May. On the left bank of the Vistula, at 4 a.m. on the 31st ult., the enemy, covered by curtains of smoke of poisonous gases which were visible nineteen miles from the Russian rear attacked our position on the Byura, and Sawka rivers. The enemy was driven back.

Peninsula Press

No. 21   Thursday, JUNE 10th. 1915   Official News.

The Fall of Przemysl.

German wireless messages, describing the fall of Przemysl on June 4th, state that the two North forts and the intermediary fort were bombarded by heavy artillery from May 30th. On the evening of June 2nd the second position was stormed, and taken with heavy losses for the Russians.

The Germans marched into the city just as the last Russians were leaving. The Austrian forces which were attacking from the South followed immediately. The Russians retreated in good order, toward the East.

According to Russian prisoners the garrison was ordered to hold the fortress to the last man, but the effect of the heavy artillery fire was so terrible that 7,000 surrendered.

Russian despatches say that the forts of Przemysl could not be defended having been destroyed by the Austrians before they surrendered the city some weeks ago.

On the Italian Front.

Rome.

On the Trentino frontier, the Italians are advancing along both banks of the River Adige, which leads direct to Trent. The village of Ala was occupied, situated ten miles from Trentino. From the Asiago plateau, on the Italian side of the frontier, the Italian artillery bombarded Fort Luserna, which hoisted the white flag, whereupon another Austrian fort in the vicinity – Fort Belvedere – turned its guns on the Luserna. This double bombardment, from friend and foe, completely destroyed the fort. The Italian troops also occupied the important position of Amaspezza near Sloro; as well as the village of Vezzano.

We occupied the pass Tre Croci and the town and valley of Cortina Damiezzo in Cadore. The Austrians on the Friuli frontier have long been strengthening with numerous guns the position on the left bank of the Isonzo commanding the fords; they also strongly hold several points on the right bank covering the town of Gorizia. The heavy rains have transformed the rivers into torrents, but the Italians continue to advance most vigorously.

Bulgaria and the War.

Sofia, June 2nd

The Bulgarian Minister at Bukharest has arrived here to report on the situation in Romania, and to receive instructions regarding Bulgaria's attitude towards an eventual understanding with Romania who is reported to have made overtures with that object.

Rome, June 2nd

The Bulgarian Minister, who is pro-German, has been transferred from Rome to Berlin.

Pro-Italian demonstrations are reported from Sofia.

The ease with which France is bearing the heavy burden of the war is shown by the statement made by the Finance Minister on June 3rd. The sum which the Chamber of Deputies was asked to vote was £287,600,000.

Progress in France.

Paris.

To the North of Arras the battle continues, the British having the advantage. The French delivered several successful attacks on both sides of the road from Aix Norlette to Sauchez and captured wide ground in the wood to the East and South of Neuville Saint Vaast. They continued to progress, reaching the centre of village. The French have captured more trenches in the centre and South of the "Labyrinth" South-east of Neuville and have advanced appreciably. All German counter-attacks were repulsed. The French attacked the enemy's positions close to a Farm House on a front of 200 metres and captured two successive lines of trenches, taking some prisoners and machine guns.

After an effective bombardment the French delivered an attack to the North of the Aisne and East of Tracy-le-Mont, with important results.

On a front of one kilometre the French took at one rush two successive lines of trenches and several German fortified positions. Violent counter-attacks were repulsed by the French who took over 200 prisoners.

In Champagne near Beausejour the French have progressed.

The attempted bombardment of Verdun, reported on the 5th has not

58

been renewed. On the heights of the Meuse and in the Vosges there have been artillery engagements.

Rheims has again been bombarded by the Germans who directed their fire especially on the Cathedral.

Prisoners in Germany.

The German military authorities have decided to transfer 15,000 French prisoners from" most comfortable camps" to labour in moor camps. The selection will be made without reference to the social status of the prisoners.

The excuse for this new "frightfulness," according to German statements, is the fact that German prisoners of war taken by the French are sent to Africa "compelled to labour in a torrid climate." Yet the Germans pretend that all they are fighting for is "a place in the sun.'

Roumania's Impatience to Join the Allies.

The "Petit Journal's" Bukharest correspondent telegraphs:- The news from Rome has increased the impatience to end the negotiations which are in progress with Russia. The Roumanian Government, it is said, does not consider adequate the concessions relating to Bukowina and the South of Galicia. It demands, the prolongation of the line of the river Pruth in Russian territory, as there are more Roumanians in that region than Slavs. On the other hand, the Roumanian Government is disposed to diminish her claims in the Bonato, and recognises that the Serbian Capital, situated in a strategically difficult position, must in future be protected by wide surrounding zones.

Peninsula Press

No. 22   Friday, JUNE 11th. 1915   Official News.

"We are Afraid."

The following extracts from a copy of Army Orders found on a Turkish prisoner will be read with interest:-

"Para. 11. A great deal of ammunition is being expended. This is a proof that while the enemy is losing the terror we at first instilled in him, we ourselves are afraid.

Para. 12. All Company Captains will be made responsible for stopping the waste of material, and the commanders of the fire trenches are to pay strict attention to it. The names of those who offend and harm their country's interest are to be sent here.

To C.C.'s 1st and 2nd Coys. 1st Battalion 25th Regiment in the left zone of Krithia Valley."

The Question of Munitions.

London.

At a meeting at Manchester of engineering employers and Trade Union representatives Mr. Lloyd George said the issue of the war now depended on the workshops. The Russians had suffered a severe set back in Galicia and the great German success was due entirely to their overwhelming superiority in shot and shell equipment.

Two-hundred thousand shells were concentrated on the heads of the gallant Russians in a single hour. Had we been able to apply the same process to the Germans they would have been expelled from France; we should already have entered Germany and the end of the war would have been in view. We now had more than plenty of men for the equipment available and more would respond to the call, but we wanted workshops to provide power to break a way through. He was confident that what French engineers had accomplished, British could also. The recent French victories were largely attributable to private workshops in France.

Mr. Lloyd George appealed for the help of all. He had not come to brandish great powers under the Defence of the Realm Act but these would be most useful in enabling them to organise quickly and get rid of unnecessary difficulties. It was impossible in war time to wait for every unreasonable man to become reasonable.

Austria Renews Her Pledge.

German wireless messages describes the military and political situation in Austria-Hungary as "exceedingly good." The Dual Monarchy, say the Vienna newspapers, "will faithfully continue the war until an honourable and lasting peace has been secured for Austria-Hungary and her Allies.''

Italian Advance in Austria.

Rome, June 9th.

The Italian Army continues to advance in Austrian territory and meets with feeble resistance. Two great movements are developing:- we are hammering at the defences on the plateau between Lavrone and Foloaria, South-east of Trent and are advancing along the line of the Isonzo which flows into the Gulf of Trieste. We have reached this important river and are making bridge heads preparatory to crossing.

Progress in France.

Paris, June 9th.

North of Arras there has been very heavy fighting. The converging attacks of the French on "The Labyrinth," South East of Neuville, are progressing. All German counter-attacks have been repulsed. To the South East of Hebuterne our attacks were completely successful. We have taken two German lines, capturing 400 prisoners, including 7 officers, and a large number of machine guns.

The enemy has made desperate efforts to retake the two lines of trenches captured yesterday North of the Aisne; they brought up reinforcements in motor cars from a distance of 50 miles. In spite of this, the Germans were utterly defeated and left 2,000 dead on the field. We took 200 prisoners and 6 machine guns.

On the British Front.

London, June 9th.

Field-Martial Sir John French reports that the situation on the British front is unchanged. The artillery is less active. We brought down two German aeroplanes, one by gun fire, the other in an aerial engagement with a British aviator.

Germans Massing on the Yser.

Amsterdam, June 9th.

The frontier between Belgium and Holland been been closed in consequence of the enormous movement of German troops to the Yser. Barbed electric wire has been put along the whole frontier.

The German Reply to America.

Intense disappointment is expressed at Germany's answer to the United States note on the Sinking of the "Lusitania," especially at the failure to mention President Wilson's demands. There is little concealment anywhere that the situation is grave.

The "New York 'Herald'" says that in the case of "Germany versus civilization" the United States holds a brief for civilization. Germany must respect the rights of non-combatants. The United States will not be diverted from her duty by quibbling.

The "World" says that the answer is worse than evasive. It is insincere and even petti-fogging.

The "Journal" says that Germany contends that the "Lusitania" was a warship in the same way as Louvain University and Rheims Cathedral were fortifications.

Other newspapers say the reply is an amazing insult and that nothing is left but to sever diplomatic relations.

A Quiet Meeting of Parliament.

London.

There was nothing very dramatic in the first assembly of the coalition Parliament on the 3rd inst. Many new Ministers were absent pending the passage of the bill abolishing the necessity for re-election. Nevertheless there was much novelty in seeing Liberals and Unionists on the same benches and ex-ministers who were Privy Councillors occupying the Opposition bench.

Peninsula Press

No. 23   Saturday, JUNE 12th. 1915   Official News.

Germany and the United States.
Mr. Bryan Resigns.

New York, June 11th.

Mr. Bryan, Secretary of State, has resigned. He is at variance with the Cabinet as to the attitude that ought to be taken toward German defiancy of the laws of humanity. Mr. Bryan wants arbitration. The President wants action.

A wireless message from New York says, great astonishment was manifested in Washington in consequence of Mr. Bryan's resignation, when it became known that the note to Germany was written in a friendly tone and in no wise closed the door to a peaceful solution.

Washington, June 11th.

President Wilson and Mr. Bryan differ on two points.

Mr. Bryan wishes the question of submarine attacks to be investigated by an International Commission under the Arbitration Treaty negotiated by the United States with thirty countries, although Germany is not a signatory of the Treaty.

Mr. Bryan also maintains that Americans have no rights over an Imperial State if they travel in the war zone after the German warning!

It is understood that the whole Cabinet supports President Wilson's view:- that arbitration is impossible unless Germany previously agrees to discontinue the indiscriminate destruction of merchantmen.

Mr. Lancing has been appointed Interim Secretary of State.

German Submarine Sunk

London, June 10th.

Mr. Balfour, First Lord of the Admiralty, announced in the House of Commons that another German submarine has been sunk. Six officers and twenty-one men were captured.

£30 a Second.

Mr. Acland, Financial Secretary to the treasury, speaking in London, stated that the Government were authorising the spending of taxpayers' money at the rate of £30 a second.

Enemy Property in the United Kingdom

Lord Charles Beresford, addressing a meeting in Chelsea, said that military prisoners in Germany were being slowly murdered by starvation and foul treatment. At the end of the war those responsible would be got hold of, and he hoped every one of them no matter how exalted and powerful their position, would be hung up on the scene of their barbarities. (Loud cheers). He made three proposals. The first was that every penny belonging to a German in the British Empire should be confiscated. (Cheers). He was informed on good authority that there was German property to the value of £84,600,000 in this kingdom and £500,000,000 in the Empire as a whole. Let us seize all we can now, and make the Germans pay up also at the end of the war. His second proposal was the internment of all wealthy Germans in this country. (Cheers). He would keep these people behind barbed wire until our men in Germany were treated as honourable prisoners of war. His third proposal was the confiscation of all the German mercantile ships in the Empire. (Cheers).

British Casualties.

London, June 10th.

Mr. Asquith informed the House of Commons that the British Casualties in Flanders and the Dardanelles up to the end of May, were:- Killed 3337 Officers; 47,015 men - Wounded 6,498 officers, 147,472 men. Missing 1,180 officers, 52,617 men.

Italian Advance.

Rome, June 11th

Operations continues with the object of dislodging the Austrians from their position on the right bank of the Isonzo and establishing bridgeheads. The enemy favoured by the nature of the ground, resisted stubbornly and strengthened their fortifications. 500 Austrian prisoners were taken. Floods have broken the bridges over the Isonzo.

Advice to an Ally.

London.

Bulgaria, and Roumania have commenced negotiation with a, view to joining the Allies. The Roumanian Premier's in active communication with the Entente Powers. Relations between Austria-Hungary and Roumania are daily becoming more strained. The "Frankfurt Gazette" willing to be generous at other people's expense, advises the Austrian

Government to accede to Roumania's "just demands" for territory. The Romanian Press is full of articles urging the Government to taken advantage of the present opportunity.

There are 3,000,000 Roumanians in Hungary, the majority of whom are in Transylvania, and 300,000 in the little Duchy of Bukovina which is Austrian Crown property and lies between Galicia and the North West frontier of Roumania. The "manifest destiny" of Roumania, is to bring under her rule the greater part of the Roumania race outside her borders. Russia is already over-running Bukovino and sooner or later will penetrate into Transylvania. If Roumania does not take up arms against Austria within the next few weeks she will have resigned herself to the sacrifice of her ambitions.

Peninsula Press

No. 24   Sunday, JUNE 13th. 1915   Official News.

German Wiles and the Greek Elections.

When your enemy begins to spread political falsehoods broadcast you may be sure he is feeling the pinch somewhere. Germans have always been clumsy amateurs in diplomacy, and their latest effort shows how little they have learned from their failures.

The activity of the German wireless service has been remarkable during the last few days. We have just received a despatch the purpose of which is to sow dissension among their enemies. So obvious is its mendacity; so disingenuous are its arguments that not even a child could be deceived.

We are told, for example, that the Russians, who have checked the Austro-German advance in Galicia, are preparing to sue for peace. The authority for this statement is the "Vossicbe Zeitung," which has long been distinguished for the fertility and audacity of its inventions. All party leaders of the Duma met on Saturday and unanimously resolved to petition the Government to appoint a Coalition Cabinet. This proposal to follow the prudent example of Great Britain is interpreted by the German "reptile press" as having for its main object "the downfall of Goremykin's Ministry which advocates unceasing war." To bolster up this absurd conclusion, the "Vossiche Zeitung" reports that next day M. Goremykin, President of the Council, General Sukhomlinof, Minister of War, M. Bark, Minister of Finance, and Count de Fiedericks, Minister of Imperial Household, had audience of the Czar and "two hours excited discussion" while M. Rodshanko, President of the Duma, "visited the Grand Duke Nicholas at Army Headquarters and later the Grand Duke sent a long private letter to the Czar."

Having disposed of Russia, the German official report turns its attention to Greece, keeping in view, we may be sure, the general election which takes place to-day. The Greeks are informed that the Chief of their General Staff is of opinion that "the ultimate victory of the Central European Powers over all enemies is more assured than ever." This it is added, "was predicted by him from the outset, without finding credit."

Servia is selected as the next victim. This unhappy country which has suffered so much and so long from the intrigues and ambitions of

Austria, is now asked to believe that Italy, not Austria, is her real enemy. "Austro-Hungary," says the German wireless report, quoting from the "Munich Post," "is hostile not toward Servia, but toward the party of assassins and the degenerate reigning family. A happy future is assured to Servia if she will liberate herself from the corrupt reigning clique, restore Macedonia to Bulgaria and accept Albania from the Bulgarians!" Servia, we are informed, "is utterly dissatisfied with the attitude of the Allies who have sacrificed Servian interests. Italy, instead of creating a diversion in favour of Servia by entering Bosnia invades Albania with all her available troops and puts before her Allies the unpleasant task of expelling her from that country!"

Next comes Holland whose sympathies with Germany have been alienated by the fate of Belgium. The German wireless tells us that with one exception, the Dutch newspapers brand the action of Italy as "highway robbery."

The United States, having decided that action, and not apologies and excuses, is demanded by the sinking of the "Lusitania," does not escape the universal censury. A Stockholm newspaper is summoned to the aid of the Kaiser's Government and lectures the citizens of the Republic in this fashion:- "Violent language against Germany on the "Lusitania." question is improper for a country partaking of the crime. By permitting its own citizens to shield ammunition transports, America has lost the moral right to complain. America is unable to hurt Germany more than she has done already by the delivery of munitions of war to the Allies. President Wilson's attitude means vigorous partizanship for England against Germany. He is doing nothing to frustrate England's starvation policy."

With the guilessness that characterises them in diplomacy, the Germans close their report by disputing the prophecy that "starvation may compel Germany to beg for mercy." Having appealed to the United States to save them from starvation at the hands of Great Britain, and having attempted to justify piracy and the murder of civilians at sea by the plea of threatened starvation, the German Government assure the whole world that "the condition of their country is one of plenty and that meat, flour, potatoes and all the necessities of life are in abundance."

American Note to Germany.

New York, June 12th.
Mr. Gerald, United States Ambassador, delivered at the Foreign Office on Friday, the second American note on the sinking of the "Lusitania."

This note, which insists that Germany shall cease her acts of piracy and murder of civilians on the high seas, led to the resignation of Mr. Bryan, Secretary of State, as announced in yesterday's "Peninsular Press."

Austrian Defeat.

Rome, June 11th.

The Austrians lost 200 killed, 400 wounded and 220 prisoners in the fighting on the 7th and 8th inst., for possession of Foiekofel on the Carnia frontier. On the night of the 9th, the Austrians re-attacked the position to which they attach great importance, but were repulsed with heavy losses. Severe fighting continues along the river Isonzo, the enemy resisting stubbornly. We occupied the citadel on the heights dominating Monfalcone, North of the Gulf of Trieste where we took 500 prisoners.

Russian Successes

Amsterdam, June, 11th.

The German official report to-night admits Russian successes in the North and South. Bringing up reinforcements from the North-east, the Russians checked the enemy's encircling movement on Dubissa, compelling the Germans to retreat to a new line. Russian reinforcements are advancing from the South and South-east of Lemberg.

Desperate Fighting in France.

Paris, June 11th.

We have captured the village of Neuville after most desperate hand-to hand and house-to-house fighting. The Germans retired, abandoning a field gun, several machine guns and much material. One thousand German dead were counted. The enemy's attack on Beausejour in Champagne was repulsed. Many German dead were left on the field.

Peninsula Press

No. 25   Monday, JUNE 14th. 1915   Official News.

The Munitions Question

London

Mr Lloyd George asked the Lancashire factories to supply a quarter of a million explosive shells per month. The workmen have promised to supply a million. Addressing the meeting in Manchester, Mr. Lloyd George said that the issue and perils were great and that nothing could pull us through but the united efforts of every man in the Empire. Never before had our troops shown greater courage and endurance, and it would be horrible to think that they should fail owing to our neglect.

Within four hours provisional arrangements were made in Manchester for the production of war material. It is expected that within a month all the large firms, and in time all engineering firms in Lancashire, will be making shells by day and night. The leaders of the workers state that the men will most willingly devote their entire energies and place them at the disposal of the firms. They are anxious to have the war service badge. Mr Appleton, Secretary of the Federation of Trade Unions, said that all welcomed the definiteness of Mr. Lloyd George's speech and regretted it was not made eight months ago.

British Chemical Shells

In the House of Lords the other day Lord Kitchener described the effects of the poisonous gases used by the Germans, and said that it would be necessary to take steps in order to avoid a great disaster. A telegram from London informs us that Sir T. Brunner has publicly announced that the great chemical works of Brunner, Mond and Company have undertaken to make chemicals for shells.

Invasion of Albania

Rome, June 12th

Servian and Montenegrin troops have occupied ten towns in Albania including Tilano. The fall of Durazzo in now expected.

Roumania Restless

Bucharest, June 6th

There was a great demonstration here today, when 30,000 persons sang the Marseillaise and the Garibaldian hymn. They marched to the Italian

Legation, where the speakers said they hoped Roumania would follow the example of her Latin sister, Italy, in order to realise the national ideal.

A meeting of the Conservative party denounced the Germanophile party's attitude and its leader, Marghiloman, who left the meeting. It is expected that Lahovarif, who is a supporter of the Triple Entante, will be elected leader.

London, June 6th

The Bucharest correspondent of the "Berliner Tagblatt" telegraphs to his paper in a very pessimistic strain regarding the attitude of Bulgaria and Roumania towards Germany and Austria.

Americans Insulted in Germany

Many Americans have arrived in Switzerland from Germany. It is stated that Americans are now openly insulted in Germany. The American colony in Berlin have been warned unofficially that it would be well to hold themselves in readiness to leave the country.

United States and Submarine Policy

Washington, June 12th

The second American note delivered on Friday to the German Government states that, the delimitation of the war zone may operate as an abbreviation of American rights. The United States Government expects Germany to adopt measures to respect and safeguard American lives and ships. (Wireless).

Russians Drive the Enemy Across the Dneister

Petrograd, June 12th

Russian troops have inflicted a serious check on the Germans on the Dneister. The enemy's forces crossed the river near Zuravno, between Premysl and Stanslan, where the Russians took the offensive and drove them back. (Wireless).

Further Progress in France

Paris, June 12th

The French official report announces further successes in the labyrinth, South-east of Neuville. We drove the enemy back East of the labyrinth, near the high road to Arras and Lille.

Bulgaria and Turkey

German newspapers are betraying uneasiness as to the attitude of Bulgaria towards Turkey. The "Koenische Zeitung's" Sofia correspondent telegraphs that a considerable stir is now apparent throughout Bulgaria. In political circles there seems to be a desire to demand a rectification of the southern frontier, namely a straight line from Enos to Media. If this demand is refused a return to the frontier line stretching to the river Maritza is desired.

The same journal states that last Saturday the Allies despatched a note to the Bulgarian Government, the contents of which have given great satisfaction to Bulgaria. This statement is confirmed by the "Cologne Gazette" which adds that there are great movements of troops in Bulgaria.

Mr Asquith at the Front

Mr Asquith, while on a visit to the front was much amused at the sight of "Tommies" waiting their turn for a warm bath in a brewery. They were shouting and plunging into the steaming tubs like schoolboys. Recognising the visitor, the men jumped out of their baths and surrounded him giving cheer after cheer. Mr Asquith was visibly moved by their enthusiasm, though the humour of the situation changed his mood to one of hearty laughter, in which all the men joined. During his visit to the hospitals he was struck by the astonishing spirit of optimism which prevailed.

German Socialists Discontented

London, June 7th

A report of a meeting in the Reichstag has leaked out at which German Socialists complained of the dearness of food and the badness of bread, although millers were earning huge dividends. The prohibition of protest meetings and he muzzling of the press were also denounced as was the hard treatment meted out to miners, who were sent to the trenches if they complain of low wages. One speaker said that if the workmen submitted to such gross injustice they could not be human beings.

Peninsula Press

No. 26   Tuesday, JUNE 15th. 1915   Official News.

Successful Night Operation.

Since our success of the 4th, which has much impressed the Turks, Divisional Generals have been impressing on their Brigades that trench warfare can be made offensive, and the offensive spirit maintained even when it was not possible - for various reasons - to make any general advance.

On the night of June 11th and 12th, a successful night operation was carried out by two regiments of the 87th Brigade, who made a simultaneous attack on an advanced Turkish trench from two sides. The assaulting party of one regiment gained the trench, but were bombed out of it. It was taken a second time but again our troops had to retire. At two o'clock in the morning of the 12th, having sent for a fresh supply of bombs from the neighbouring Brigade, a third assault was made, this time successfully. These assaults were led by two fine young officers, brothers, of the name of Inglis. At the same time the assaulting party of the Second Regiment rushed a sniper's post and gained a Turkish communicating trench, pushing on to within 30 yards of the advanced post captured by the First Regiment. These two posts are now established and connected by a trench. The following morning a counter-attack was made by the Turks, 50 of them rushing forward with bombs. This party came under the machine-gun fire of the Naval Motor Machine-gun Squadron and were practically wiped out, at least 30 dead being visible close in front of our trenches. The following night, with a view to advancing our left flank trenches into line with the advanced post captured the previous evening, an officer's patrol went out by night to the position reached on the 4th June by the 14th Sikhs. They found it occupied by two Turks only, and the party returned bringing with them a maxim gun belonging to the 14th Sikhs which had been abandoned on the 4th June when the machine-gun detachment were annihilated. They also brought in 3,000 rounds of ammunition.

Luxury in German Trenches.

Some of the German trenches in front of our line from Festubert to Ricbebourg l'Avoue were wonderful constructions in concrete. They were fitted with electric light and fans, and with mechanism worked by electric power for draining them. The necessary power was obtained from electric plant at the coal mines in the La Bassee area. In one trench our men profited for several hours by the electric light, but eventually the enemy severed the wires and so cut off the current. Most of the trenches were provided with machines guns embedded in cement, in concrete casemates.

Hand Grenade Fighting.

Paris, June 14th

The French official report says:-

In the region North of Arras there has been, a heavy artillery engagement. On the plateau of Lorretta, the Germans along the whole section Aix Noullette-Ecurie have tried by a violent bombardment to prevent the organisation of the positions captured by us. Our artillery replied against the trenches and German batteries. After severe fighting with hand grenades we captured the station of Sauchez, East of Labyrinthe. In spite of violent German efforts we have maintained all recently gained positions near the farm of Tout Vent, South-East of Hebuterne. This morning the Germans made a counter-attack which was easily repulsed.

Earmarking Enemy Assets.

It is estimated that in the United Kingdom there is German property estimated at £84,000,000. Mr. Lloyd George was asked in the House of Commons whether legislation would be introduced to prevent the payment of money to any enemy country until such enemy country has given guarantees for the payment of its debts to England. Mr. Lloyd George replied that it is the intention of the Government to prevent German and other hostile country's assets from leaving England until proper provision is made for securing corresponding British assets now in the hands of the enemy.

"Story of a Brilliant Irishwoman."

The "Continental Times" a German newspaper publishes a "vivid account of a visit to a camp of Irish prisoners by a brilliant Irish-woman" whose name is given as "M. Leonard Marshall." The camp is at Limburg and the writer visited it on St. Patrick's Day, with the help of "kind German friends" and the "ever gracious" military authorities.

She attended high Mass, which was said by "the chaplain Father Crotty [sic] - an Irish Dominican priest sent over specially from Rome by his Holiness the Pope." She writes:-

"More than 2,000 Irishmen are on the field, formed into a square, rows upon rows of Irish faces; touzled heads of fiery red hair, snub noses, and eyes of violet blue. Refined, clear cut features bearing the stamp of race – dark hair and eyes as grey as the morning skies.

From the highest to the lowest I love them all. The hot-headed, warm-hearted Irish!" She describes Sir Roger Casement as "our hero and our hope," and also thinks highly of the Kaiser, of whom, indeed, she "predicted year's ago that one day the world would feel his greatness." She told the French prisoners in the camp "how it pained her to see the French fighting for the hereditary foes of their race! She concludes with the remark:-

"When Redmond and his traitor crew are wiped off the earth, mayhap we shall be victoriously singing "Deutschland uber Alles," on free Irish soil."

PENINSULA PRESS,

| No. 26 | TUESDAY, JUNE 15th, 1915. | Official News. |

Successful Night Operation.

Since our success of the 4th, which has much impressed the Turks, Divisional Generals have been impressing on their Brigades that trench warfare can be made offensive, and the offensive spirit maintained even when it was not possible —for various reasons—to make any general advance.

On the night of June, 11th and 12th, a successful night operation was carried out by two regiments of the 87th Brigade, who made a simultaneous attack on an advanced Turkish trench from two sides. The assaulting party of one regiment gained the trench, but were bombed out of it. It was taken a second time but again our troops had to retire. At two o'clock in the morning of the 12th, having sent for a fresh supply of bombs from the neighbouring Brigade, a third assault was made, this time successfully. These assaults were led by two fine young officers, brothers, of the name of Inglis. At the same time the assaulting party of the Second Regiment rushed a sniper's post and gained a Turkish communicating trench, pushing on to within 30 yards of the advanced post captured by the First Regiment. These two posts are now established and connected by a trench. The following morning a counter-attack was made by the Turks, 50 of them rushing forward with bombs. This party came under the machine-gun fire of the Naval Motor Machine-gun Squadron and were practically wiped out, at least 30 dead being visible close in front of our trenches. The following night, with a view to advancing our left flank trenches into line with the advanced post captured the previous evening, an officer's patrol went out by night to the position reached on the 4th June by the 14th Sikhs. They found it occupied by two Turks only, and the party returned bringing with them a maxim gun belonging to the 14th Sikhs which had been abandoned on the 4th June when the machine-gun detachment were annihilated. They also brought in 3,000 rounds of ammunition.

Luxury in German Trenches.

Some of the German trenches in front of our line from Festubert to Richebourg l'Avoue were wonderful constructions in concrete. They were fitted with electric light and fans, and with mechanism worked by electric power for draining them. The necessary power was obtained from electric plant at the coal mines in the La Bassee area. In one trench our men profited for several hours by the electric light, but eventually the enemy severed the wires and so cut off the current. Most of the trenches were provided with machines guns embedded in cement, in concrete casemates.

Hand Grenade Fighting.

Paris June, 14th
The French official report says :—
In the region North of Arras there has been a heavy artillery engagement. On the plateau of Lorrette, the Germans along the whole section Aix Noullette-Ecurie have tried by a violent bombardment to prevent the payment of money the positions captured by us. Our artillery replied against the trenches and German batteries. After severe fighting with hand grenades we captured the station of Souchez, East of Labyrinthe. In spite of violent German efforts we have maintained all recently gained positions near the farm of Tout Vent, South-East of Hebuterne. This morning the Germans made a counter-attack which was easily repulsed.

Earmarking Enemy Assets.

It is estimated that in the United Kingdom there is German property estimated at £84,000,000. Mr. Lloyd George was asked in the House of Commons whether legislation would be introduced to prevent the payment of money to any enemy country until such enemy country has given guarantees for the payment of its debts to England. Mr. Lloyd George replied that it is the intention of the Government to prevent German and other hostile country's assets from leaving England until proper provision is made for securing corresponding British assets now in the hands of the enemy.

"Story of a Brilliant Irishwoman."

The "Continental Times" a German newspaper publishes a "vivid account of a visit to a camp of Irish prisoners by a brilliant Irishwoman" whose name is given as "M. Leonard Marshall." The camp is at Limburg and the writer visited it on St. Patrick's Day, with the help of "kind German friends" and the "ever gracious" military authorities.

She attended high Mass, which was said by "the chaplain Father Crotty (sic)—an Irish Dominican priest sent over specially from Rome by his Holiness the Pope." She writes:—

"More than 2,000 Irishmen are on the field, formed into a square, rows upon rows of Irish faces; tousled heads of fiery red hair, snub noses, and eyes of violet blue. Refined, clear cut features bearing the stamp of race—dark hair and eyes as grey as the morning skies. From the highest to the lowest I love them all. The hot-headed, warm-hearted Irish!" She describes Sir Roger Casement as "our hero and our hope," and also thinks highly of the Kaiser, of whom, indeed, she "predicted years ago that one day the world would feel his greatness." She told the French prisoners in the camp "how it pained her to see the French fighting for the hereditary foes of their race! She concludes with the remark:—

"When Redmond and his traitor crew are wiped off the earth, mayhap we shall be victoriously singing 'Deutschland uber Alles,' on free Irish soil."

R.E. Printing Section, G.H.Q., M.E.F.

Peninsula Press

No. 27   Wednesday, JUNE 16th. 1915   Official News.

M. Venizelos Heads the Poll.

(From our Special Correspondent.)

Panagbia, Tuesday.

The final returns of the Greek elections have not yet reached the capital of the island of Imbros. From telegrams already received it is certain, however, that M. Venizelos will return to power with a large majority.

M. Venizelos recently left Greece and became a voluntary exile in order that he might not embarrass his successor in the Government. His proposal to make terms with Bulgaria as a preliminary step toward. intervention in the war met with opposition from King Constantine. M. Venizelos thereupon resigned. The electors have given him an emphatic recall and have endorsed his policy of intervention.

The American Note.

A German wireless message received yesterday profess general satisfaction with the American Note on the sinking of the "Lusitania," And the acts of piracy committed by German submarines. "It is not an ultimatum," says the message, "as was predicted by British newspapers. On the contrary, it leaves open the way to friendly discussion and an understanding satisfactory to both sides."

German newspapers are reported to be especially pleased with President Wilson's offer to meditate between Germany and Great Britain.

Bulgaria Protests.

London, June 7th.

The Bulgarian Government has seized at Sofia some German railway trucks which appeared to be empty, but were found to contain contraband of war which was being sent to Turkey.

Bulgaria has protested in Constantinople against the act of the Turkish authorities, who have seized Bulgarian goods in the provinces.

Three German Warships Damaged.

Petrograd June 7th.

Russian submarines reported the approach of German destroyers and battleships in the Gulf of Riga. The Germans retired on the advance of the Russian fleet. German hydro-planes afterwards made an abortive attack and were driven off by Russian artillery. The German fleet again approached Russian shores yesterday, and was attacked by submarines. The Russians also successfully laid mines in the route of the enemy. Three German warships are known to have been sunk or damaged. An enemy submarine sank the transport "Yenissei"; thirty two of the crew were saved.

Anglo-Italian Agreement.

London.

Mr. McKenna and the Italian Minister of Finance have discussed proposals for financial co-operation. The conference disclosed the complete agreement of the two Governments and their resolution to co-operate in the use of financial resources in the same ungrudging spirit as in the use of the naval and military forces.

"We Want to go Home."

That some of the enemy are not enjoying themselves in Flanders is shown by the following message which was recently flung into our trenches:- "We are too few to attack, too many to retire, and too proud to surrender: but we all want to go home."

The Only Way.
A Bishop's Warning.

The Bishop of Pretoria, after spending a month at the front in France and Flanders writes on May 25th; "It was the most glorious month I have ever spent, and I want, if I can, to pass on to others a few of the impressions which were burnt into my soul during that time-for the days are crititical. I have never doubted that the spirit of our troops was as fine as men told us it was, but I never realised how fine it was until I lived in it and with it. It beggers description: it is amazing. It is all the more so when you realise, as you do when you are up at the front, that this spirit is there in spite of the fact that the men who show it feel it in their bones that somehow the nation is not backing them as the nation could and should. That, I am convinced, is the feeling right through the Army in France and Flanders; and the reason is not far to seek.

After recording some of his impressions, Dr. Furse, puts this question: "Is this new Government going to tackle this business on the same ridiculous principles of voluntary service as heretofore, or in the only way in which it can be tackled with any hope of ultimate success? Is it going to tell the nation at once that we can't win this war and shall uselessly sacrifice thousands of lives, unless the Government has the power given to it to call upon the services of every single man, woman and child, if need be, for whatever each individual is most capable of doing directly or indirectly for the one object before us-the smashing of the enemy? The men at the front are waiting for the answer, and so are thousands of men and women here at home."

The Bishop concludes his stirring appeal to the conscience of the Government and the people in these words:- "The nation will welcome national service because the temper of the nation is different from what it was. Recent events have clearly shown, even to the most phlegmatic, that we are in a perfectly real sense up against the Devil incarnate. What else is it when we are fighting against an enemy who will stop at nothing, however mean and cruel, and disgusting; an enemy who will use gas, sink Lusitanias, put arsenic in running streams, and sow disease? Mere abuse won't tame this Devil or drive him out, but a nation serving will. National Service will be welcomed once the nation learns the truth that thousands of the finest and most gallant lives that the Empire has ever produced are being thrown away because the nation has not yet realized that it is at war.

There is only one way to make the nation realize this fact, and that is by bringing every member of it under the direct orders of the State for one purpose and one purpose only. Nothing else matters to day."

Exploding a Zeppelin.

London.

Flight Lieutenant R. Werneford attacked a Zeppelin at 3 o'clock on the morning of the 7th inst., between Ghent and Brussels. From a height of 6,000 feet be dropped six bombs. The Zeppelin exploded and fell to the ground, where it burned for a considerable time. The force of the explosion caused the monoplane to turn turtle but the pilot succeeded in righting his machine. He had to make a forced landing in the enemy's country, but was able to re-start his engine and returned safely.

Peninsula Press

No. 28   Thursday, JUNE 17th. 1915   Official News.

Honour for General D'Amade.

General d'Amade, who was till recently in command of the French Expeditionary Force in the East, is mentioned in Army Orders for his dis-embarkation of troops at Kum Kale and at Sedd-el-Babr in the teeth of a strongly entrenched enemy greatly superior in numbers and equipped with formidable artillery. He succeeded, the order states, in solidly establishing his forces on the southern portion of Gallipoli only as a result of repeated attacks, in which be personally took the most brilliant part. Such a result obtained with young troops, most of whom had never seen fire, was due to his lofty conception of duty and to his personal ascendancy over his men, to whom he communicated his tenacity and indomitable energy.

(Morning Post. Paris Correspondent, May 30th.)

Continued Progress in France.

Paris, June 16th.

The French official report says;-

In the secticn North of Arras during Sunday night the French repulsed several German attacks on the trenches and strengthened the captured positions East of Lorette. On tbe right of these positions we have advanced about 160 yards. South of the Labyrinth the fight in this section has been continuous. South-east of Hebuterne the French have stopped a counter-attack with artillery fire. This attack was followed by a violent bombardment in the region of Quennivieres Farm. The French have advanced slightly and inflicted serious losses on the enemy. The artillery fight has been violent and a German attack on the positions captured on June 6th, was completely repulsed. A long range German gun fired on Compiegne but did no damage of any sort. In Lorraine the French have advanced their line in front of the Forest of Barroy.

Mr. Bryan's Conscience

Mr. Bryan, who resigned his position as Secretary of State owing to differences with the Cabinet over the diplomatic Note to Germany on the Sinking of the "Lusitania," wrote to President Wilson:-

"Obedient to your sense of duty and actuated by the highest motives, you have prepared for transmission to Germany a note in which I cannot join· without violating my duty to the Country. The issue involved is so momentous that my remaining in the Cabinet will be as unfair to you as to the cause nearest to my heart, namely, the prevention of war."

President Wilson replied deploring the resignation which he accepts with feelings of personal sorrow only because Mr. Bryan insists upon it. President Wilson dwells on the delightful association with Mr. Bryan for the past two years during which their judgments had agreed until now, and says "even now we are not separated in object but only in methods.'

The "Breslau" Damaged.

It is officially reported from Petrograd, on the 18th inst., that two Russian destroyers engaged the Turkish cruiser "Breslau" near the Bosphorus and severely damaged her. On the same day the Turks claim that their cruiser "Midilli" sank a Russian destroyer in the Black Sea.

Bomb Throwing Competition.

The following is the programme of a competition at Anzac:-
Commencing at 3 p.m.
JUDGES:- Major Row, Major Cribb, Capt. Griffiths.
TIMEKEEPERS:- Capt. Jervis, Lieut. Robertson, Lieut. Mead.
CONDITIONS:- Each company will enter 8 teams of 3 men. The two trained N.C.O.s of each company to take 4 teams each and to act as observers with periscopes.
1st PRACTICE.
2 Jam Tin Bombs - 5 second fuse.
2nd PRACTICE.
2 Percussion Bombs.
3rd PRACTICE.
1 Gun Cotton Bomb (Lothiniere) 6 sec. fuse.
All competitors will throw from the trench

POINTS:- Hits (i.e. inside enemy's trench). 2 points for each direct hit, 1 point for each hit inside a space of 3ft. either in front or rear of enemy's trench.
EXPOSURE:- Judges will rule out of action any thrower exposing any part of head or body. Teams completing practice with absolutely no exposure will have 1 point added to total score.
TIME:- Timekeepers will stand in rear of each thrower and record any bomb thrown after "fuse time" has elapsed ruling out of action 2 men for every bomb so thrown.
TRAJECTORY:- In practice No. 2 the Judges will, at their discretion, award points for trajectory.
PRIZES:- 1st Prize. 20 packets of cigarettes and 1 tin Marmalade; 2nd Prize. 16 packets cigarettes and 1 tin Marmalade; 3rd Prize. 12 packets cigarettes.

Mexican Anarchy.

Mexico is almost forgotten in the great war, but it is still seeking trouble. President Wilson has issued a manifesto declaring that the United States cannot punish the anarchical conditions in Mexico to continue indefinitely. She calls upon the faction leaders in Mexico to unite and organise a Government, otherwise the United States will intervene.

PENINSULA PRESS.

No. 28　　　　THURSDAY, JUNE 17th, 1915.　　　　Official News.

Honour for General D'Amade.

General d'Amade, who was till recently in command of the French Expeditionary Force in the East, is mentioned in Army Orders for his dis-embarkation of troops at Kum Kale and at Sedd-el-Bahr in the teeth of a strongly-entrenched enemy greatly superior in numbers and equipped with formidable artillery. He succeeded, the order states, in solidly establishing his forces on the southern portion of Gallipoli only as a result of repeated attacks, in which he personally took the most brilliant part. Such a result obtained with young troops, most of whom had never seen fire, was due to his lofty conception of duty and to his personal ascendency over his men, to whom he communicated his tenacity and indomitable energy.

(Morning Post. Paris Correspondent, May 30th.)

Continued Progress in France.

Paris, June 16th.

The French official report says:—

In the section North of Arras during Sunday night the French repulsed several German attacks on the trenches and strengthened the captured positions East of Lorette. On the right of these positions we have advanced about 100 yards. South of the Labyrinth the fight in this section has been continuous. South-east of Hebuterne the French have stopped a counter-attack with artillery fire. This attack was followed by a violent bombardment in the region of Quennivieres Farm. The French have advanced slightly and inflicted serious losses on the enemy. The artillery fight has been violent and a German attack on the positions captured on June 6th, was completely repulsed. A long range German gun fired on Compiegne but did no damage of any sort. In Lorraine the French have advanced their line in front of the Forest of Barroy.

Mr. Bryan's Conscience.

Mr. Bryan, who resigned his position as Secretary of State owing to differences with the Cabinet over the diplomatic Note to Germany on the Sinking of the "Lusitania," wrote to President Wilson :—

"Obedient to your sense of duty and actuated by the highest motives, you have prepared for transmission to Germany a note in which I cannot join without violating my duty to the Country. The issue involved is so momentous that my remaining in the Cabinet will be as unfair to you as to the cause nearest to my heart, namely, the prevention of war." President Wilson replied deploring the resignation which he accepts with feelings of personal sorrow only because Mr. Bryan insists upon it. President Wilson dwells on the delightful association with Mr. Bryan for the past two years during which their judgments had agreed until now, and says "even now we are not separated in object but only in methods."

The "Breslau" Damaged.

It is officially reported from Petrograd, on the 13th inst., that two Russian destroyers engaged the Turkish cruiser "Breslau" near the Bosphorus and severely damaged her. On the same day the Turks claim that their cruiser "Midilli" sank a Russian destroyer in the Black Sea.

Bomb Throwing Competition.

The following is the programme of a competition at Anzac :—

Commencing at 3 p.m.

JUDGES :—Major Row, Major Cribb, Capt. Griffiths.

TIMEKEEPERS :—Capt. Jervis, Lieut. Robertson, Lieut. Mead.

CONDITIONS :—Each company will enter 8 teams of 3 men. The two trained N.C.O.s of each company to take 4 teams each and to act as observers with periscopes.

1st PRACTICE.
2 Jam Tin Bombs—5 second fuse.

2nd PRACTICE.
2 Percussion Bombs.

3rd PRACTICE.
1 Gun Cotton Bomb (Lotbiniere) 6 sec. fuse.

All competitors will throw from the trench.

POINTS :—Hits (i.e. inside enemy's trench). 2 points for each direct hit, 1 point for each hit inside a space of 3ft. either in front or rear of enemy's trench.

EXPOSURE :—Judges will rule out of action any thrower exposing any part of head or body. Teams completing practice with absolutely no exposure will have 1 point added to total score.

TIME :—Timekeepers will stand in rear of each thrower and record any bomb thrown after "fuse time" has elapsed ruling out of action 2 men for every bomb so thrown.

TRAJECTORY :—In practice No. 2 the Judges will, at their discretion, award points for trajectory.

PRIZES :—1st Prize. 20 packets of cigarettes and 1 tin Marmalade; 2nd Prize. 16 packets cigarettes and 1 tin Marmalade ; 3rd Prize. 12 packets cigarettes.

Mexican Anarchy.

Mexico is almost forgotten in the great war, but it is still seeking trouble. President Wilson has issued a manifesto declaring that the United States cannot punish the anarchical conditions in Mexico to continue indefinitely. She calls upon the faction leaders in Mexico to unite and organise a Government, otherwise the United States will intervene.

R.E. Printing Section, G.H.Q., M.E.F.

Peninsula Press

No. 29   Friday, JUNE 18th. 1915   Official News.

"The Shortest Path to a Triumphant Peace"
Mr. Churchill on the Dardanelles Campaign.

The following is an extract from Mr. Winston Churchill's great speech to his constituents at Dundee on June 5th:-

"I have two things to say to you about the Dardanelles. First, you must expect losses both by land and sea; but the fleet you are employing there is your surplus fleet, after, all other needs have been provided for. Had it not been used in this great enterprise, it would have been lying idle in your southern ports. A large number of the old vessels of which it is composed have to be laid up, in any case, before the end of the year, because their crews are wanted for the enormous reinforcements of new ships which the industry of your workshops is hurrying into the water. Losses of ships, therefore, as long as the precious lives of the officers and men are saved, as in nearly every case they have been - losses of that kind, I say may easily be exaggerated in the minds both of friend and foe.

And military operations will also be costly, but those who suppose that Lord Kitchener (loud cheers) has embarked upon them without narrowly and carefully considering their requirements in relation to all other needs and in relation to the paramount need of our Army in France and Flanders - such people are mistaken and, not only mistaken, they are presumptuous.

THE PRIZE IN VIEW

My second point is this. In looking at our losses squarely and soberly, you must not forget, at the same time, the prize for which you are contending. The Army of Sir Ian Hamilton, the Fleet of Admiral de Robeck, are separated only by a few miles from a victory such as this war has not yet seen. When I speak of victory I am not referring to those victories which crowd the daily placards of any newspapers I am speaking of victory in the sense of a brilliant and formidable fact, shaping the destinies of nations and shortening the duration of the war. Beyond those few miles of ridge and scrub on which our soldiers, our French comrades, our gallant Australians, and our New Zealand fellow subjects are now battling, lie the downfall of a hostile Empire, the destruction of an enemy's fleet and army, the fall of a world-famous capital, and probably the accession of powerful Allies. The struggle will be heavy, the risks numerous, the losses cruel; but victory when it

81

comes will make amends for all. There never was a great subsidiary operation of war in which a more complete army of strategic, political, and economic advantages has combined, or which stood in truer relation to the main decision which is in the central theatre. Through the narrows of the Dardanelles and across the ridges of the Gallipoli Peninsula lie some of the shortest paths to a triumphant peace. That is all I say upon that subject this afternoon; but late, on, perhaps, when the concluding chapters in this famous story have been written, I may be allowed to return again to the subject.

National Service and German Confidence.

The newspapers at home have started a campaign in favour of National Service. Among the few journals that oppose the movement as "a fad and not a real ucturial need" is the "Nation " which answers itself in a parallel column by quoting "from a very competent and friendly correspondent abroad" the following remarkable account of the present position and intentions of Germany:-

"They ...... tell me frankly that the Germans are more than ever confident of victory. Every man who can carry a rifle or help to kill will count. All the male population between 14 and 60 will eventually be called out to fight. The Kaiser has never been so popular, and every atrocity is hailed as a new glory. The greater the number of nations against them the greater their triumph will be. That is the genuine feeling in Germany. Depression and murmuring are unknown. There is no doubt that food is cheaper there than in Switzerland and Italy. We must understand that the job is a stiff one and the end far off, even if new countries do intervene."

On the Russian Front.

Since the beginning of May one and a half million Austro-Germans have been trying to cut the Russian Army in two, to drive one half North and the other East. According to German wireless messages of the 15th inst. General Mackensen's army has advanced on a broad front thirty miles North of Przemysl and stormed all the Russian positions, taking 16,000 prisoners.

The latest Russian reports, dated the 13th, state that after furious bombardments and repeated attacks West of Shawli, the Germans reached the Russian entanglements only to be driven back, leaving piles of dead before the trenches. The Russians continue to advance near Dubissa and have made successful night attacks, capturing a number of prisoners, guns and other booty. In Galicia the enemy attempted to cover their retreat with armoured trains and motor cars, but the accuracy of the Russian artillery fire compelled them to withdraw hurriedly.

After retiring from Stainslau, the Russians developed an offensive movement in the direction of Obtique (?) and took 1,200 prisoners.

When the Germans were driven back over the Dneister, the Prussian Guard sustained heavy loses and left behind ten pieces of artillery and sixteen machine guns.

Canada and the War.

A memorandum issued by the Canadian Government, says: "Up to the present nearly thirty-six thousand officers and men have been despatched Overseas by the Canadian Government. It is anticipated that by the 1st of July the number will reach approximately seventy thousand. More than five hundred nurses have also gone. The recruiting, enlistment, and organisation of additional forces is steadily proceeding, and this is all the more necessary by reason of the very heavy casualties which have been sustained by the Canadian division during the past five weeks in the fighting at Langemarck and vicinity. The gallantry, resourcefulness, and tenacity of the Canadian troops during these battles have never been surpassed."

Peninsula Press

No. 30   Saturday, JUNE 19th. 1915   Official News.

A Visit to the Turks in the Peninsula.

The following extracts from the reports of a correspondent - presumably American - who has visited the Turkish positions in the Gallipoli Peninsula will be read with interest. The reports which have reached London by way of Bucharest appear in the "Daily Telegraph" of June 7th.

THE FIRST BOMBARDMENT.

Writing from the town of Gallipoli, on May 23rd, the correspondent says:-

"The mosque is a blackened mass of ruins, and the burnt-out buildings that spot the town show the work of the big English guns. Yet, Gallipoli is by no means destroyed. That the initial bombardment was justified is patent from the fact that the Headquarter Staff of the Turkish Army was stationed here. At that time it was the base for the troops operating further down the Peninsula, and while undefended in the sense that no forts exist, still it was certainly a legitimate point of attack. No shell has fallen here for some time, and gradually the frightened people are finding their way back to their homes. The base has been changed to a place which I cannot name. Here a camp on the hillside comes to the water of the quiet bay, where some twenty transports lay. It was night again when we reached here. The moon shed its light on the busy scene. Caiques, almost spilling boxes of ammunition over their high sides, made trip after trip from ship to shore."

ONLY THE SHELL OF A CITY.

From Chanak on May 25th the same correspondent writes:-

"We row past Maidos, a collection of roofless, shattered houses. The empty windows stared down on us like eye-sockets in so many skulls.

Chanak is only the shell of a city. Beyond the white houses that line the sea front there is nothing except in the direction of Kalid Bahir, from which it is separated by only a few hundred yards of water. When you actually see this narrow passage, swept by over 50 eight-inch guns mounted thirty feet above the water, the folly of attempting to force it by the old methods is patent. That the Allied Fleet suffered as little as it did is a miracle.

As every inch of the surface of the waters is plotted on the artillery maps in the forts, it needs but a moments' calculation to get the exact range of any ships entering the zone. As the main land operations are taking place across on the Gallipoli Peninsula, Chanak is the only base for the supply of the Coast Defence Troops stationed on the Asiatic side. Besides these there is but a comparatively small force of infantry holding Kum Kale. A training camp is established lower down the coast.

Admiral Von Usedem, the German Commander, a gentleman with a kindly eye and courteous manner, and wearing the Order Pour le Merite, lives in a well-concealed camp, but sea-planes circle around Chanak, daily dropping spheres of death. Admiral Melton shares with Admiral Von Usedom command of the zone, and his chief aid[*sic*] is my friend Prince Reuss. His mother would not recognise him wearing a fez.

He gave me an outline of the situation here from his side, but obviously I cannot write of his confidences. Yet it is no breach to say that the Germans are supremely satisfied with the outlook as far as the forts guarding the Narrows are concerned. The arrival of a German submarine in Saros is what the Germans are congratulating themselves on to-day. They tell me she torpedoed the "Triumph." Struck at 12.30, not a vestige of the battleship could be seen above water at 1 o'clock.

This morning three shots fell in fort Namazieh, across the Narrows, without doing any harm. Indirect fire of this kind, however, is telling against the morale of the fortress troops.

From the hill at Kodjadah you can look down on both the English and Turkish trenches, which at points are not more than 10 yards apart. An unending line of troops and transports moves along the coast roads to the support of the Turkish position. The supply of men seems to be without end. It is not the lack of soldiers that worries General Liman Von Saunders as he rides along the trenches from the Dardanelles to the Agean Sea. All the Turkish army is an armed camp. But the daily supply of ammunition diminishes.

Continued Progress in France.

Paris, June 18th.

The French official report issued today is as follows:-
North of Arras the French have advanced to the East of Lorette, to the South-west and South of Sauchez and in the Labyrinth, taking 300 prisoners and some machine guns. South of Arras, the Germans have violently bombarded the positons which they lost near the farm

Tontvent but delivered no infantry attack. At the farm Quentestiere, after having repulsed several counter-attacks we have advanced our line to the North-west of the trenches already taken, capturing 100 prisoners of whom two were officers. The town of Rheims has been bombarded, the Germans dropping 100 shells of which several were incendiary. Ten shells fellon the Cathedral.

In the Vosges the French have made an important advance on both banks of the Fecht and are entirely masters of the heights dominating the valley of the Fecht North of Sondernach and Metzeral. On the South the French have advanced also between the two branches of the upper Fecht and on the heights between the valley of the Fecht and that of the Leuch.

On the 15th inst., bombs were dropped on Nancy, Saint Die and Belfort by German aviators. At Nancy a few civilians were injured.

(Wireless).

Karlsruhe Bombed.

Amsterdam, June 17th.

It is announced from Berlin that five airships bombed Karlsruhe. Several people were killed and much damage was caused to numerous places.

[Karlsruhe is about 80 miles as the crow flies from the nearest French frontier·].

Volunteers for the Italian Army.

According to the information of the "Agenzia Nazionale," the enlistment of volunteers in the National Army has already been attended with excellent results, demonstrating the intense enthusiasm for the war that reigns throughout Italy,[sic] On 31st May, already over 200,000 men belonging to all classes and ages, had asked to enlist. It is believed that this number will soon be doubled.

Peninsula Press

No. 31   Sunday, JUNE 20th. 1915   Official News.

The Greek Elections.

The result of the Greek elections gives M. Venizelos a clear majority of 68 votes over all possible combinations. The returns are as follow:-

Venizelcs	189
Gounaris	90
Theotokis	12
Independants	24
	315

The Government, of which M Gounaris is Prime Minister, has decided not to resign just now on the ground of the King's health.

His Majesty, according to a telegram of the 18th inst., is now out of danger.

The election was fought on the question of intervention or non-intervention in the war. M. Venizelos is in favour of intervention on the side of the Allies. He resigned the Premiership in March because the King and the General Staff were opposed to his policy. He was succeded by M. Gounaris who maintained that the country would not consent to make territorial concessions to Bulgaria in order to secure her cooperation in the war.

M. Theotokis who has twelve followers in the new Chamber, is opposed to intervention for fear of the Bulgars and Slavs.

King Constantine, in an interview not many weeks ago, said that if M. Venizelos returned to power "we will work together harmoniously as before, for the realization of Greece's national aspirations."

M. Venizelos, shortly after his resignation, went into voluntary exile at Mytelene. He will now return to Athens to lead his majority in the Chamber. M. Gounaris, though defeated, will not meet Parliament until July 20th so that no decision can be taken till that date.

Turk's Disappointed with their Bombardment.

At about seven o'clock on Friday night the Turks shelled with heavy howitzers and field guns the trenches of the 87th Brigade. They were also reported to be massing for attack in the ravine, but did not come on and only fire fighting ensued which died down at 9 p.m.

On the left of the 42nd Division, our attack was not successful and the Turks gained some ground.

During the night all the lost ground was re-taken. At 2.30 a.m. the 29th Division made a successful attack on the Turkish trench East of the nullah and improved and connected it with their line. A heavy counter-attack on this position was driven back with heavy loss to the enemy by enfilading fire from the Royal Naval Division trench West of the nullah.

Prisoners state that the Turks expected that their bombardment with high explosive shells would have cleared us out of our trenches. They were much disappointed at so little impression being made in this respect, although the trenches were so damaged.

Three hundred dead Turks lay in front of the 87th Division alone. The enemy lost heavily from our machine gun fire and shrapnel.

German Wireless News for Neutrals.

Germans are adepts at presenting a military situation in a light that may attract, even if it does not convince. The following report on the position in the Gallipoli Peninsula is an example of the art they are cultivating so assiduously at a time when certain neutral states are supposed to be making up their minds. Our men in the fighting line will be able to judge of its spirit as well as its facts. If, as the report says, the Turks are "confident," we are more than confident; we are certain. Constantinople, June 5th.

From the "Courier," Berlin.- "The Forces of the Allies in the Gallipoli Peninsula at Ari Burnu (Kaba Tepe) and Sidd el Bahr are in the greatest danger and in a position of futility owing to the withdrawal of the bombarding fleets, due to German submarines, and the consequent extreme difficulty of maintaining communications oversea from the Aegean Islands.

The English position is at present desperate. Their inability to land heavy artillery was at first compensated by the fleet guns, but the withdrawal of the ships at Ari Burnu (Kaba Tepe) leaves the shore forces resting almost on the water's edge, without means of meeting the heavy attacks of Turkish artillery on the surrounding heights. These conclusions reached after a week in the Turkish field under Field-Marshal Liman von Sanders, Commander-in-Chief. The Turks are fighting with confidence, aided by a few German machine gun squads. The furthest distance the English have advanced at Ari Burnu (Kaba Tepe) is 1,000 yards from the shore, and at Sidd el Bahr about two miles.

I have seen the forts at Chanak, and Kalid Bahr they are still intact. The net result of the English Dardanelles action at present is almost nil.

The general impression in Constantinople and Berlin, is that the attack as at present conducted is a "fizzle," due to the ineffectual bombardment of March 18th, the insufficient size of the landing forces and the failure to embroil Bulgaria against Turkey." (Wireless).

Amsterdam, June, 18th

The German official reports acknowledge a reverse at Ypres where the British attacked in strong force. At La Basse the British advanced with four divisions against the West Phalians reinforced by the Prussian Guard. In Galicia the Germans claim to have made progress West of Lemburg and admit Russian successes between the Dneister and Zurano. (Wireless)

Italian Successes.

Rome, June 18th.

Our troops are gradually occupying the dominating points in the Trentino. In Carnia the fighting is intense. At Monte Nero we rushed the Austrian positions at dawn and took 800 prisoners.

In the air raid on Karlsruhe 180 bombs were dropped on the Castle, the arms factory and the station. Of the 28 French aeroplanes all returned except two.

Peninsula Press

No. 32 Monday, JUNE 21st. 1915 Official News.

No Strike in Munition Factories

London, June 18th.

It is understood that Mr. Lloyd George's Munitions Bill gives no compulsory powers over workmen, though it restricts Trade Union rules, suspends strikes and prohibits lock-outs.

Progress in France.

London, June 18th.

Field-Marshal Sir John French reports that fighting continued on Wednesday in Co-operation with the French attacks on Arras. All the German first line trenches East of Ypres remain in our hands, though we were unable to retain the second line of trenches occupied in the morning. Our artillery was very effective.

In the region North of Arras, there have been violent artillery duels lasting all day, but the French have retained in all cases the positions recently captured from the Germans.

Paris, June 20th

In Alsace, the French have consolidated the positions captured on the 10th and continue to advance. French patrols have penetrated as far as the outskirts of Metzeral. The French are holding ground on both banks of the Fecht and now threaten with their artillery and infantry the enemy's communication between Metzerel and Munster. They have also succeeded in capturing more prisoners as well as machine guns and a very large quantity of ammunition and spare parts for rifles.

Why Germany Has No Friends.

The "Leipziger Volkszeitunq," an important socialist journal, has a remarkable article on the demoralisation of Germany:

The sentiments of the people of Holland, Scandinavia and the United States of America have remained favourable to England and hostile to Germany even since the announcement of reprisals against the war methods of German submarines. This state of feeling is so opposed to what was hoped that it forces to reflection. To-day, as yesterday, the small States of Europe do not feel English domination to be a humiliating constraint, but the solid basis on which rest their own independence and the equilibrium of Europe. In their eyes England, not for democratic principles, but because she was clearly conscious of her own interests, has always opposed the strongest European Power of the day and has supported the weaker against the stronger - in 1814, Prussia against France, and 1915 France against Prussia. Say, if you will, that the weak in the European concert have by the sacrifice of all their physical and economic forces, laid the foundation of the wealth and power of England, it is none the less true that, whatever her reasons, England has been the protectoress of small nations.

To the power of persuasion of these historic souvenirs there is only one decisive reply: the democratisation of Germany. Germany must outbid England: assure by democracy the national independence of the other States: and facilitate by free trade their junction with the buoyant economic organisation of Germany

Another Submarine V.C.

His Majesty has been pleased to confer on Lieut.-Commander Nasmith the V.C., on the officers of the submarine the D.S.C., and on the crews the D.S.M.

Lieut. Nasmith recently made a daring and successful submarine raid in the sea of Marmora where he sank one Turkish gunboat one ammunition ship and three supply ships.

Fierce Battle in Galicia
Petrograd, June 18th.
The battle in Galicia continues with undiminished fierceness. The enemy was driven back in disorder on the 11th inst. between the river Tysmieoica and the Styran Dneister front. Above Jurarnod the Russians took 746 prisoners. The enemy crossed the Dneister on the 15th inst. above and below Nymevik. Those who crossed above the town were destroyed, while those who crossed below were unable to advance.

Fatal Accident to Lieut. Warneford
Paris, June 19th
Sub-Lieut. Warneford was killed while testing an aeroplane in Paris.
On the 8th inst. this officer attacked a Zeppelin between Ghent and Brussels at a height of 6,000 feet and dropped six bombs. The Zeppelin exploded, fell to the ground and burned for a considerable time. The force of the explosion caused the aeroplane to turn turtle. Lieut. Warneford managed to right the machine and had to make a forced landing in the enemy's country, but was able to restart the engine and returned safely.

An Unwelcome Visitor.

The "New York Herald" in an editorial article commenting on the announcement that Herr Dernburg, the German Emperor's personal representative, has decided to remain indefinitely in America says; "May be he desires to save his skin which is no concern of Americans. May be the German Government believes that his presence is beneficial in case relations become strained, which is our concern. His stay is an insult to the United States, he having meddled with internal affairs, carried on propaganda against our neutrality and declared, when the nation was mourning that the Americans who were lost in the "Lusitania" had themselves to blame because she was rightly torpedoed as an enemy ship. Coldblooded, untruthful, egotistical and intolerable, Herr Dernburg's room is desired and not his presence which is just as objectionable silent as noisy. Has he no sense of shame or no feeling of propriety?"

Peninsula Press

No. 33   Tuesday, JUNE 22nd. 1915   Official News.

Germans Approaching Lemberg.

According to German Embassy report, General Mackensen's Army broke through the Russian lines near Magierow, about 25 miles North-west of Lemberg. The Russian positions on both sides of the Lemberg road were stormed and the main positions entered. Since 8 a.m. to-day (Sunday), says the report, the Russians along the whole front are retreating in the direction of Lemberg and thousands of prisoners have been taken, North and South of the city.

The French in Alsace.

Paris, June 21st.

The official report states that:-
North of Arras, the Ford de Buval, which was obstinately defended by the Germans has been carried by assault. The French captured some machine guns.

In the direction of Souchez, the French have taken several trenches and 300 prisoners, including 12 officers. A German battalion succeeded in capturing two French outposts in front of Embermenil. The French immediately counter-attacked and re-occupied the positions.

In Alsace the French advance continues. They have also taken Anlasswasden which lies between the two branches of the river Fecht, and on the right bank of the eastern branch they have captured the heights of St. Hilger, and advanced towards Landesback. The French have bombarded the station at Munster and exploded some magazines. They have occupied Metzeral which the Germans set on fire before evacuating.

Why Not?

According to a message from Chiasso, the Republic of San Marino is seriously debating whether it should remain neutral or declare war against Germany, Austria and Turkey. San Marino in the hills near Rimini, on the Adriatic, is entirely surrounded by Italian territory, yet it forms an absolutely independent state. Its area is 82 square miles; its population is 10,652, and it has an army of about 1,000 men.

The Republic was founded in the 4th century by a pious mason of Dalmatia, and is governed by a council of 60, of whom two are elected

Regents for six months. San Marino made a treaty of friendship with Italy in 1909.

"Gott Strafe England."

A Saxon nursing sister sent home to her relatives accounts of visits paid by the German Emperor and Empress to the military hospital to which she is attached. Several of these letters are printed in the "Allgemeine Chemnitzer Zeitung" and among them is the following:-

"Her Majesty (the Empress) passed through two surgical wards and then inspected the operating room, which is fitted up extremely well. Over the door are painted the words 'Gott Strafe England' God Punish England.' The Empress said: 'Children, that is the one motto, "Gott Strafe England."

Campaigning in South Africa.

General Botha's force – so successful in its operations in German territory – has experienced a variety of hardships and discomforts; more trying perhaps than the actual fighting. A member of the force, writing after a month's continuous trek says: "we have done night marches galore – in fact have mostly trekked at night – marches in dust and heat and marches at freezing point, with an icy wind such that one could feel neither one's stirrups nor reins, marches in darkness and rain and marches in the most glorious moonlight. We left the desert with a temperature of 100 degrees in the tents, and climbed up to a high plateau at 5 000 feet level with temperature very near the freezing point, with all tents and most blankets left behind at the base. By now, however, we are rapidly accumulating transport, things are not (mostly German), off as might appear"

"Everything has been taken away – people stock, supplies, and all – worst of all there is practically no grazing for animals. This is of course a very serious thing for us, as want of sufficient water and food for the animals neccesarily holds us up. The general is getting impatient at his inability to give the enemy a knock. The Germans however, don't appear to be at all keen to come to grips – they are indeed an elusive foe. They are, of course, very weak in numbers, so it is their game to delay us as much as possible, and to fight only when it suits them."

Why Americans Wish England Well

Mr W. D. Howells, a former Editor of the "North American Review" writing in the hundredth anniversary number says:-

"We cannot, indeed, cast our lot with the Allies, but our will must be with them always, because they are in the right if there is any such thing as right or wrong. If it is wrong to build up a ruthless power by a system

of world wide espionage, to fortify a bad cause by every art of treachery and deceit, and then to use that power with arrogant disregard of all intentional traditions, and all laws of religion and all the impulses of humanity, Germany is wrong and England is right and that is why we must wish England well, whatever becomes of our questions and protests."
(Mr Howells wrote before the sinking of the Lusitania.)

The Pope Declines to leave Rome.

In view of the new situation created for the Pope by the war between Italy and Austria, the Spanish Premier has offered the Pope the hospitality of Spain, placing at his disposal the Palace of the Escorial as accommodation for His Holiness, the Cardinals, and the Vatican officials.

The Pope in reply expressed his deep sense of the kindliness of the Premier's suggestion, but declined the offer, stating that he has no intention of leaving Rome at present.

Peninsula Press

No. 34   Wednesday, JUNE 23st. 1915   Official News.

A Substantial Success.
The Haricot Taken.

After 24 hours heavy and continuous fighting we have achieved a substantial success. At 4.30 on Tuesday morning, General Gouraud began an attack upon the line of formidable works which run along the Kereves Dere. By noon the 2nd French Division had captured all the Turkish 1st and 2nd line trenches opposite their front, including the famous Haricot redoubt. On their right the 1st French Division, after some hard fighting, also captured the Turkish trenches opposite their front, but were heavily counter-attacked and forced to fall back. A second time this Division advanced to the attack and stormed the position but once more it was forced to retire.

In view of the possibility that the failure of the 1st Division might compel the 2nd Division to retire from their hardly-gained ground, General Gouraud then ordered a third attempt to be made. The bombardment of the Turkish trenches was therefore resumed, the British guns and howitzers lending their aid to the French artillery as in the previous attacks. At about 6 p.m. a fine attack was launched and 600 yards of Turkish first line trenches captured.

Heavy counter-attacks during the night, especially at 3.30 a.m., failed to dislodge the French troops from their positions. The Turkish losses were considerable, one battalion in particular being spotted by aeroplane and practically wiped out by the "75s" before it could scatter. Some 50 prisoners including one officer remained in our hands.

The elan and contempt of fire shown by the young French drafts were especially remarkable.

The French battleship St. Louis did excellent service during the fighting against the Asiatic batteries.

Surprising Constantinople.

London.

An "eye-witness" of the visit of one of our Submarines to Constantinople has reached Costanza. He had taken a boat at 5.30 a.m. from Pera to Stambul and suddenly noticed at sixty yards from the landing place a stick upright in the water moving towards the bridge.

The sight was amazing as the current ran in the opposite direction. He then saw a white trail in the blue-green water and guessed it was a torpedo. A moment later there was a shattering explosion and an enormous column of water. He saw the army transport Stanboul settling by the stern. A second explosion followed amidships. Nothing was visible for a few minutes but a mass of wreckage. Then a third torpedo hit the Custom House quay, but did not do much damage. There was a terrible commotion on shore, the police and soldiers distractedly firing off rifles. The submarine gleamed for a moment in the sun, an officer was seen in the look out and then it sank. Then the batteries on the hill showered shells for half an hour, a sheer waste of ammunition.

2,000,000 Men on War Work.

Replying to Mr. Chiozza Money, who asked whether we have two million men of military age engaged in making munitions of war, or whether this number includes workers of all ages and sexes, Mr. Lloyd George says: "The figures quoted represent an estimate of the number of male workpeople of all ages engaged on Government work."

Russia Confident.

Petrograd, June 14th.

(Official). The struggle has now reached extreme intensity. The Germans have nearly doubled their troops in the field since the beginning of the war and the possibility of a further increase in their infantry is doubtful. The attacks of the Allies have compelled the Germans to keep on both fronts larger forces than originally intended. The unshakable unity and growing power of the Allies augurs well for future success.

Continued Progress in France.

Paris, June 22nd.

The French official report received by wireless says:-

North of Arras the French have made fresh progress towards Sauchez, capturing several trenches. Near Dompierre, West of Peronne, a German attack, preceded by the explosion of several mines, was completely checked by artillery and musketry fire. West of the Argonne, the French have repulsed a violent attack and taken some prisoners. On the heights of the Meuse, they have captured two lines of enemy trenches and maintained their position in spite of violent counter-attacks. Sixty prisoners were taken of whom two were officers.

In Lorraine near to Revillon the French captured the enemy's line along a front of about 1,500 yards. A strong column attempted a counter-attack and was repulsed. In the district of Bonhomme the French captured by assault the spur East of Bonhomme and reached the boundaries of the village. In the valley of the Fecht the French have passed the cemetery of Metzeral. To the South-west, they have also gained ground, and taken 500 prisoners, including 5 officers and 11 N.C.O.s.

Significant German Move.

The "Gaulois" notes a fact which, if not of a military nature, is still very significant. The Germans in Aisne and Artois had sown the fields with corn, hoping themselves to reap the harvest. A new order has gone forth to plough the sown fields and destroy the springing corn. This brutal command proves that the invaders have lost their belief in a lengthy occupation of French soil.

New Use for Racecourses.

Taking advantage of the cessation of racing, the Home Office, in conjunction with the Law Authorities of the Crown, has formulated a scheme for using several of the English racecourses that have up-to-date buildings as concentration camps for aliens. It will be remembered that Newbury was acquired last autumn for this purpose. Gatwick has now been requisitioned by the Government, and, as soon as the necessary alterations have been made, will be used for the internment of Germans and Austrians.

Peninsula Press

No. 35   Thursday, JUNE 24th. 1915   Official News.

Another Trans-Atlantic Liner Threatened

London June 23rd

The liner "Cameronia," which arived at Liverpool yesterday, was attacked by a submarine during her voyage from New York. Although under full steam the liner found it impossible to elude the submarine and tried to ram it. To avoid the steamer, the submarine submerged and was not seen again. The "Cameronia" had a number of prominent American passengers on board. The incident has been reported to the United States Ambassador.

De Wet Sentenced.

General De Wet, who was tried for treason, has been sentenced to five years imprisonment. He attempted to raise a rebellion in South Africa and led an armed force against the Government. His failure was speedy and the redoubtable soldier who so often eluded capture in the Boer War was soon made a prisoner.

Encouraging Reports From France

Paris June 23rd

Fourteen shells, fired by heavy long range guns, have fallen in Dunkirk. A few civilians were killed.

The Belgians have captured a German trench.

French airmen have bombarded German aviation parks, setting fire to four hangars and hitting two aeroplanes and a captive balloon.

In the Arras sector all the German attacks have been repulsed, except in one case South of Souchez, where the enemy succeeded in retaking a small portion of trenches.

East of Argonne a violent German attack forced the French first line to bend back, but an immediate counter-attack enabled the French to regain almost entirely their original position.

On the heights of the Meuse, in the sector of Calonne, the French have captured some new trenches. In Lorraine, they have extended toward the North their position on the ridge of Reillon and occupied the hills South-east of Rembois. Two counter-attacks were repulsed and some prisoners were taken.

In Alsace the French have captured Metzeral and passed North and South of the village.

Some prisoners and three machine guns were taken.
(French official report, received by wireles).

German Version
The German wireless report, dated Tuesday, says: Against the German front, North of Arras, there were only cannonades. An infantry charge, North of Souchez, was repulsed. At Moulin Sous Equivont, a local French night attack failed.

On the Western border of the Argonne, the Germans took several French lines of defence. The French had heavy losses. Six officers and 523 men were taken prisoners. On the heights of the Meuse, the French made five strong charges against the German positions. The charges broke down under our fire. East of the high road the enemy invaded the German position, but were chased out and lost 70 prisoners.

In the Vosges the French attacks in the valley of the Fecht and southward were repulsed with much bloodshed. To avoid unnecessary losses, the Germans evacuated by night the village of Metzeral which had been reduced to a heap of ruins by the French artillery.

On the Russian Front
Petrograd June 21st.
In various areas, except Galicia, the Russians have got the upper hand. A brilliant feat of the Russian Cavalry near Lemberg is reported. They charged the forces advancing in the direction of Rawaruska (North of the city) and cut up and routed them. The enemy attempting to force the passage at Grodek were repulsed.

A wireless message of yesterday's date reports that the Russians are making a stand outside Lemberg.

Russian submarines have sunk a large steamer and two sailing vessels between Enkroli and Kerken.

The Russians are progressing between the Dneister and the Pruth.

The German official report of the 21st inst., states: "We have stormed Grodek and Zomalno (?)"

(Grodek is 16 miles West by South of Lemherg. Zomalno is probably meant for Komarno, which is 22 miles Sonth-west of Lemberg).

"Austro-German troops are pursuing the Russians and have advanced to Zolkiew, approaching Lemberg." (Zolkiew is 25 miles North).

"…troops repulsed Russian charges South-west-near Zilieroy and Bessarabian frontier, with heavy losses for the enemy."

"Between Pangui Vegerow about 9,500 Russian prisoners, and eight field pieces and 26 machine guns were taken. North-west of Syuale and East of the Upper Dubissa, several strong Russian attacks failed."

Italian Success.
Rome, June, 22nd.

The battle for the heights across the Isonzo, commanding Plava, was a great success. The Italians crossed the river on pontoons at dawn and attacked with the bayonet.

Italy is being handicapped by severe weather conditions.

(Wireless)

The German wireless also of June 22nd says: Two new charges near Plava were repulsed. The enemy has been thrown from the ………….. position

On the 19th an Austrian destroyer successfully shelled Monopoli, North of Brindisi, and seaplanes damaged the railway depots.

The Munitions Question.

It is officially announced that Mr. Lloyd George, Minister of Munitions, travelled to Boulogne on Saturday last and had a meeting with the French Under Secretary for War. It was arranged that there should be an exchange of views between the Allies on the question of the output of munitions.

The War Loan.

The new war loan is being subscribed eagerly by the general public. Among prospective subscribers were all classes, including naval and military officers. Over one million was subscribed by Cardiff mine owners and coal exporters.

Peninsula Press

No. 36   Friday, JUNE 25th. 1915   Official News.

The Fall of Lemberg.

News has reached us of the retaking of Lemberg, an important town about fifty miles East of Przemysl.

A German wireless message states that the capture of Lemberg "has caused universal rejoicing at Constantinople, and flags are out everywhere."

A mutilated German wireless report begins as follows:- "These attacks made us master of important positions and much booty was taken. Among the Russians recently taken prisoner some have declared that men of fifty years have been called out for war service and have been armed with old and rusty rifles. Among the recruits recently called out in several places "Stop the War" meetings have been held."

NOTE.- The Russians, having withdrawn from Eastern Galicia before strong Austro-German armies with a preponderance of heavy artillery, made a splendid defence on the line of the river San, to the South of the Dneister and in the valley of Pruth. The enemy succeeded in crossing to the North of Jaroslav, and, after stubborn resistance, forced the Russians to abandon Przemysl, the forts of which had been rendered useless by the Austrians before they surrendered the city to the Russians, on March 22nd. Przemysl was re-occupied by the Austro-German armies on June 4th and the advance on Lemberg began without delay. The enemy is said to have 1,500,000 troops on this front.

How Germans Report Our Successes.

The value of German reports may be measured by contrasting the following report with the account we gave on Wednesday. On the 21st and 22nd our French comrades captured two lines of Turkish trenches and the famous Haricot redoubt. This is how the success is reported by the Germans:-

"On June 21st, the enemy, supported by heavy artillery and recent large reinforcements, instituted several attacks which lasted until after midnight and have been, on this occasion, finally shattered. The enemy, who suffered very heavy loss, were driven back to their old positions.

An enemy battery which had just been placed in position was knocked to pieces at Ari Burnu on the 20th."

According to a report from Athens the Allies have discovered and confiscated in the island of Calymnos a large quantity of benzine which is supposed to have been for German use. Calymnos is a small island to the North of Rhodes in the Aegean Sea. It is one of the twelve islands occupied by the Italians during the Turco-Italian war.

The age of recruits for the new army of 800, 000 has been raised to 40 years. The number of men in the United Kingdom between the ages of 19 and 40, including those who have already volunteered for the Army and Navy, is 7,889,000. Of these nearly one half are unmarried.

On the West Front.

Paris, June 24th.

The French official report, received by wireless, says:-
North of Arras, between Sauchez and Ecurie, there has been an extremely violent artillery engagement. The Germans launched further counter-attacks, one near the cemetery at Neuville; the other near the Labyrinth: both were completely repulsed. West of the Argonne, near the road from Denaville to the Chateau Pionsville, the fight developed into a hand grenade duel. The Germans made a determined attempt on the night of the 21st, to retake the positions they lost at Colonne, and eventually succeeded in reoccupying a small portion of their old second line of trenches. Fresh attacks made by the Germans at Lemtry were repulsed and the French retain all the captured positions and have taken more prisoners.

In the Vosges, at La Fontenelle, the Germans on the evening of the 22nd, threw 4,000 shells on to the French positions, and, after advancing, succeeded in setting foot in a part of the defences. The French have since then retaken practically all the positions lost, the Germans now holding on to the extreme end of one of the walls. The French captured 146 prisoners, including 8 officers. On the banks of the Fecht the French have occupied Sundernagh and have advanced.

Should the Japanese come to Europe?

M. Pichon, who was for a time Foreign Minister of France and is a member of the Senate, has long been advocating Japanese intervention in Europe. Writing in the Paris "Journal," of which he is editor, M. Pichon says: "In 1900 Japan played a leading part in putting down the Boxer movement, fighting shoulder to shoulder with the armies of Europe. Without her help the legation staffs and the personnel of the Christian missions in Pekin might all have perished. This alone should have sufficed to prove that Japan did not wish to isolate her cause from that of the Western nation, but stood ready to join those willing to fight for the ideals to which she owes the form of her institutions and the new direction given to her destinies. Japan has just given further proof of this by taking the side of justice and the free peoples against barbarism and oppression; by undertaking to dislodge Germany from Chinese soil which the latter had wrongfully and forcibly annexed. The feat of arms of Tsingtau adds new lustre to the military annals, already so long and brilliant, of the "Land of Valour," whose acts are now beyond count.

Is Japan to confine herself to this one act in the present great conflict? I am of those who believe that she could bring to us on the European continent help of incomparable value; and I am convinced that the Japanese Government would ask nothing better than to respond to the call of the Triple Entente if her help is asked for further battles."

PENINSULA PRESS.

| No. 36 | FRIDAY, JUNE 25th 1915. | Official News. |

The Fall of Lemberg.

News has reached us of the retaking of Lemberg, an important town about fifty miles East of Przemysl.

A German wireless message states that the capture of Lemberg "has caused universal rejoicing at Constantinople, and flags are out everywhere."

A mutilated German wireless report begins as follows:—" These attacks made us master of important positions and much booty was taken. Among the Russians recently taken prisoner some have declared that men of fifty years have been called out for war service, and have been armed with old and rusty rifles. Among the recruits recently called out in several places 'Stop the War' meetings have been held."

NOTE.—The Russians, having withdrawn from Eastern Galicia before strong Austro-German armies with a preponderance of heavy artillery, made a splendid defence on the line of the river San, to the South of the Dneister and in the valley of Pruth. The enemy succeeded in crossing to the North of Jaroslav, and, after stubborn resistance, forced the Russians to abandon Przemysl, the forts of which had been rendered useless by the Austrians before they surrendered the city to the Russians, on March 22nd. Przemysl was re-occupied by the Austro-German armies on June 4th and the advance on Lemberg began without delay. The enemy is said to have 1,500,000 troops on this front.

How Germans Report Our Successes.

The value of German reports may be measured by contrasting the following report with the account we gave on Wednesday. On the 21st and 22nd our French comrades captured two lines of Turkish trenches and the famous Haricot redoubt. This is how the success is reported by the Germans:—

"On June 21st, the enemy, supported by heavy artillery and recent large reinforcements, instituted several attacks which lasted until after midnight and have been, on this occasion, finally shattered. The enemy, who suffered very heavy loss, were driven back to their old positions.

An enemy battery which had just been placed in position was knocked to pieces at Ari Burnu on the 20th."

According to a report from Athens the Allies have discovered and confiscated in the island of Calynnos a large quantity of benzine which is supposed to have been for German use. Calymnos is a small island to the North of Rhodes in the Aegean Sea. It is one of the twelve islands occupied by the Italians during the Turco-Italian war.

The age of recruits for the new army of 300,000 has been raised to 40 years. The number of men in the United Kingdom between the ages of 19 and 40, including those who have already volunteered for the Army and Navy, is 7,899,000. Of these nearly one half are unmarried.

On the West Front.

Paris, June 24th.

The French official report, received by wireless, says :—

North of Arras, between Souchez and Ecurie, there has been an extremely violent artillery engagement. The Germans launched four counter-attacks, one near the cemetery at Neuville ; the other near the Labyrinth : both were completely repulsed. West of the Argonne, near the road from Donaville to the Chateau Pionsville, the fight developed into a hand grenade duel. The Germans made a determined attempt on the night of the 21st, to retake the the positions they lost at Colonne, and eventually succeeded in re-occupying a small portion of their old second line of trenches. Fresh attacks made by the Germans at La mitry were repulsed and the French retain all the captured positions and have taken more prisoners.

In the Vosges, at La Fontenelle, the enemy on the evening of the 22nd, threw 4,000 shells on to the French positions, and, after advancing, succeeded in setting foot in a part of the defences. The French have since then retaken practically all the positions lost, the Germans now holding on to the extreme end of one of the walls. The French captured 140 prisoners, including 3 officers. On the banks of the Fecht the French have occupied Sundernagh and have advanced.

Should the Japanese come to Europe ?

M. Pichon, who was for a time Foreign Minister of France and is a member of the Senate, has long been advocating Japanese intervention in Europe. Writing in the Paris "Journal," of which he is editor, M. Pichon says : " In 1900 Japan played a leading part in putting down the Boxer movement, fighting shoulder to shoulder with the armies of Europe. Without her help the legation staffs and the personnel of the Christian missions in Pekin might all have perished. This alone should have sufficed to prove that Japan did not wish to isolate her cause from that of the Western nation, but stood ready to join those willing to fight for the ideals to which she owes the form of her institutions and the new direction given to her destinies. Japan has just given further proof of this by taking the side of justice and the free peoples against barbarism and oppression ; by undertaking to dislodge Germany from Chinese soil which the latter had wrongfully and forcibly annexed. The feat of arms of Tsingtau adds new lustre to the military annals, already so long and brilliant, of the "Land of Valour," whose acts are now beyond count.

Is Japan to confine herself to this one act in the present great conflict ? I am of those who believe that she could bring to us on the European continent help of incomparable value ; and I am convinced that the Japanese Government would ask nothing better than to respond to the call of the Triple Entente if her help is asked for further battles."

R.E. Printing Section, G.H.Q., M.E.F.

Peninsula Press

No. 37   Saturday, JUNE 26th. 1915   Official News.

£3,000,000 a Day.

Mr. Asquith, in moving the vote for £250,000, 000 the fifth credit since the outbreak of war, said that from April to June 12 the daily cost of the war was £2,660,000. While the future army and navy expenditure would expand slightly, the financial obligations to our Allies would increase the daily cost to at least £8,000,000.

The Prime Minister finished his speech with these words: The formation of a National Government will demonstrate, not only to the Empire, but to the whole world that Britons are resolved whole heartedly and without party distinction to prosecute the war with every moral and material force. (Cheers). It is impossible to overestimate the value of the entry of Italy. I have always emphasised the gravity of the task and my confidence in the ultimate issue. I deprecate the blind counsel of hysteria and panic. (Cheers). Our paramount duty is to obtain the willing and organised help of every Briton. (Cheers). When our cause has been vindicated and once more there is peace on the earth may it be recorded on that proudest day in the annals of the Empire that there is no workshop which did not take a part in the common struggle or an unearned share in the common triumph." (Loud and prolonged cheers).

Mr. Dillon, speaking on behalf of the Nationalists, was loudly cheered on affirming their honest and sincere desire to aid the new Government to carry the war to a triumphant conclusion.

The Brussels Air Raid.

Among the German airships destroyed at Evere was Zeppelin No. 38. An eyewitness at Evere says that a tremendous German cannonade brought out the townspeople, who eagerly watched the contest when the British aeroplane manoeuvred. The people shouted for joy when the German shells missed. The Germans were attempting to remove the airship, which was a Zeppelin not a Perseval, when, suddenly, the airman dived and threw three bombs, which exploded most violently. Then there was an explosion and a flare.

When the Zeppelin was blown up the Bruxellois in indescribable joy sang the "Marseillaise" and the "Brabanconne." The Germans lost their heads and sent cavalry to charge the crowds. Five Taubes were also burned in the hanger and nineteen German soldiers killed.

Peace Meetings in Germany.

A Reuter's telegram says; Information has reached Petrograd that peace meetings have been held in many German towns in consequence of the appalling German losses in Galicia, where, it is stated, one army of 150,000 men was annihilated and re-created in the course of a single month.

Slatin Pasha.

Slatin Pasha, the famous prisoner of the Mahdi, who was many years a trusted servant of the British in Egypt; is an Austrian by birth. When war was declared between Great Britain and Austria, he resigned his position under the Sudan Government. A telegram from Zurich states that Sir Rudolph von Slatin Pasha has volunteered for active service with the Austrian army and has gone to the Italian front.

The Trans-Caucasian Campaign.

A Russian communique sums up the operations on the Caucasian and the Persian fronts since March the 8th, 1915. The Turkish offensive, which was led through Persian Territory, has been completely defeated, the army, composed of regulars and irregulars, under the command of Halil Bey, whose headquarters were at Urumiah, being completely routed and dispersed.

The Russians are advancing on Tabriz and Dilman. They have occupied Urumiah, Ushnu and the Turkish territory as far as Van and Melazghert, including a portion of Moush.

The Turkish offensive along the River Tchorouk was checked and broken in spite of desperate resistance. The Russians are now occupying Ardosht Ide, capturing quantities of war material. The Russians have also made great captures at Van, including twenty-five fortress guns and quantities of powder and provisions as well as the Government treasury.

Not a Life Saved.

The humaneness of the British Navy and the methods of the enemy are sharply contrasted in an Admiralty return showing the number of rescues that have been effected from sunken warships. Between August 5th and May 2nd, 1202 men were saved from German warships, including submarines. These figures include only rescues made by the British ships engaged. In several cases members of the enemy crews were saved by other means. Many of those who were subsequently made prisoners are not taken into consideration. Some 30 or 40 who were picked up, supplied with provisions and a compass and directed to Heligoland, are not included.

The Germans have rescued nobody. Six officers and 76 men of the destroyer Maori, who were rowing in their own boats after their vessel had sunk, and one officer and twelve men in boats from the Crusader, have, however, been made prisoners by the enemy.

German Official's Predicament.

There is no limit to German insolence writes the Washington Correspondent of the "Morning Post."

On the very day on which the "Lusitania" was torpedoed Count Bernstorff asked the State Department to secure from the British Government a safe conduct for the German Consul-General at New York who wanted to return home.

The Department having passed the request on to the British Embassy, the Embassy replied that "it was inconsistent for Count Bernstorff to ask for a safe conduct from the British Government as he had published advertisements warning Americans of the danger they incurred by travelling on British ships, and further, that as the German Consul-General in New York was known to have taken s leading part in the anti-British propaganda in the United States, it was hardly likely that the British Government would care to facilitate his return to his own country." So the Consul-General remains in New York to keep company with the melancholy Herr Dernburg, which is the most impressive tribute to British sea-power that Germany has rendered. Herr Dernburg, also anxious to leave, has to linger in New York because Great Britain refuses to regard his precious person as inviolate and all the German Emperor's ships cannot help him.

Peninsula Press

No. 38   Sunday, JUNE 27th. 1915   Official News.

Progress in France.

Paris, June 26

North of Arras the French have made fresh progress between Angier and Sauchez. A German counter-attack was repulsed in the Labyrinth. On the heights of the Meuse near Calonne the Germans delivered a very violent attack along the whole French front. This was accompanied by asphyxiating bombs and burning liquids. Having succeeded in penetrating into a part of their old second line of defences occupied by the French, they were repulsed by means of an energetic counter-attack. At midnight they again attempted to seize the position but were repulsed with heavy losses. In Lorraine they have tried twice to retake their lost positions but without success; in each case they were completely repulsed. They also delivered two attacks against the French trenches at Seichalserhrapf. The Germans bombarded the outskirts of Metzeral and the crests to the East of the village where the French advance had sensibly increased.

Yesterday a German aeroplane threw five bombs into the Sanatorium at Zuydcoote but did no damage.

The Retaking of Lemberg.

A Petrograd Communique says that the Russians abandoned Lemberg on the 22nd inst. and continue to retire on a new front.

The Austro-German offensive in the direction of Lemberg was arrested on the 21st and on the following night by stubborn fighting which cost the enemy dear. As, however, the Austro-Germans had succeeded in advancing toward the town of Zolkiew it was decided to evacuate Lemberg.

Russian cavalry sabred three companies West of Rewa Raska.

A wireless message dated the 24th states that the battle continues on the Dneister, where the Russians took 1,000 prisoners.

A later report says that on Tuesday and Wednesday the enemy tried to advance along the railway but failed. A desperate battle is proceeding in front of Juravia-Demesykovitz and is developing in our favour. Great German forces crossed to the left of the Dneister, on Wednesday in the

Kyaing district, but were driven back to the river.

The Austrians crossed to the left bank of the Martynaco, but were flung back. On Tuesday the Russians took the offensive on the Dneister, South of Mynioff and approached the strongly fortified position of Mount Byniennia. At dawn on Wednesday they stormed the position held by the enemy who fled in disorder. The Russians entered their works and bayonetted almost the whole garrison.

Military Honours.

The following military honours for service in the field are announced in the Birthday list:-

Grand Cross of the Bath; General Sir Douglas Haig.

K.C.B.; Major-General E. Graham Tool, Major-General F. J. Davies, Major-General Remy H. Wilson and Major-General H. F.M. Wilson

Grand Cross of St. Michael and St. George:-
General Sir Horace Smith-Dorrien, Lieut.-General Sir J. Wilkocks, Lieut.-General Sir J. Maxwell and Major-General Sir W. Birdwood.

V.C. Lieut.-Colonel Doughty-Wylie and Captain J. H. Walford. These two officers organized and led the attack through the village of Sidd-el-Bahr during the landing operations in the Gallipoli Peninsula. Both were killed at the moment of victory.

Fighting in Albania.

Rome, June 25th.

The Montenegrin army arrived on the outskirts of Scutari on the 22nd. The Albanians offered a feeble resistance.

NOTE.- Both Montenegro and Servia are showing activity in Albania, a country in which Italy has special interests.

Items of Interest.

The Admiralty announce that H.M.S. "Roxburgh," a cruiser completed in 1905, was torpedoed in the North Sea on the 20th inst. The damage was not serious and the cruiser was able to proceed under her own steam. There were no casualties.

The number of prisoners taken by the French in the district of the Fecht, since June 14 is: 25 officers, 58 N.C.O.s and 588 men.

In the House of Commons Mr. Asquith announced that the total naval casualties were, killed; officers 549, men 7,696, wounded: officers 181, men 2,262; missing: officers 74; men 2,785.

PENINSULA PRESS.

No. 88   SUNDAY, JUNE 27th 1915.   Official News.

Progress in France.

Paris, June 26

North of Arras the French have made fresh progress between Angier and Souchez. A German counter-attack was repulsed in the Labyrinth. On the heights of the Meuse near Calonne the Germans delivered a very violent attack along the whole French front. This was accompanied by asphyxiating bombs and burning liquids. Having succeeded in penetrating into a part of their old second line of defences occupied by the French, they were repulsed by means of an energetic counter-attack. At midnight they again attempted to seize the position but were repulsed with heavy losses. In Lorraine they have tried twice to retake their lost positions but without success : in each case they were completely repulsed. They also delivered two attacks against the French trenches at Seichalserhrapf. The Germans bombarded the outskirts of Metzeral and the crests to the East of the village where the French advance had sensibly increased.

Yesterday a German aeroplane threw five bombs into the Sanatorium at Zuydcoote but did no damage.

The Retaking of Lemberg.

A Petrograd Communique says that the Russians abandoned Lemberg on the 22nd inst. and continue to retire on a new front.

The Austro-German offensive in the direction of Lemberg was arrested on the 21st and on the following night by stubborn fighting which cost the enemy dear. As, however, the Austro-Germans had succeeded in advancing toward the town of Zolkiew it was decided to evacuate Lemberg.

Russian cavalry sabred three companies West of Rewa Ruska.

A wireless message dated the 24th states that the battle continues on the Dneister, where the Russians took 1,000 prisoners.

A later report says that on Tuesday and Wednesday the enemy tried to advance along the railway but failed. A desperate battle is proceeding in front of Juravia-Demesykovitz and is developing in our favour. Great German forces crossed to the left of the Dneister, on Wednesday in the Kyaing district, but were driven back to the river.

The Austrians crossed to the left bank of the Martynaco, but were flung back. On Tuesday the Russians took the offensive on the Dneister, South of Mynioff, and approached the strongly fortified position of Mount Byniennia. At dawn on Wednesday they stormed the position held by the enemy who fled in disorder. The Russians entered their works and bayonetted almost the whole garrison.

Military Honours.

The following military honours for service in the field are announced in the Birthday list :—

Grand Cross of the Bath ; General Sir Douglas Haig.

K.C.B. ; Major-General E. Graham Tool, Major-General F. J. Davies, Major-General Henry H. Wilson and Major-General H. F. M. Wilson.

Grand Cross of St. Michael and St. George :— General Sir Horace Smith-Dorrien, Lieut.-General Sir J. Willcocks, Lieut.-General Sir J. Maxwell and Major-General Sir W. Birdwood.

V.C. Lieut.-Colonel Doughty-Wylie and Captain J. H. Walford. These two officers organized and led the attack through the village of Sidd-el-Bahr during the landing operations in the Gallipoli Peninsula. Both were killed at the moment of victory.

Fighting in Albania.

Rome, June 25th.

The Montenegrin army arrived on the outskirts of Scutari on the 22nd. The Albanians offered a feeble resistance.

NOTE.—Both Montenegro and Servia are showing activity in Albania, a country in which Italy has special interests.

Items of Interest.

The Admiralty announce that H.M.S. " Roxburgh," a cruiser completed in 1905, was torpedoed in the North Sea on the 20th inst. The damage was not serious and the cruiser was able to proceed under her own steam. There were no casualties.

The number of prisoners taken by the French in the district of the Fecht., since June 14 is : 25 officers, 53 N.C.O.s and 538 men.

In the House of Commons Mr. Asquith announced that the total naval casualties were, killed; officers 549, men 7,696; wounded: officers 181, men 2,262; missing: officers 74; men 2,785.

R.E. Printing Section, G.H.Q., M.E.F.

Peninsula Press

No. 39   Monday, JUNE 28th. 1915   Official News.

German Reverse in Galicia.

The rejoicings in Germany over the victory at Lemberg were damped by tonight's Berlin communique admitting reverses in the Russian theatre of war and that they have been compelled to evacuate ground in Galicia which had been captured on Wednesday.

The German advance near Lemberg has been arrested and a battle is in progress which is developing favourably for the Russians. A large body of the enemy who had crossed the Dneister were driven back.
(Rinella Press, June 27)

Albanians Appeal to Italy.

Mursa, a tribal chieftain, has been acclaimed president of the Albanian Government.

Rome despatches state that the Servian advance guards have established themselves at El Basan and Tirana and in the outskirts of Durazzo.

Montenegrin troops have occupied the famous Tarabosc hill which dominates the town of Scutari and have taken possession of the customs house on the River Bojana and of the barracks outside the town on Monte Verde.

They are threatening Scutari from both sides.

The Albanians of Scutari are demanding the immediate occupation of this town by the Italians. The Italian Consul, has obtained an assurance from the Montenegrins that they will respect Scutari.

[NOTE.- Scutari is the largest town in Albania, containing over 30,000 inhabitants. The population is mixed Christian and Moslem though the former is largely predominate. The Christians are Roman Catholic and consequently not friendly to the Montenegrins who are Orthodox. During the Balkan war, it will be remembered that Scutari was captured by the Montenegrins but that Austria-Hungary would not agree to their retaining it and King Nicolas withdrew his troops under protest.]

"After the War is Over."

The Director of the Military Museum at Constantinople has lately issued the following notice:-

"The public are hereby informed that the 700 British mitrailleuses and 300 French cannon captured during the battle of Ari-Bournou at Gallipoli by our heroic troops, in the course of bayonet charges in which they drove into the sea and drowned more than twenty thousand of the enemy, will be on exhibit in the foreign gallery of the museum immediately after the cessation of hostilities."

On the Western Front.

Paris, June 27th.

The French advance in the district of Arras is checked by the state of the ground which in places has been rendered impossible by recent storms. A heavy artillery duel took place North of Sauchez and Neuville, while East of the Labyrinth there was a fight with hand grenades.

East of Albert, at Le Boiselle, the Germans fired two mines without result.

Between the Oise and the Aisne, especially round Queanevieres, there have been artillery engagements; and West of the Argonne a few hand grenade fights have enabled the French to advance slightly.

In the Champagne and Argonne Sectors, the battle of the mines continues, the French having the advantage, capturing four machine guns and a large quantity of rifles, cartridges and grenades.

A German attack in the Vosges was repulsed

Italian Progress.

The Italians are progressing in the Tyrol. Their guns continue to smash the fortifications at Mallionghetta. (Rinella Press, June 27).

Turks in the Argentine.

The Turkish subjects at Buenos Aires have presented an address to the Argentine Foreign Minister refusing to be represented by the German Consul.

Submarine v. Submarine.

The Italian submarine "Medusa" which carried out useful and daring reconnaissances, was torpedoed by an enemy submarine. An officer and four of the crew were rescued and are prisoners.

The "Medusa" was built in 1914. It had a displacement of 250 tons and a speed of eight knots under water and 14 above. This is the first time in the history of naval warfare that a submarine has sunk one of its own kind.

The Munitions Problem.

London, Wednesday.

A conference of Trade Union representatives pledged themselves to support Mr. Lloyd George's scheme for transferring men from commercial work to munition factories. It was also decided to do everything to prevent disputes throughout the country.

The New Derby and Oaks.

The New Derby was run at Newmarket in fine weather. O'Neill rode Gadabout. When fairly in sight Pommern drew to the front. Maintaining his lead to the end he won in a canter.

(Newmarket). 17th June. The result of the New Oak's was:- Snow Marten 1, Bright 2, Silver Tagg 3. Eleven ran. Won by four lengths; a head between second and third. Betting 20-1 Snow Marten; 7-1 Bright; 11-4 Silver Tag.

Peninsula Press

No. 40   Tuesday, JUNE 29th. 1915   Official News.

Au Drapeau !

There was an impressive parade on Thursday night at Sidd-el-Bahr for the presentation of Legions of Honour and Medailles Militaires to French Officers and men in the Expeditionary Force.

A small body of troops was drawn up in hollow square, with bayonets sparkling in the light of a full moon, and in the centre of the square stood the brave officers and men who were to receive their great honour. Behind them was a line of officers and chevaliers of the Legion, with drawn swords, waiting to greet those whose names were now to be inscribed on the roll of fame.

Punctually to the minute, General Gouraud, the French Commander, came on to the ground, accompanied by Lieut.-General Hunter Weston, commanding the British 8th Corps. The bugles rang the general salute and then to each gallant officer, N.C.O. and man General Gouraud presented the distinctions, stating in a few well chosen words the particular acts of bravery and devotion which had won the reward.

The whole M.E.F. will rejoice to know that chief among those whom their country has delighted to honour was Colonel Girodon who, unfortunately, owing to his wound was unable to be present to receive the high honour of "Commander of the Legion" so admirably earned in the fine affair of the 21st inst.

Austrian Reverse in Galicia.

A wireless message says that a Vienna communique admits that the Russians have pierced the Austrian front between the Dneister and the Pruth.

German Submarine Sunk.

Amsterdam, Tuesday.

A German submarine sank near Borkum, after an explosion on board. The commander and two of the crew were saved. (Rinella Press).

Canada's 150,000.

General Hughes, Canadian Minister of Defence, is making an appeal for an additional 85,000 soldiers. The new contingent will be composed of

27 regiments of infantry and six batteries of artillery, recruited from all parts of the Dominion. Four Highland regiments will be included. This new force will bring the number of soldiers raised in Canada for active service to more than 150,000. (Daily Graphic).

Norway has lost 27 ships, Sweden 24, and Denmark 14 since German submarines started their piracy against unarmed merchantmen.

(London Paper).

Petrograd, Tuesday.
The Russian Minister of War has resigned. (Rinella Press).

On the West Front.
Paris, June 28th.
North of Arras the Germans succeeded in reaching the sunk road from Ablain to Angres, along a front of about 200 yards. North of the Oise and of the Aisne, near to Quennevieres, after a fight with grenades, a small body of Germans tried to advance from their trenches and were easily repulsed. At Bagattelle, in the Argonne, the Germans made a very violent attack early in the night of 26th and 27th, and, after a fierce fight were finally repulsed. On the heights of the Meuse, East of Calonne, the Germans made an attack which was repulsed everywhere except in one small portion of trenches. The fight continued during the whole night. The French positions and gains have been maintained.

In Lorraine, after having thrown incendiary shells on Arracourt, the Germans attempted a, coup de main on the village but the attack was defeated. On June 25th, French aviators dropped 20 shells of which ten were 155's on the railway station of Douai and the neighbourhood. The station of Douai appears to have been seriously damaged.

(Official report).

"Come and Surrender!"
Having boasted that they had driven us into the sea, the Teutonized Turks are seeking to beguile us into submission. At Anzac the other day a German aeroplane was seen to drop some papers which were carried by the wind into the Turkish trenches. The Turks tied a couple to the tail of a bomb and delivered the strayed leaflets into our lines. It was a proclamation inviting us to surrender on the grounds that our British men-of-war have abandoned us to our fate and we are "exposed to certain perdition by starvation or thirst." Australians and New Zealanders are informed that "Greedy England made you fight under a contract. You may confide in us for excellent treatment. Our country disposes of ample provisions. There is enough to feed you well and

make you feel quite at your comfort. Don't further hesitate. Come and surrender!"

As the German directors of the conscience and the arms of Turkey did not succeed in their efforts to distribute this invitation to a meal we have no hesitation in giving it the wider publicity of the "Peninsula Press."

Suppressing the Peace Maker.

Amsterdam, Tuesday.
The German Socialist newspaper, "Vorwaerts" has been suppressed for publishing articles advocating peace.   (Rinella Press).

Captain Disguised as Cook.
The Captain of the German auxiliary cruiser, Prince Eitel Fredrich, which was interned by the United States authorities, has been arrested on board an Italian steamer in the Straits of Gibraltar. The Captain was disguised as a cook.   (Reuter).

Peninsula Press

No. 41   Wednesday, JUNE 30th. 1915   Official News.

Gaining Ground in the Peninsula.

The plan of operations on Monday was to throw forward the left of our line South-east of Krithia, pivoting on a point about one mile from the sea, and after advancing the extreme left for about half a mile, to establish a new line facing East on ground thus gained.

This plan entailed the capture in succession of two lines of Turkish trenches East of the Saghir Dare and five lines of trenches West of it. The Australian Corps was ordered to co-operate by making a vigorous demonstration. The action opened at 9 a.m. with the bombardment, by heavy artillery of the trenches to be captured. The assistance rendered by the French in this bombardment was most valuable. At 10.20 our Field Artillery opened fire to cut the wire in front of the Turkish trenches and this was effectively done. Great effect on enemy's trenches near the sea and in keeping down his artillery fire from that quarter was produced by the very accurate fire of H.M.S. "Talbot", "Scorpion" and "Wolverine". At 10.45 a small Turkish advanced work in the Saghir Dere, known as the Boomerang redoubt, was assaulted. This little fort was very strongly sited, protected by extra strong wire entanglements and has long been a source of trouble.

After special bombardment by French mortar, and while the bombardment of surrounding trenches was at its height, part of the Border Regiment, at the exact moment prescribed, leapt, from their trenches as one man like a pack of hounds streaming out of cover, raced across and took the work most brilliantly. The artillery bombardment increased in intensity till 11 a.m. when the range was lengthened and the infantry advanced.

The infantry attack was carried out with great dash along the whole line. West of Saghir Dere the 87th Brigade captured three lines of trenches with little opposition. The trenches were full of dead Turks, many buried by the bombardment, and one hundred prisoners were taken in them. East of the ravine two battalions of Royal Scots made a fine attack, capturing the two lines of trenches assigned as their objective, but the remainder of the 156th Brigade on their right met with a severe opposition and were unable to get forward.

At 11.30, the 86th Brigade, led by 2nd Royal Fusiliers, started the second phase of attack West of the ravine. They advanced with great steadiness and resolution through the trenches already captured and on across the open, and taking two more lines of trenches reached the objective allotted to them, the Lancashire Fusiliers inclining half-right and forming line to connect with our new position East of the ravine.

The northernmost objective had now been attained, but the Gurkhas pressing on under the cliffs captured an important knoll still further forward, actually due West of Krithia. This they fortified and held during the night making our total gain on the left of precisely one thousand yards. During the afternoon the 88th Brigade attacked a trench, a small portion of which remained uncaptured on the right, but the enemy held on stubbornly, supported by machine guns and artillery and the attacks did not succeed.

During the night the enemy counter-attacked the furthest trenches gained, but was repulsed with heavy loss. A party of Turks who penetrated from the flank between the two lines of captured trenches, were subjected to machine gun fire at daybreak, suffered very heavily and survivors surrendered. Except for a small portion of the trench already mentioned, which is still held by the enemy, all and more than was hoped for from the operation has been gained. On the extreme left our line has been pushed forward to a specially strong point well beyond the limit of the advance originally contemplated. The line gained is being consolidated and is much more advantageously sited than that previously held. The enemy's casualties are reported to be very severe. Our casualties were about 2,000, the greater proportion of which are slight cases of which 250 were at Anzac in the useful demonstration made simultaneously there.

All engaged did well but certainly the chief factor in the success was the splendid attack carried out by 29th Division whose conduct in this, as on previous occasions, was beyond praise.

Quiet on the Western Front

Paris 29th

The official report issued last evening says:- Along the whole front the day was comparatively quiet. North of Sauchez, at Neuville and Rochincourt, there was an Artillery duel. Arras has again been bombarded with heavy guns. Between the Oise and the Aisne artillery engagements are proceeding in favour of the French. In the Argonne and on the heights of the Meuse, along the trench of Calonne, the Germans have not renewed their attack after the check of last night.

During the morning of the 27th a French airman succeeded in throwing five bombs on the Zeppelin sheds of Friedrichshaffen. His motor failed and during the return journey he had to come down at Rheinfezden, in Swiss Territory.

To Repeat the Crime of Rheims.

Not content with destroying historic buildings at Rheims, Louvain and Arras, the German Vandals are casting malicious eyes on St. Mark's, Venice, and on Milan Cathedral. The "Vossische Zeitung" has already made the discovery that wireless telegraphic apparatus and anti-aircraft guns have been placed on these famous churches, and that the Austrians would be justified in making air attacks on them.

The Austrians were not slow to take the hint. One of their aeroplanes aimed a bomb at St. Mark's. Luckily, it fell in the Royal Garden a few yards from St. Mark's Square.

(Egyptian Gazette).

City Men as War Workers.

The authorities at the Royal Arsenal, Woolwich have accepted the offer of a number of city business men to devote their Sundays to helping in the manufacture of munitions. A similar offer has been made by salesman of Smithfield. The work allotted to these amateur munition makers will, of course, be of a simple, though not less valuable, character, and, as time goes on, each will be given the duties for which he proves best fitted. Each man will be paid at the standard rates for the work he is doing. (London Paper).

Peninsula Press

No. 42   Thursday, JULY 1st. 1915   Official News.

Australians and New Zealanders in Action.

Further details have now been received with regard to the part played by the Australian and New Zealand Army Corps in the operations of Monday.

This Army Corps, as we said yesterday, was instructed to undertake operations with a view to preventing the enemy on its front from detaching troops to the Southern area. Between 11.30 a.m. and 12 noon, the action was opened by H.M.S. "Humber," "Pincher" and "Chelmer" engaging the enemy's heavy guns and trenches. At 1 p.m. three and a half squadrons of the 2nd Light Horse Brigade moved out on the right of the position, advancing some 700 yards when the enemy was encountered in strength. On their left, two companies of the 9th Battalion, 3rd Brigade, advanced under cover of supporting fire of neighbouring troops and from trenches and reached a line close to the Turkish trenches, 700 yards in front of our line. Meanwhile our artillery engaged the enemy's reserves collecting in the ravine opposite the right centre, shelling them effectively with guns and howitzers. Along the remainder of the front, the enemy was kept engaged by rifle fire and bomb attacks which drew heavy rifle fire and artillery fire. About 2.30 p.m., indications were seen of a massing of enemy's troops for a counter-attack against the left of our advanced troops. Howitzer fire being turned on, the enemy's attack failed to develop in any strength and a weak attack was repulsed by machine gun fire.

The retirement of advanced troops was begun at 3 p.m. well covered by rifle, machine gun and artillery fire and the troops were all back in the trenches by 4.30 p.m., except on the extreme right, where they were in by 5.30.

The enemy's casualties cannot be estimated but our machine guns found targets in the open on several occasions and many Turks were seen to fall. The artillery also did considerable execution against reserves caught moving up in the open towards areas previously registered. The Naval gun fire also gave valuable assistance. All indications showing that the enemy was in a state of confusion and apprehension, and was keeping the trenches fully manned, two demonstrations were made after dark at 8.45 and 11.30 p.m. with flares, star shell and destroyer bombardment. Both successfully drew heavy fire from the enemy.

The 8th Corps report 180 prisoners taken since the morning of the 28th, namely 88 of 16th regiment, 139 of 33rd regiment and 8 of 126th regiment. A Circassian prisoner carried a wounded private of the Royal Scots into our lines under fire.

Russian Fleet in the Black Sea

Since our engagements on May 10th with the "Goeben" and on June 11th with the "Breslau," now under repair, these Turkish war ships have not appeared in the Black Sea. We captured a steamer on June 15th and since then all traffic have been stopped in the Elreqli-Zongouldick region. On June 23rd and 27th we burned eight sailing vessels, most of which were carrying benzine, explosive shells, petrol and provisions from Roumania and Bulgaria.

(Russian Official Report).

The Submarine "Blockade."

What an insignificant effect Admiral van Tirpitz's much-advertised "blockade" of Great Britain by German submarines is having upon our overseas trade is shown by the returns at exports and imports during May.

Our imports for the month, amounting to £71,644,000, showed an increase of £12,545,000 on the same month of last year, when there was no war to interfere with international exchange. Of this increase over £8,000,000 represents articles of food, drink and tobacco. The month's exports, valued at £38,618,000, were the largest registered since the commencement of the war.

Taking the whole five months of the present year, the value of the goods imported into the United Kingdom country is £85,601,000 greater than in the corresponding period of last year.

(Daily Telegraph).

The Policy of Greece.

The King of Greece, who has been suffering from pleurisy, is now convalescent.

M. Venizelos, who secured a majority at the recent elections, has authorised a statement that he is convinced that any policy, except supporting the Entente Powers, would be disastrous to Greece. (Reuter).

The Greek Parliament will not meet till the 20th, M. Gounranis, the defeated Premier having put forweard the King's illness as a reason for delaying the assembling of the Chamber.

The Germans in Africa.

The Press bureau announces that the expedition against Port Bukoboan on the Western shore of the Victoria Nyanza, the base of the German operations, is of considerable importance. The expedition sailed from Kisumu on the 26th of June, commanded by Brigadier-General Stewart. The British force along the river Kagera, co-operated. The operations have been successful and the troops are returning, after destroying the fort, the wireless station and many boats and machine guns.

Pretoria.

General Botha is advancing North into German South West Africa, occupying Ogwarongo, Okanyande and Waterburg, one hundred miles from Bloemfontein. (Rinella).

America and Germany.

Washington.

The State Department says that Germany will give a favourable reply to the last American note on the sinking of unarmed merchant-men. (Rivella [*sic*]).

German Attempt to Control American Munition Factories.

The New York "Sun" learns "authoritatively that German agents sought to buy stock in order to control the big factories which are working day and night on war contracts, failing which they began a widespread plan to influence labour leaders and forment strikes.

This scheme to prevent delivery of guns and ammunition to the Allied Powers was engineered by the German Government. Count Bernstorff, the German Ambassador, explained to a conference of German bankers in New York that there was "no limit to the amount of money available."

The conspiracy is not likely to succeed. Apart from the fact that the Germans would not be able to find the means of making gigantic payments in the present state of their financial relations with the United States, the promoters of such a scheme would be liable to prosecution under the Anti-Trust Act."

Peninsula Press

No. 43   Friday, JULY 2nd. 1915   Official News.

Another Success on our Front.

The operations of Monday, June 28th, already reported, have led to still further success, this time on our right. On Tuesday afternoon we received reports of hostile columns visible from Anzac, moving West from North of Achi Baba and South from Kilid Bahr, towards the Turkish right flank, indicating that the enemy was massing for counter-attack against the position we captured on the previous day.

The Commander-in-Chief requested the Vice-Admiral to send two destroyers to assist in repelling counter-attack in case of need and informed General Gouraud of the situation, suggesting that the enemy's movement might facilitate any operations he might have in contemplation.

Meanwhile, at Anzac, two mine galleries in front of the right centre were blown in during the evening, after which the enemy subjected our trenches for two hours to heavy rifle and machine gun fire with some artillery fire. After a lull and another outburst of fire, a determined attack was made with the bayonet against the left of the position. This attack was repulsed with heavy loss to the enemy, all Turks who reached our trenches being bayonetted and a few prisoners taken.

The enemy's casualties are difficult to estimate, but 300 killed seems a modest estimate, one hundred lying close to our trenches and 60 more visible from our outpost. On the Southern front, the Turks, as anticipated, made a concerted attack along the coast against our Northernmost trenches. H.M.S. "Wolverine" got searchlights and guns on to the main body and must have caused heavy loss. Further East, the attack was pressed closer under heavy artillery fire but was finally checked about 40 yards from our parapet. Bomb attacks and intermittent shelling long continued but no further general attack was made.

The enemy's losses were heavy, the ground being thick with dead and wounded Turks, probably 500 in all. Our casualties in this part were about 175 since noon on Tuesday.

On the Royal Naval Division front there was heavy rifle and machine gun fire during the night, but no attack was made in the centre.

At about 6.30 a.m. on Wednesday the French moved out and by 7.20 had taken a strong system of entrenchments immediately in front of the left centre of the line, called by them the "Quadrilateral." The consolidation of the "Quadrilateral," was begun at once. The casualties are reported at only about 75. The 42nd Division reported a number of Turks seen driven out of the trenches by the French bombardment and much execution was done during their retreat.

Subsequently trenches prolonging the "Quadrilateral" to the South were captured after more serious fighting, thus completing the capture of all that part of enemy's line required to round off the gains made by the French on the 21st ult. The enemy's losses were very considerable.

Stubborn Fighting on the Dneister.

Petrograd, June 30th.

A stubborn battle continues to he fought on the Dneister. On the 27th the enemy was repulsed everywhere with heavy losses. East of Lemberg on the 28th, great forces of the enemy made desperate attacks on the left of the Dneister and were defeated.

The advance of great forces of the enemy between the sources of the river Vieprz, near Lublin, continues. On Sunday and Monday our rearguard in the region of Tomazoff repulsed several desperate attacks. Reinforced by fresh German troops on the Dneister the enemy endeavoured to throw into confusion the Russian retiring on Grailalipa. Their attacks failed and their losses were enormous.

(Renilla Wireless).

On the Western Front.

Paris, July 1st.

Violent artillery fire and some infantry action marked the night in the region North of Arras. The French have advanced slightly North of the chateau of Carleal, and to the South of Cabaret Rouge a German attack has been repulsed. In the Upper Vosges the French retook and on the 29th ult., all the positions they had previously occupied East of Metzeral. At two o'clock in the morning the Germans attempted a fresh attack which was easily repulsed.

(Official report).

Peace Demonstrations in Berlin.

Berne.

The Berne Correspondent of the "Morning Post" writes:-
Since March 18th, when, as I telegraphed, a great women's demonstration for peace took place in Berlin, the police and the

authorities have evidently dreaded a similar manifestation of feeling, being well aware that a strong desire for peace exists among certain classes of the population, especially the women. When the Reichstag met on May the 18th, the building was guarded by police, and the public were excluded from the street along which the deputies had to pass. On the Reichstag re-assembling on May the 28th, after the Whitsuntide recess, still greater precautions were taken, great numbers of police and plain clothes detectives, and afterwards a force of mounted police, being stationed around the Reichstag building. Nevertheless, a crowd of about two thousand, mostly women, managed to assemble just before the meeting of the Reichstag in front of the building, and, despite the police, who took many persons into custody, contrived to make a demonstration. Three Social Democrats who showed sympathy with the women were also arrested, and are still under arrest. The Wolff Bureau lost no time in telegraphing instructions to all the German newspapers to say absolutely nothing about these occurrences, which explains the fact that it is only now that the news has reached me.

Peninsula Press

No. 44   Saturday, JULY 3rd. 1915   Official News.

The Attack that Failed.

Further details have now been received of the attack made by the Turks on the night of the 29th-30th ult. At about 2 o'clock on Wednesday morning the searchlights of H.M.S. "Scorpion" discovered half a Turkish battalion advancing near the sea, North-west of Krithia. The "Scorpion" opened fire and few of the enemy got away. Simultaneously, the enemy attacked the knoll we had captured due West of Krithia, advancing from the nullah in close formation in several lines. The attack came under artillery and enfilade rifle fire and the enemy lost heavily. The foremost Turks got within 40 yards of the parapet, but only a few returned.

The Turks made several heavy bomb attacks during the night, our troops being twice driven back a short distance. In the early morning we regained these trenches by bayonet attack and they have since been strengthened. At 5.30 a.m. 2,000 Turks moving from Krithia into the ravine were scattered by machine gun fire. The operations reflect great credit on the vigilance and the accurate shooting of H.M.S. "Scorpion." The Turkish losses in the nullah and ravine are estimated at from 1,500 to 2,000 dead. At about 10 p.m. on Wednesday the Turks again attacked with bombs a portion of the most northerly trench captured by us on the 29th.

An officer of the Gurkas being wounded (not dangerously as it turned out) the men became infuriated flung all their bombs at the enemy, and then charging down out of the trench, used their kukris with great effect. About dawn the Turks once more attempted an attack over the open but nearly the whole of these attacking forces, about half a battalion, were shot down; and a final bomb attack, though commenced, failed utterly.

A further report from Anzac of the enemy's attack on Tuesday and Wednesday last, on our right flank states that the action commenced with very heavy fire from midnight till 1.30 a.m. to which our men replied only by a series of cheers. The Turks then launched their attack and came right on with bayonet and bombs. Those who succeeded in getting into our saps were instantly killed, the remainder being dealt with by bomb and rifle fire from the 7th and 8th Light Horse. By 2 a.m. the enemy broke and many were killed while withdrawing. The enemy's attack was strongest on his right. They were completely taken aback by a concealed sap constructed well ahead of our main line, and their dead are lying thickly in front of this. Some got into the sap and several got across it, and all these were wiped out by fire from the main parapet farther back. Following the defeat of this attack, the enemy attacked at 3 a.m. on our left and 30 men came over the parapets in front of the right of Quinn's Post. These were duly polished off.

Prisoners brought in state that three fresh battalions were employed in the main attack which was made by the personal order of Enver Pasha who, as they definitely assert, was present in the trenches on Tuesday the 29th ult.

Wednesday was very quiet at Anzac, except for heavy musketry fire along our left and centre during the storm in the evening. Latest report of enemy casualties on 29th, estimates them at between 400 and 500 actually seen to fall on those areas alone that are exposed to view and exclusive of any loss inflicted by our bombardments of reverse slopes and gullies in which reserves are known to be collecting.

It is manifest with what apprehension the Turks regard out latest gains and how bravely they have tried to neutralize them and at what cost.

On the West Front.

Paris, July 2nd.

After a continuous bombardment which lasted three days, the Germans attacked the French positions in the Argonne, between the road from Binarville and the Four-de-Paris. Twice driven back, they eventually succeeded, after a third attempt, in setting foot in some parts of the French lines near Bagatelle, and were repulsed everywhere else after a very fierce struggle. Two fresh attacks against the trenches to the East of the road from Binarville were defeated. A violent attack in the neighbourhood of Metzeral was completely repulsed, the Germans suffering heavy losses.

(Official Report by wireless).

Letters to a Turkish Soldier at the Front

The following characteristic letters, written to a Turkish soldier at the front, will be read with interest:-

"To my dear son-in-law, Hussein Aga. First, I send you my best salaams and I kiss your eyes. Your mother Atrf also kisses your eyes. Mustafa also kisses your eyes and Mrs. Kerim also sends her salaams. Your daughter Ayesha kisses your eyes. Should you inquire after our health, thank God I can tell you we are a health, and I pray God we may continue to be so. Your letter of the 4th February we have received.

Your mother kisses your eyes and Abdullah kisses both your hands. Your brother, Bairham's wife, has died – may your own life be long – but before dying she brought into the world a child. The child also has died.

What can I say about the decrees of God? Your brother Bairham has also been taken as a soldier. We pray God that his health may he preserved. The money you sent has arrived. Thank God for it, for money is scarce these days. Everybody sends salaams: everybody kisses your hands and your feet. God keep you from danger."

     Your Father
      Falk.

To my dear husband, Hussein Aga. I humbly beg to inquire after your blessed health. Your daughter sends her special salaams and kisses your hands. Since you left I have seen no one. Since your departure I have no peace. Your mother has not ceased to weep since you left. Your daughter declares that she is enceinte and weeps all day. We are all in a bad way. Your wife says to herself "While my husband was here we had some means." Since your departure we have received nothing at all. Please write quickly and send what money you can. All your friends kiss your hands and your feet. May God keep you and save us from the disasters of this war.

     Your Wife
      Fatima.

Peninsula Press

No. 45   Sunday, JULY 4th. 1915   Official News.

On Our Front.

SOUTHERN SECTION.- Thursday night was quiet on the French front, but on our extreme left, part of one of the newly captured trenches, held by the 10th Gurkhas, was subjected to a heavy bomb attack which caused the evacuation of that part of the trench. This was subsequently recaptured by the Inniskilling Fusiliers and is held. On Friday evening, Turkish guns commenced a heavy bombardment of the two furthermost trenches recently captured on our left and on the cliff to the North of them. The bombardment lasted half an hour and was immediately followed by an attack from the ravine North of our position against our extreme left. Promptly dealt with by the guns of H.M.S. "Scorpion" and heavy rifle and machine gun fire from our trenches, the attack died away.

NORTHERN SECTION.- During the night of Friday there were some bursts of fire from the Turkish trenches, which shows them to be still apprehensive of attack. A half-hearted attack with bombs was delivered against a party covering the work on advanced trenches on our left.

On the French Front.

Paris, July 2nd.

The French official report issued to-day says:-
The artillery fire has been very violent North of Arras and near Ypres. From Souchez to the North of the Aisne the Germans made a bomb attack against the French position. The attack failed completely.

Near La Boiselle and before Dompiere French mines broke up the enemy's organisation. From the Argonne it is confirmed that on the 30th of June, between the Binarrille Road and the Four de Paris the Germans made an attack with the intention of breaking the French line. The first trenches were reached only because of the heavy artillery and the use of asphyxiating shells, but the Germans were stopped by the strength of the second line and then thrown back by infantry counter-attacks which established themselves along the front about 200 yards from the first French line. Three fresh attacks were instantly checked and in the wood of Le Pretre a German attempt was also defeated.

Austro-German Advance in Galicia.

Petrograd, July 3rd.

The enemy's offensive East of Lublin, between the rivers Vieprz and Bug, on the front Zamose and Ashal, continues. We repulsed attacks on the river Bug and Gutarlalipa on Monday and Tuesday. Noticing the enemy crossing the Dneister near Halicz, North of Stanislau, we took the offensive and drove them back, taking 1,000 prisoners.

A squadron of German warships, including one battleship, four light cruisers and several destroyers, tried to make a landing at Widau. The attempt failed. One of the enemy's destroyers was sunk by a mine. Our destroyers, protecting Widau, forced the German squadron to retreat.

(Renilla Wireless)

Organising the Country.

Mr. Lloyd George, introducing the Munitions Bill, declared that where the Allies were making progress at any point of the line, it was due to the superiority of munitions. The Allies had the superiority in men both in numbers and quality. He had been told that the enemy was turning out a quarter of a million shells daily. We could surpass even that if we worked in earnest. Indeed, if Great Britain in the next few months could produce as much as France, then the Allies would have an overwhelming superiority in the first great essential of victory.

The country, said Mr. Lloyd George, had been organised into ten munition areas each managed by a committee of local business men, assisted by an expert and a representative of the War Office and Admiralty.

Mr. Lloyd George concluded by emphasizing the need for skilled labour to double the output of machine guns. Every available machine gun would be of vital necessity if Germany swung her forces from East to West.

(Reuter).

Austria's Early Preparation.

After heavy storms the general attack has been resumed with greater violence. The Italians are finding stronger and better organised resistance on the part of the Austrians whose numerous defences were prepared years before the outbreak of war and include many lines of entrenchments, tunnels, galleries, caves concealing artillery excavated in the rocks, false trenches meant to deceive the enemy and also ditches and traps innumerable forming a complete labyrinth. During the fighting on the spurs of Monte Nero a shot from an Italian big gun fell on a rock trench and the debris swept half a company of Austrians over a precipice. Many Austrian regiments have been sent back from Galicia as some Slavs and Czechs refused to fight against the Italians. One battery was discovered carefully firing in the air. (Reuter).

Floreat Etona.

Eton has given many of her sons to the service of the country. How many there are under arms it is impossible to say, but there is a published record, compiled by Mr. Vaughan, of those on active service. In the latest edition there are 2,210 names. Of these 821 have been killed or have died of wounds, 482 have been wounded, and 216 have been mentioned in dispatches. Among the names of the killed is that of Captain Francis Grenfell, who was one of the first to gain the Victoria Cross in the war. The names of three other holders of the Victoria Cross appear, and all three have died at the front – Lord Roberts. Brigadier-General Fitz Clarence, and Brigadier-General J. E. Gough.

Women and War.

London.

There has been a remarkable increase recently in the employment of women throughout the country, in every class of work including banks, railways, farms and tramways. The Government has been the pioneer in the movement which found work for a vast number of women in shell making. Government is now engaging women to act as postmen and messengers.

Mr. J. J. Thomas, Labour Member for Derby, speaking at Nottingham to railway workers, said that he was convinced that female labour had come to stay, but it must not be used to reduce the status of men.

(Reuter).

Peninsula Press

No. 46 Monday, JULY 5th. 1915 Official News.

Instructive Extracts from Turkish Orders.

The following extract from Turkish orders shows that the Turks have passed the limit of their resources in trained men and have to fall back on recruits who join the ranks without any preparation:-

"The men of the 1st and 2nd Companies of the 127th Regiment, in order to learn how to load and fire the rifle and to take aim, must have their practice cartridges in small quantities."

The Turk is a stubborn defender of prepared positions, though there are times when he fails to satisfy his leaders, who complain of trenches "lost through carelessness." Colonel Rifaat, who commands the 11th Division, declares that "it is our principle not to lose any trenches captured from the enemy." To enforce this principle, he has issued the following order:-

"Henceforth commanders who surrender these trenches from whatever side the attack may come, before the last man is killed, will be punished in the same way as if they had run away. Especially will the commanders of units told off to guard a certain front be punished, if instead of thinking about their work, supporting their units and giving information to the higher command, they only take action after a regrettable incident has taken place. I hope that this will not occur again. I give notice that if it does I shall carry out the punishment.

I do not desire to see a blot made on the courage of our men by those who escape from the trenches to avoid the rifle and machine-gun fire of the enemy. Henceforth, I shall hold responsible all officers who do not shoot with their revolvers all the privates who try to escape from the trenches on any pretext.
   (Sd) Comander of the 11th Division
    Colonal Rifaat

The Commander of the 1st Battn.
The contents will be communicated to the officers and I promised to carry out the order till the last drop of our blood has been shed.
Sign and return.
   (Sd) Hassan
     Commander of the 127th Regt
(signatures of Company Commanders follow)

On the West Front.

Paris, July 3rd.

The French official report, received by wireless, says:-
The day has been marked by renewed activity of the German artillery, particularly in Belgium. At Roclaincourt and on the front from the Somme to the Aisne, the French have attacked the German trenches on the right bank of the Aisne, in the district of Soupir and Troyan, as well as in Champagne. In the Argonne the day has been quieter and the Germans since their last checks have made no infantry attacks. On the heights of the Meuse, near Calonne, the artillery fire continued. In the Vosges there have been some artillery actions at Fontennelle and at Hartmansweiler.

Another Submarine Raid.

After an absence of twenty-four days one of our submarines has returned. She has torpedoed a large steamer in Panderma in the Sea of Marmora and sunk ten sailing vessels, of which seven contained grain, foodstuffs and petrol, and one was loaded with 100 tons of granite blocks.

The Struggle in Galicia.

London.

The progress of the retreat of the Russians and their ability to continue hitting back at the pursuing forces, will be closely watched in the coming days. It is certain that the Germans will not be deterred by occasional blows from endeavouring to carry out their plan, namely to separate the central and southern Russian armies and to deal a smashing blow. So far, this object has not been accomplished, but it is in nowise abandoned.

Experts are confident that the Grand Duke will hold the armies together at any cost, will never hesitate to retreat if it serves his purpose, and will make the enemy pay dearly for every yard of territory he gains.

(Reuter's Special Service).

A Disinfected Prince.

According to the "Berliner Tageblatt" the Kaiser's third son, Prince Adalbert, who is an officer in the Navy, recently visited the eastern theatre of war and spent some time in the trenches. On his departure he was provided, in accordance with the regulations, with the following certificate:- "It is hereby declared that his Royal Highness Prince Adalbert of Prussia has been disinfected and is at present free from vermin."

133

"Charm versus Kultur."

Herr Arnold Schroer, Professor of English Language aad Literature at the Commercial Academy of Cologne, publishes in the "Koenische Zeitung," a noteworthy article, on the question: Why has England so much more success among the neutrals than Germany?

One must not, says the Professor, underrate England's strength, which lies in the English character. Every nation which has had to deal with England has been deceived by her. Yet every one of them has been again captivated by her so soon as she made friendly eyes. England's charm has a hold on them, whether they admit it or not, and this is a fact with which we must reckon...... In order to break this charm, it is not enough to defeat the English Army and Navy, nor is it enough to show the world by academic arguments that the German idealistic philosophy is more valuable than the utilitarian philosophy of the English. The charm must be understood and then if possible, defeated by a still stronger charm.

To this is added another trait of the English character, which, though excluded, like all morality, from English politics, nevertheless is fully valid in English private life, and is best characterised by the word fairplay.

Peninsula Press

No. 47   Tuesday, JULY 6th. 1915   Official News.

Enver Pasha at the Front.

We stated on Saturday that Enver Pasha was present in the trenches of the Northern Section on 29th June and personally ordered the attack delivered on that night. This is confirmed by the statement of an intelligent Armenian prisoner captured on that date. According to him, stringent orders were recently issued that no further attacks were to be made because, if Turks remained on defensive, the British would be forced to attack and would suffer as severely as the Turks had hitherto suffered. But Enver Pasha, when he arrived in the Northern Section, overrode this instruction and orders were received by the prisoner's regiment that the Australians were to be driven into the sea.

We have received further details of the counter-attack delivered by Turks on our left in the Southern Section at 6 p.m. on Friday, the 2nd inst. After a heavy bombardment of our advanced positions by high explosive and shrapnel, lasting half an hour, the enemy infantry advanced but were driven back to the main nullah about, a mile to our front by the accurate shooting of H.M.S. "Scorpion" and by our rifle and machine gun fire. At about 7 p.m. the Turkish artillery recommenced their bombardment, under cover of which two battalions emerged from the nullah to the North-east of our most advanced trench and commenced an attack across the open, advancing in two regular lines. At the outset very effective shrapnel fire from the 10th Battery, R.F.A., caused great execution among the attackers. The Gurkha supports then advanced, and, there being insufficient room in the trenches took up a position on some excavated earth in the rear, whence a deadly rifle fire was poured into the advancing lines.

Turkish officers could be seen endeavouring to get their men forward, but they would not face the fire and retreated in disorder, after suffering heavy casualties. Well defined lines of dead can now be seen on ground over which the attack took place. How great importance the enemy attaches to the advanced position gained by us can be judged from his continual determined counter-attacks. The ground in front of our trenches in every direction can be seen covered with Turkish dead, and patrols sent out at night report that the valleys and ravine are also full of them.

There can be no possible doubt that the enemy's losses have been very heavy. Their total casualties between 28th June and 2nd July are put down at 5,150 killed and 15,000 wounded. The number of killed is approximately correct, while the wounded is an estimate based partly on the knowledge of the number already reported to have arrived in Constantinople and partly on experience of the proportion of wounded to killed in previous engagements.

Since the 29th of June the total amount of Turkish arms and ammunition collected is 516 rifles, 51 bayonets, 200 sets of equipment, 126,400 rounds of ammunition and 100 bombs.

The following charm was found on the body of a dead Turk:-
"My God, I ask you for the sake of Moses who talked with you, and for the sake of helping the Prophet, to keep this monument from snakes and scorpions."
NOTE:- The "Monument" referred to most probably deceased's grave stone.

Reported Naval Action.

A Rinella wireless message, the date and place of origin of which cannot be deciphered, states:-
"A naval action took place off the East coast of Gothland at 6.30 a.m., July 2nd. The warships later steamed Northwards, but at 10 o'clock four cruisers were fighting a running action near...... German destroyers laden with wounded arrived at Matthammarsvik in East Gothland.

The German minelayer "Albatross" was chased by four Russian cruisers and driven ashore East of Gothland. Twenty-two of the crew were killed and twenty-seven wounded."
NOTE:- Gothland is an island off the coast of Sweden, South of Stockholm.

The Munitions Bill.

London, July 4th.
The Munitions Bill has passed the House of Lords and become law.
(Rinella Wireless).
NOTE:- The object of this Bill is to organise and expedite the manufacture of munitions of war. It invests the newly created Minister of Munitions (Mr. Lloyd George) with extraordinary powers to prevent strikes.

Italy and Turkey.

The Rome correspondent of the "Daily Telegraph" writes: Political

136

circles are beginning to consider the eventuality of declaring war against Turkey in order to end an embarrassing situation. The Italian Ambassador in Constantinople, Signor Ganoni, is prevented from telegraphing to Rome.

The "Idea Nazionale," the organ of the Nationalists, demands that Italy should participate in the action in the Dardanelles.

News from Constantinople states that Turkey greatly dreads the intervention of Italy. It is probable that this intervention would exercise an influence on the Balkan States, which are still hesitating between neutrality and intervention.

A Tribute to France.

A certain Dr. Hana Delius, who has been touring France, according to his own confession, on a forged passport, describes, in the Berlin "Lokal Anzeiger" his impressions of the popular attitude towards the war. He writes:-

To speak plainly we shall deceive ourselves if we think the French nation is already exhausted and dispirited. And we will not, like the French, build hopes and expectations on a deception as to the resisting power of our enemies. We want to know the truth, in order to measure our patience and our powers according to facts, just because in this war, above all others, the thing is to stick it the longest. I have spoken in France with innumerable people in every profession and every grade of society, with politicians, savants, and journalists, with coal heavers, waiters and cabbies, with people of the middle-class, private soldiers, and officers. I have visited hospitals and seen wounded men straight from the battlefield. Above all, I have interrogated the women, society ladies, and women of the people. In fine, I have carefully investigated popular feeling, as it is manifested in the streets and public places - and I have arrived at the conclusion that we must guard ourselves against underestimating the remarkable moral strength which the French nation is displaying in this war. The French are now by no means weary or discouraged. On the contrary, my impression is that their confidence has perhaps reached its highest point, which is hoped will soon be passed. For until then there will be no prospect of peace.

Peninsula Press

No. 48   Wednesday, JULY 7th. 1915   Official News.

Another Turkish Failure.

NORTHERN SECTION.- On Monday night two mines were successfully exploded. The night was quiet, but at 4 a.m. the enemy started a heavy bombardment of the trenches which raised hopes of an attack. All guns previously used against us and some new ones were in action, but the bombardment died away about 6 a.m. without doing much damage. No attack followed. During the bombardment about 20 11.2 shells were dropped from a Turkish battleship in the Straits.

SOUTHERN SECTION.- During the night the Turks kept up a heavy musketry fire along the whole line, but did not leave their trenches. At 4 a.m. their batteries, both in Asia and on the Peninsula, started the most violent bombardment of our beaches and trenches that has yet been experienced. It was calculated that up to 10.30 a.m. the Asiatic batteries firing on these beaches had expended 1,000 rounds from several kinds of ordnance, 700 rounds falling on Lancashire Landing alone. At least 5,000 rounds of artillery ammunition were expended by the Turks in their bombardment. Meanwhile, this shelling of our lines on the Peninsula, which began at 4.10 a.m., proved to be preliminary to a general attack on our front with special efforts at certain points. The principal effort was made at the junction of the Royal Naval Division section with that of the French. Here, at 7.30 a.m., the Turks advanced out of their trenches, drove back the advanced troops and assaulted a portion of our line held by the Royal Naval Division. Some 50 Turks gained a footing in our trench, where, nevertheless, some men of the R.N.D. held on. Our supports and the men who bad retired counter-attacked immediately and hurled the Turks out of the trench again.

The enemy's dead at this point are 300; 20 bodies counted close to the parapet and the balance in the centre between the two lines. Another attack on the right of the 29th Division section was practically wiped out by rifle and machine-gun fire from the 29th and 42nd Divisions and the Turkish dead here are 150.

On our left the Turks massed in the nullah north-east of our newly captured trenches and attempted several attacks, but none of these was able to get home owing to steadiness of our troops and effective artillery support. Here, too, the Turkish losses are reported to be exceedingly heavy.

To sum up, Monday's attack seems to have been one of those periodical attempts to "drive us into the sea" which take place when fresh Turkish reinforcements arrive. The troops which attacked are identified as having come from Adrianople. Not only has the result been a complete failure but, while our losses were negligible and no impression has been made on our line, the enemy has added a large number to his recent very heavy casualties, and it seems plain, from the disjointed nature of his attacks that he is finding it difficult to drive his infantry forward to face our fire. The bombardment died down towards 11 a.m. though it was resumed at intervals.

Subsequently to the first attack the Turks seemed to be massing for an attack upon the French, but any such intention, was dissipated by artillery fire.

America and British War Loan.
(Rinella Press.) New York, July 4.

New York bankers, headed by Messrs. Morgan, are negotiating the flotation of a loan for £20,000,000 for the British War Loan.

German Attempt to Assassinate Mr. Morgan.
(Rinella Press). New York, July 4.

Mr. J. P. Morgan, the well-known American financier was shot at. The wounds are not serious and his condition is favourable.

Mr. Morgan's assailant is of German descent and gives the name of Frank Holt. He is a teacher of German at Cornell University.

German Attack on the American Capitol.
(Rinella Press). Washington, July 4.

An explosion damaged the Senate wing of the Capitol at Washington. No one was injured.

New York, July 4.

Frank Holt, who tried to kill Mr. J. P. Morgan, has confessed that he placed the bombs which damaged the Capitol.

Wireless Messages.
On the West Front.
Eiffel Tower, July 6th.

After a violent bombardment the Germans made two attacks North of Arras. Both were repulsed. In front of Sauchez the Germans left their trenches en masse, armed with grenades, and were forced to retire, leaving many dead. The second attack was in the Labyrinth and was immediately checked. In the Argonne there has been fighting with grenades and bombs, without any infantry action.

On Sunday the enemy attacked along a front of four or five kilometres, and, after an artillery bombardment, succeeded in reoccupying about one kilometre of his former lines which the French had taken. Notwithstanding the vigour of their attack, the Germans were unable to advance any further.

German General Headquarters, July 4th. In the Argonne our troops continued their offensive. Our captures have risen considerably. In the first two days of June (? July) we took 2,656 prisoners, including 87 officers, 72 trench mortars, one quick firing gun and 25 machine guns.

On the heights of the Meuse, the enemy, despite previous failures, four times renewed his attempt; to retake the lost positions at Eparges. We easily defeated these attacks. North-West of Regnieville, we captured the French positions over a front of 600 yards and took from the enemy a small wood, North of Fey-en-Haye.

Our aeroplanes were very active yesterday. They dropped bombs, near Harwich, on the Landguard fort and on an English destroyer flotilla; at Darnbarle, on the railway, and at Remeremant, on the sea front.

An English aeroplane in flames fell over the Dutch border. A German aeroplane forced a French aviator to come down at Schlucht.

The enemy dropped bombs on Bruges without doing any military damage.

Peninsula Press

No. 49   Thursday, JULY 8th. 1915   Official News.

Wireless Messages.

German Battleship Sunk.

We have received the following details of the naval engagement eported in Tuesday's "Peninsula Press."

(Rinella Press).

Petrograd, July 4th.

In the Baltic on the 2nd inst., a Russian submarine blew up a battleship of the Deutschland type.

The Russian cruiser squadron off Gothland engaged two German light cruisers and some destroyers. One German cruiser was badly damaged and ran ashore, while the other ships retreated. An hour later the Russian squadron encountered the German cruiser "Roon," with light cruisers and destroyers. The action lasted half-an-hour. The enemy's ships retired Southward and were joined by another light cruiser. The Russian squadron again attacked and the enemy took to flight.

A German submarine attacked the Russian ships but failed.

The Russian casualties were insignificant.

(Official)

On the Russian Front

(Rinella Press).

Petrograd, July 3rd.

The enemy established contact with us along the river Swipinca and Porand. Advance in the North between the rivers Sirepregana and Bug. We captured 2,000 prisoners and several machine guns. On Thursday evening the enemy established himself on the left bank of Guila Lipa (South-east of Lemberg).

(German Wireless).

General Headquarters, July 4th.

Eastern front: Situation is unchanged

141

South-eastern front: General von Linsengen's army is in full persuit attacking the Zlota Lipa lines (North-east of Stanislau). Three-thousand Russians were captured. Under this pressure, the enemy is leaving his positions between Narajov and North of Prxemyslany (50 miles South-east of Lemberg). Between Kamionka and Koxlov (North-east of Lemberg) the situation is unchanged. General von Mackeusen's army is advancing to the attack.

Between the Vistula and the Piliea (which joins the Vistula 30 miles South of Warsaw) nothing of importance has occurred.

The Western Front.

Eiffel Tower, Paris, July 6th.
The day of the 5th has been comparatively quiet, except for German artillery fire between the Meuse and Moselle. Bois Le Pretre particularly has been subjected to a very heavy bombardment by heavy artillery. The night of the 5th-6th was full of incidents. In Belgium the British, supported by French artillery, captured some German trenches South-west of Pilkem. There was violent fighting around the station of Sauchez which remained in our hands in spite of repeated attempts of the enemy to dislodge us. The town of Arras was bombarded all the night. In Argonne there has been constant fighting with grenades and bombs. Our artillery has checked all German advances. On the heights of the Meuse, the Germans twice attacked the French positions East of the trench of Calonne and were completely repulsed. In the district of Bois Le Pretre the Germans made two attacks which were completely broken up by infantry and artillery fire which inflicted very heavy losses.

How the Turks Report "Victories."

The following is taken from the Turkish newspaper the "Sabah," of June 14th. It purports to describe the unsuccessful attack made by the Turks on the night of June 3rd and our attack on the following day.

"The late battles at Sedd-el-Bahr and Ari Burnu which probably formed the most violent engagements that have taken place in the Chanak Kale theatre, ended in our favour and the defeat of the enemy, thanks to the courageous self-sacrifice of our officers and men.

The English and French began the attack in the afternoon of Friday, May 22nd (June 3rd) and tried to support this attack by firing some 6,000 shells. At the same moment their ships joined in but from fear of submarines very soon withdrew under cover. Our troops met the enemy's attack with a, very heroic counter-attack, and our left wing defeated the enemy's right wing. The English and French were unable to make any headway on this day, and we took five mitrailleuses. The enemy's troops in the Ari Burnu zone attacked on Saturday night. The next day the result of the battle that went on until noon was that our troops completely drove back all attacks and captured many rifles, bombs and trenches. The enemy's losses in the engagement here were more than 3,000.

In the direction of Sedd-el-Bahr however, the battle was still going on on Saturday. Our right wing having taken the other· trenches was advancing. Finally, on Monday, our troops at Sedd-el-Bahr made a violent counter-attack shouting as they went the centuries old cry of "Allah Allah." This bloody engagement which lasted four hours, and in which everyone from the highest to the lowest rank participated with the greatest valour, ended in our complete favour and our troops drove the enemy back into his former positions taking 12 machine guns. These guns are today being used against the enemy.

The enemy, defeated and demoralised, retired, having suffered very heavy losses. These losses are estimated at over 15,000. In fact a great many hospital ships were seen coming and going during the engagement.

The battle of the 23-24th May (4-5th June) will form one of the most glorious pages of our military history. During this engagement, our soldiers of every rank displayed the very greatest bravery and courage, and even when the battle was raging most violently the most perfect order and discipline was maintained in the army.

Whilst the enemy was pouring shells on us, and attacking, our soldiers were fighting with the greatest coolness and sanfroid. They might indeed have been on the parade ground.

The War in South West Africa.
(Rinella Press).

Pretoria, July 4th.

General Botha has occupied Totavia, in German South-west Africa.

143

Peninsula Press

No. 50   Friday, JULY 9th. 1915   Official News.

Wireless Messages.
(Rinella Press).
Sinking of the "Deutschland."

Petrograd, July5.
The "Deutschland" was leading the German squadron at the entrance to Danzig harbour when she was blown up by a Russian submarine on the 2nd inst.

A Russian destroyer rammed a German submarine while she was attempting to approach the Russian warships.

Note:- The "Deutschland" was one of the pre Dreadnought battle fleet. She was launched in 1905 and her tonnage was 13,040.

Several Austrian Battalions Captured.

Petrograd, July 5th.
We captured several Austrian battalions in the local attack in the direction of Radom (about 70 miles South of Warsaw).

There was fierce fighting on the 2nd and 3rd inst., between the rivers Vistula and Bug. The enemy's offensive on Warzenka, (fourteen miles North-west of Lemberg) was stopped.

Later.
In the direction of Lublin, the enemy advanced on a front between Roasvik and the river Vieprez. All German attacks on the 3rd and 4th between the rivers Vieprez, Bug, Faras and Sokal were repulsed.

The enemy's offensive East of Warzenka was arrested on Sunday and on the following day their losses included 2,000 killed and 2,000 prisoners.

Submarines in the Channel.

London, July 7.
Some French destroyers shelled two German submarines in the English Channel yesterday. One submarine was struck by several shells before she disappeared.

The British steamer "Anglo-California" arrived at Queenstown after being shelled by a German submarine. Twelve of the crew, including the captain, were killed.

The Italian Campaign.

Rome, July 6th.

Italian heavy guns continue to smash Malborghetto, on the Carinthia frontier. After repeated counter attacks we gained some ground.

Later

The bombardment of Malborgetto[*sic*] and Predil continues effectively. On the Carisco plateau our offensive is developing. In the Valley of Daone the enemy attempted an attack on our position in the Pass of Campo and suffered serious losses.

In Cadore our artillery operating against the other side of the valley created great havoc. On the Carnia front an attack against our position in the rugged Pass of Schannitz is continuing. Our advance progresses slowly.

Between the 4th and 7th inst, we captured 1,400 prisoners.

On the 6th, one of our dirigibles bombarded the railway North of Opcina. On the morning of the 6th, a squadron of our aeroplanes threw several bombs on the Austrian Aviation Camp and started several fires.

Germans Use Liquid Fire.

Eiffel Tower, Paris, July 8.

British troops repulsed several counter-attacks, inflicting heavy losses on the enemy. North of Arras two German attacks have been repulsed. On the heights of the Meuse the French have retaken the portion of trench captured by the Germans on June 27th. Several German counter-attacks have been repulsed with heavy losses to the enemy. South-east of St. Mihiel the Germans have taken the offensive after a very violent bombardment, but only at one point in the region of Lavamgfery have they succeeded in gaining the French line along a frontage of about 700 yards. Everywhere else they have been driven back with very heavy loss. East of Bois le Pretre the French checked a fresh German attack which was made with the assistance of liquid fire. In the Vosges there has been fresh activity on the part of the German artillery, which has bombarded La Fontenelle, L'Helgenfirst, and from Hartmannswillerkoff to Than. (Official Report).

Organising the Nation.

London, July 7th.
(Rinella Press.)
The National Register Bill was read a second time by 353 votes to 50.

Note : This Bill provides for a census and requires every man to state his age, permanent address, occupation, whether married or single, whether he has any physical disability, and whether he is willing to enlist or to do other war work.

Persecuting the Greeks.

Notwithstanding the assurances of the Turkish Minister in Athens and the declarations of certain newspapers, the persecuting of Greeks in Turkey has not ceased. On the contrary, it has become more violent. Greeks have been driven from their homes on the shores of the Marmora on the pretext that they were giving supplies to British submarines.

(From "Le Messager d'Athenes.")

The "Lusitania" Note.

(Reuter), London.
The German reply to President Wilson's Note on the sinking of the "Lusitania" is generally forecasted as follows:-

Germany admits that the information she had gained concerning the presence of guns, troops and munitions on the "Lusitania" was erroneous. Germany proposes that Great Britain should allow vessels charged with food-stuffs to reach German ports. Germany is ready to enter into negotiations with the American Government to take measures so that passengers may be protected against danger.

Germany refuses categorically to accede to the proposal that her submarines should cease to attack merchant ships.

A Shirkers Bill in France.

(Reuter), Paris.
A remarkable bill was debated in the Chamber on Thursday. It contains measures for ousting shirkers from safe billets and imposes penalties varying from two to five years imprisonment on men in the army having "soft jobs" and on their protectors. It provides that men who are indispensable for the manufacture of munitions working in the public service shall not be removed from their posts.

146

Peninsula Press

No. 51   Saturday, JULY 10th. 1915   Official News.

Messages Received by Wireless.

Washington officials agree that the United States cannot approve Germany's proposals. The concessions Germany is willing to make are insufficient.

The Austrian communique says that Russians have taken the offensive North of Kramik against the Archduke Joseph's Army.

The Russian communique mentions continuous desperate fighting on the 6th between the rivers Vistula and Vieprez. In the direction of Lublin, the Russians forced the enemy to take the defensive and captured 2,000 prisoners and several maxims. On the 5th the enemy attacked many points between Kamianka and Gloriany but heavy losses compelled him to suspend the movement.

Eiffel Tower reports on the 9th July: North of Arras, several rather violent infantry actions developed between Any and Sauchez. North of the Bethune-Arras Road a German attack, preceded by a heavy bombardment, was completely repulsed. North of the station of Sauchez the French made an attack which allowed them to approach nearer the village. They captured a line of German trenches after having exterminated the defenders and advanced beyond it, capturing some prisoners and a gun. In the Argoune, musketry and artillery fire continued throughout the night of 7th and 8th.

At daybreak in the district of Marie Therese, the Germans attempted to leave their trenches and were driven back

On the heights of the Meuse there was a violent bombardment of the French position at Eparges. In the forest of Apremont after fighting which continued during the portion of the morning of the 7th, the infantry action reported above was broken off. The Germans who suffered considerable loss made no gains at any point. In the Western portion, Bois le Petre, the French during the day of the 7th recaptured 200 metres of trenches.

(Extracts from Newspapers).

Mr. Long, in introducing the Bill for a National Register, said that its object was not to coerce labour, but to secure complete and satisfactory organisation. The nation must ascertain minutely the extent of its resources. Besides maintaining an army and navy, its paramount duty was to maintain the industrial and financial position. The Bill would provide machinery to procure the maximum output at a minimum cost. There would be compulsory registration of all males and females aged from fifteen to sixty-five who would give their age and employment. They would be asked to volunteer for special work besides their ordinary occupation. This would enable Government to take full advantage of the service of everybody. (Egyptian Gazette).

In the New Zealand Parliament Mr. Massey announced that the Government was prepared to form a National Military Ministry for the duration of the war. Thus the whole of the energies of the country would be concentrated on the prosecution of the war. Sir. J. Ward asked for time to consider the proposal. (Times of Egypt).

A Captain writes to the "Spectator":-
The following facts witnessed by me during the last German attacks upon our portion of the line might help people at home to realise the strength of the poisonous gases used by the enemy. As far back as two miles from the firing lines the poplar trees in full leaf were entirely stripped of all foliage, clipped as naked as in winter. The grass for over a hundred yards in front of the enemy's trenches was turned bright yellow from where the gas attacks were made. This, by the way, is now most useful to the gunners and aeroplane observers. A cat, the pet of a Highland Regiment, was killed by the fumes in less than an hour (one mile behind the first line). Her sad death might, however have been averted had she been sensible and kept on the respirator presented to her.

In the debate on the supplementary vote for an additional 50,000 men for the Navy Mr. Macnamara said they were not required for the immediate manning needs of the fleet. We had under arms and in training all the men wanted at present. No difficulty was expected in supplying future needs, but recruiting was so good that the number provided for in the estimates for present needs, namely 250,000 was exceeded and the Admiralty were bound to ask Parliament for authority to cover the additionals. Mr. Lambert emphasised that the navy's control of the seas was a masterly situation. We had ample supplies, reserves and ammunition. The vote was adopted.

(Egyptian Gazette).

The "Egyptian Gazette" publishes an interview with an Italian who recently arrived at Alexandria from Beyrout:-

148

"Despite reports to the contrary, perfect tranquillity prevails in Syria. Never within living memory have the Moslem and Christian populations been in such full accord. The Mohammed are entirely disgusted with the war and their dissatisfaction is becoming increasing apparent daily.

"As soon as an Allied warship is sighted from the coast the inhabitants crowd on the sea-shore in constant expectation that the long desired occupation would at last be carried into execution. The appearance of a French aeroplane over Beyrout and the Lebanons was the occasion of unrestrained popular enthusiasm. No apprehension whatever was entertained as to the aeroplane's bad intentions as the people were aware that the Allies would never follow Germany's barbaric example in dropping bombs on non-combatants. Several arrests, however of innocent persons and notables were made by the Turks on the pretext of "Francophile sentiments." Djemnl Pasha is the supreme military governor of Syria. He has "carte blanche" to act as he pleases. In company with his German advisers he is constantly moving between Jerusalem and Damascus; he scarcely ever ventures near the coast. The General is a Turk to the backbone, ignorant, obstinate and arrogant. He is averse to the interference of his Prussian associates whom he greatly dislikes."

Peninsula Press

No. 52   Sunday, JULY 11th. 1915   Official News.

Wireless Message.

The only message we received by wireless yesterday was the French report:-

Eiffel Tower reports for July 10th:-

In Belgium a German attack was repulsed with very heavy loss. Between Angres and Sauchez the Germans attacked on all sides and were repulsed, and North of the station of Sauchez a very violent German counter-attack only succeeded in re-occupying a hundred yards of the original 800 yards of front lost by them. Between the Meuse and the Moselle, the night of 8-9th was full of incident. Between Feyeuhaye andl Bois le Pretre the French recaptured about 150 yards of trenches lost on July 4th. Near Carmes, the enemy attacked after a bombardment with bombs and liquid fire, and after having succeeded in reaching our advanced trenches, were thrown out except in some small portions. In the Vosges, the French gained a marked success after having driven the Germans out of a portion of the old work which they captured on June 25th. On June 22nd, the French captured all the German defensive works from the hill South-east of Lafontenelle as far as the Laurois-Moyon Maukir Road.

The French captured 10 officers and 767 unwounded men belonging to seven different battalions.

(Extracts from Newspapers).

A well-informed Greek conespondent writes:

"There has been a lavish expenditure of German gold in Athens on a scale which can only be paralleled in recent revelations of Teutonic intrigue in Rome. The object has been to obtain the exclusion of M. Venizelos from power.

"In order to effect their object those who are a party to the intrigue have not hesitated to represent, that M. Venizelos is the enemy of the dynasty. It is suggested that the Cretan statesman is in reality anxious to establish a republic and overthrow once and for all the Royal House.

"Happily enough, the result of the recent elections has proved that the Greek nation is sound at heart, but because they have been baulked at the polls the German agents have not in any sense desisted from their project. There is a rumour, to which I hesitate to give credence, but which, nevertheless, reaches me on very good authority, that certain officers who have Teutonic leanings are preparing to kidnap M. Venizelos on the ground of his alleged republican leanings.

"I need scarcely add that accusations against M. Venizelos's loyalty are absolutely absurd, in view of the fact that it is due more to him than to any other living man that the Royal authority stands as it does today. It may be hoped that the Greek people, who understand the responsibility of freedom and independence, will know how to deal with this shameless endeavour to overpower the exercise of their free volition by force." (Daily Telegraph).

M. Millerand, the French Minister of War, speaking in the Senate about the measures taken to increase the output of armaments and munitions, said:-
"After the military mobilization, we have decreed industrial mobilization. The task was difficult but we have succeeded in nine months in increasing our production six-fold and it is still increasing, especially with regard to the production of the 75 cannon. During the first three months of 1915, the production of quick-firers doubled and the proportion is the same for all arms. We are decided to follow the enemy everywhere, no matter what arms he may employ." (Havas).

The West Indian contingent for service at the front is making good progress. Jamaica, proposes sending 500 men. Private subscriptions received reach the total of £3,551, and public feeling is growing in favour of a, Government grant. Barbados expects a Government grant of £2,500, and proposes sending upwards of 100 men. Demerara is sending a similar number on the same terms as Jamaica, but with a Government grant. The Governor of Trinidad is not prepared to make an announcement regarding the contingent from that island. (Reuter).

The Agent-General for Western Australia has received a telegram stating that there was a splendid general rainfall throughout the State from the 11th to 13th inst. inclusive, which has benefited the agricultural areas, and that rain was still falling on the 14th inst.
(Morning Post).

The Australian Commonwealth has suspended the issue of permits for the export of mutton and lamb. The 37,000 carcases recently shipped, also the meat in the ships holds at Melbourne, will go to the British Government.

(Morning Post).

Beside the normal civilian post, there was created at the beginning of the war a central military bureau at Paris for the distribution of letters and packets to the various sectors. The majority of the cards and letters confided to the military sectors are not stamped, but go as if franked on service. On December 26 the military central bureau dealt with over two and a half millions of letters. Two months later this total reached 3,420,000, and on May 26 it was 4,000,000. Some patient statisticians have attempted to make out how many objects altogether have been lately sent per day to the front. Only a certain number of days were taken, rather arbitrarily and at haphazard, but they serve to give a fair idea of the whole period. On October 30 last the administration received and distributed over 1,000,000 letters, 117,000 registered packages, 18,000 newspapers, and 80,000 post-office money orders. Seven months later, on May 26, it received close upon 14,000,000 letters, 780,000 registered parcels, and 135,000 papers, with 57,000 money orders. In less than eight months the army post had more than decupled.

Peninsula Press

No. 53   Monday, JULY 12th. 1915   Official News.

Wireless Messages.

Turkish News, July 10.

The operations of the English in this neighbourhood consist solely of movements of retreat. Their positions are confined to the shore where they are under the protection of gun boats. On the remainder of the front nothing of importance has occurred.

Imperial Turkish Headquarters.

.... of the enemy were blown up. Our artillery further caused explosions and fires among the batteries of the enemy, who are busy extinguishing them. Many of the enemy were killed by our guns.

German Press.

The Constantinople correspondent of the "Frankfurter Zeitung" writes: The Dardanelles operations within the past few days are developing very satisfactory for the Turks. They captured several important trenches on the English right. The French prisoners taken consist of youths scarcely seventeen and old veterans. All make a pitiable impression. The English show signs of lack of discipline and over exertion. Their commanders must use force in order to keep their men under control, troops in the second trench firing on those in advance where they lag behind or attempt flight.

The Press Bureau (London), says it is officially announced at Petrograd that the submarine which sank the German warship in the Baltic (reported to be the "Deutschland") was British.

Italian Press, July 10th.

Calbano: We did severe damage with our artillery to the Fort of Platzweise and fire broke out. Carnia: To-day the enemy thrice attacked our position on the hill but were repulsed with heavy loss. Our artillery continue to operate effectively against Malborghetto. Over the rest of the front there have been only slight actions and no change in the situation. At Signelanoel a great many explosive shells were fired among enemy troops operating in the Mount Nero zone. One of our aeroplanes dropped bombs on Nahresina Railway Station from a height of only 100 metres.

Rome, July 10th.

There was a naval reconnaissance in force last night in the upper Adriatic. The cruiser "Amalfi" was torpedoed and sunk. Almost everyone was saved.

Eiffel Tower, July 11.

To the North of Arras several German attempts at assaults were repulsed. The Germans continued to bombard Arras. In Champagne a German attack was dispersed with considerable loss. In Loraine the Germans attacked the French positions at Leintrey and were repulsed. Nothing else of note occurred on the front except some artillery duels, particularly in the Forest of Aprement, at Bois le Pretre and Lafontonelle. German prisoners made in the battle of the 8th instant number 1,781, of whom 21 are officers. French aviators yesterday bombarded the stations of Arneville and Bayonville, also the military barracks at Nevrey.

(Extracts from Newspapers).

Reuter's Agency has received from a well-informed Russian source the following review of the military situation of the Eastern front:
"A mere list of names and of minor or major engagements presents so many difficulties to the ordinary mind in grasping the situation that it is well to take a general view of the military position as it exists today in the Eastern theatre of war, and to regard these operations in their true perspective in relation to the task of the Allies against the common foe. No Russian would be so foolish as to admit that he prefers retreat to advance, but the thing to bear in mind – a fact often overlooked – is the real object we have in view-an object which may be truly said is being surely attained.

"This is in effect the killing of the enemy, and as long as the Austro-German armies against us lose more than we do – which is undoubtedly the case – so long shall we view the progress of events with calm assurance. Whether these loses are inflicted on this or that bank of some river is immaterial, as is also the possibility that the enemy may, as in the case of Przemysl, recapture what is really an empty shell, or even go farther and occupy other positons. Such events will not deter us from the prosecution of our grand object.

"The Russian Staff is quite aware of the object of the enemy's tremendous efforts, which is both political as well as military. Russian generals have never posed as prophets, they and their armies being sufficiently occupied in fighting for an object which will certainly be attained.

154

"A very significant fact which has attracted little notice, is the appearance of new German formations against us. The further that the enemy advances, the greater becomes his difficulty and the more he comes on equal terms with us, especially in the matter of railway communication. Let us not then talk of Russian defeats and reverses so long as the Tsars armies inflict the losses they are doing on the enemy, and continue to prevent, as they have done, the Germans from achieving their real object."

The war has touched Munich in a vital spot. The military authorities have just confiscated a large part of the malt and other raw materials used for beer making by the great breweries in the Bavarian capital. Places like the world renowned Hofbrau and other beer resorts familiar to visitors to Munich have had to close several of their largest apartments, as the daily supply of beer has been reduced to one-third of the former quantity. The life of Munich is radically affected. Several of the prominent "beer-cellars" are now closing at 7 p.m., as the ordinary evening demands for beer can no longer be fulfilled. Such places as remain open later are serving lemonade or wine. House-holders accustomed to send out for their beer must henceforth secure it on the ration-card system. The newspapers state that the Munich public is facing its trials "with good humour."

(Daily Mail).

Peninsula Press

No. 54   Tuesday, JULY 13th. 1915   Official News.

Wireless Messages.

Pretoria, July 10th.

General Botha accepted the unconditional surrender of the entire German force in South-west Africa. Practically the whole of the Citizen Army will return to the Union as quickly as time permits.

The German force which surrendered consists of 204 officers and 8,166 men, 87 field guns and 22 machine guns.

Austrian as well as Russian communiques show that the Russians have recoiled on the invaders with startling effect. Austrians admit that they have withdrawn from the North of Krasnik (South-west of Lublin).

Petrograd.

We resumed our successful offensive South of Lublin, crossing the river and dealing the enemy a terrible blow. We captured, between Monday and Thursday, 11,000 prisoners and several dozen machine guns. The enemy is retreating.

Later.

Our offensive has extended in the whole region to the South of Lublin. The enemy continues to retreat. We have taken over 15,000 prisoners.

Berlin.

The German Government's answer to the United States Ambassador at Berlin on July 8th re the Note on the sinking of the "Lusitania" points out the progress in common of Prussia and America ever since the time of Frederick the Great. Since that time Germany and America have marched hand in hand with the object of maintaining the law of capture at sea and the rights of neutrals. Germany has always held it a basic principle that war is only to be made on armed forces not on a civilian population. Germany hopes that when peace is made, or perhaps before, Maritime International law may be so arranged as to leave the freedom of the seas secure. Germany would be grateful if America would work with her hand in hand. The guilt for this breach of this fundamental law of humanity was not with Germany's Government but with the ever increasing unscrupulousness of Germany's enemy. The treatment of neutrals, in forbidding even legitimate trade, the publication of England's intention to starve Germany-these were responsible for the submarine warfare. Germany's first duty was to protect German lives. The case of the" Lusitania" shows with horrible clearness what the kind of warfare instituted by our enemies must lead to.

The Note points out that England armed her trading steamers, and suggests that, in order to make American rights more secure, Germany should be informed of the sailing of all American ships. These will then pass unmolested by German submarines, provided that the American Government holds itself responsible that no contraband is on board such ships. Contraband with England must cease. Moreover, it does not suit the German Government that many English ships should pass into American hands in order, to enjoy this immunity. The German Government will be pleased to exchange views with the President on naval warfare and hopes that their common efforts will soon reach a satisfactory agreement,

One of many similar letters received by General Sir Ian Hamilton.

816, Albert Road,
Albert Park
Melbourne.
20-5-1915.

Dear Sir,
Forgive the liberty I am taking in writing to you, but I feel very proud of our "Australian Boys at the Dardanelles," and must tell you so. I am an "Australian Girl," so you can understand how interested I am in all they do, they have been sorely tried and have not been found wanting so far. I envy every soldier I meet and wish I were a boy.

I am only a working girl helping to make the great coats for the soldiers, it is the only thing I can do to help. I know we will win.
    I am, Dear Sir,
        Respectfully Yours
        Daphne Abbott.

Alexandria.
While the Sultan was going to prayers a bomb was thrown and fell at the feet of his horses but did not explode. The criminal escaped.

Press Bureau, London
Several thousands Turks, with 20 guns and a large number of Arabs, attacked a small British force on the 6th inst. in the Aden hinterland. The British maintained their position until night when they joined a column marching to reinforce Labazi Haomed.

Sir John French reports that since July 6th the enemy made repeated attempts to retake the lost trenches North of Ypres but all counter-attacks were stopped by successful co-operation of our artillery with French artillery. The enemy fell back along the canal enabling us to extend our gains and capture a machine gun and three trench mortars. The enemy's losses were severe.

On the night of the 9-10th the Belgian troops repulsed a German attack on the right bank of the Yser in front of the Maison du Passeur. On the evening of the 10th the British troops repulsed a German attack. In this attack the Germans at first succeeded in setting foot in some of the advanced line of trenches but a counter-attack drove them out immediately. A 37 m.m. gun, 4 machine guns and a large number of rifles and ammunition fell into the hands of the French.

A series of violent explosions occurred in the powder factory at Hounslow. One person was killed.

Norwegian papers state that the Hamburg-American line has made a declaration of bankruptcy.

Peninsula Press

No. 55   Wednesday, JULY 14th. 1915   Official News.

Wireless Messages.

Petrograd, July 12th.

The Russians are more than holding their own in the battle of Galicia. Heavy fighting is taking place around Hialand village, near Bystrzitza, 80 miles South of Lublin. The enemy has taken the offensive at Zlouatiasa. The garrison at Osiowich made sorties on Friday night and destroyed the enemy's saps.

Eiffel Tower, Paris July 18.

In the sector of Arras, the Germans, after throwing a large number of asphyxiating projectiles, made an attack to the South of Souchez at about midnight and were driven back. A second attack at about 2 a.m. enabled them to occupy the cemetery and a few portions of adjoining trenches. Fierce fighting with grenades took place in the trenches of the "Compact," South-east of Neuville St. Vaast without appreciable gain for either side. On the plateau North of the Oise, the artillery duel was particularly violent. In the Argonne there was fighting with bombs and mines. In the Woevre the Germans have violently bombarded Fresnes en Woevre with heavy artillery and made several attacks, one near Sault en Woevre and the others in the forest of Apremont. All these attacks have been entirely repulsed. In the Vosges the Germans exploded a mine close to the French positions South west of Ammertzville and then made an attack with several companies. The attack was repulsed with heavy losses and we captured some prisoners.

German Press, July 11th.

In the East we carried out some successful sapping. Between Ailly and Apremont some isolated bayonet fights took place. In the Le Pretre forest we improved our new positions by means of an assault. Since July 4th in the fighting between the Meuse and the Moselle 1799 prisoners, among them 21 officers, 3 field guns, 12 machine guns, and 16 trench mortars have been captured. At Leintrey, night attacks of the enemy against our outposts have been repulsed.

Yesterday evening, the enemy, after a long artillery preparation, attacked the heights of Cambres and succeeded in reaching our lines, but, were driven out again. In Ailly wood, the enemy's infantry in an attack on our position broke under our artillery fire. In a little wood to the South of Amevez Weibet the enemy's positions were taken over a front of 500 metres. Our troops, then, as previously arranged, fell back to our former position unmolested by the enemy, taking with them some prisoners.

EASTERN FRONT:- We stormed the enemy's outpost positions over a front of four kilometres.

SOUTH-EAST FRONT:- The position of German troops is unchanged.

Official statistics of the wounded treated in home hospitals in August 1914 show that nearly 85 per cent were discharged fit for service at the front, while 8 per cent died. For 1915 the statistics give the complete recoveries at 91 per cent and the deaths 1.5 percent.

Hamburg-American line denies Scandinavian reports of its insolvency.

Italian Press News, 11th July.
In the Terragnolo Valley (Adige) our troops with fine elan attacked the enemy's positions during the night of the 9th. Two strong enemy attacks were launched against our positions at the head of the Franza Valley. They were repulsed. On the heights of Boits our alpine troops silently scaled Mount Tophant and surprised the enemies forces in the valley of Travananza capturing their position and taking many prisoners. In the Isonzo zone the enemy has brought up a large number of guns of medium calibre but our artillery is replying to it with increasing efficacy. On the night of the 10th violent attacks on our recently won positions at Altipiano were checked at once.

(Extracts from Newspapers).

The New York correspondent of the "Times" gives the following details of the attack made by "a weak-minded creature of German sympathies and apparently of some German blood" on Mr. J. Pierpoint Morgan, the American financier:-
Holt arrived at Mr. Morgan's residence yesterday morning after travelling by the midnight train from Washington, where he had deposited a bomb in the reception room at the Senate, which was wrecked by the explosion. Holt waited to ascertain that the bomb actually exploded and then took the train for New York, where be changed into the train for Glen Cove. He arrived at Mr. Morgan's residence just before 9 o'clock. The banker was at breakfast with the British Ambassador, Sir Cecil Spring Rice. Holt, who carried two revolvers and several sticks of dynamite, asked to see Mr. Morgan,

saying that he was an old friend. The butler refused to admit him. Holt drew a revolver, and the butler, having led him into the library away from the breakfast-room shouted, "Upstairs, Mr. Morgan, upstairs."

STRUGGLE WITH THE ASSAILANT.

Mr. Morgan, followed by his guests, ran up the back stairs to inquire into the cause of the disturbance, and wss returning by way of the front staircase when Holt, waving his revolvers and shouting, "I've got you now, Mr. Morgan," rushed towards the banker. Mrs. Morgan placed herself before her husband, but was pushed aside as Mr. Morgan charged the man, knocking him down. Holt, however, had fired two shots. Mr. Morgan, though shot, caught the assassin by the wrist and, with the aid of Sir Cecil Rice, disarmed him. Holt was momentarily stunned by a blow from the butler.

As soon as the man was secured Mr. Morgan walked to the telephone and called to a local physician to come at once. He then telephoned to his mother, telling her that he was wounded but not seriously, and asked her not to be alarmed if she heard sensational reports.

Holt was conveyed to the police station where he answered questions put to him in a tone of great hauteur, declaring that he was a Christian gentleman, who had determined to reason with Mr. Morgan in the hope of inducing him to use his influence with American manufacturers to stop the exportation of munitions of war. He argued that any man who failed to do his utmost to prevent the wholesale murder in Europe was guilty of murder. "I have no confederates," he said, "and I had no intention of shooting Mr. Morgan. I merely wanted to frighten him, but be rushed at me, and the bullets with which I hoped to scare him, hit him." With typical German assurance, he paid a tribute to the bravery of Mr. Morgan, stating that if the moral courage of the banker were equal to his physical courage he might do some good in the world.

Peninsula Press

No. 56   Thursday, JULY 15th. 1915   Official News.

Wireless Messages.

His Majesty has sent his congratulations to General Botha and his forces on the success of their operations in German South West Africa.

On the 4th instant, the monitors "Severn" and "Mersey" ascended Refugi river in East Africa and engaged the Konigsberg, aeroplanes "spotting" and directing the fire. After six hours the Konigsberg was heavily on fire. She continued firing one gun, but was finally silenced.

A fresh attack on the 11th completed the destruction. Our casualties were 4 killed 6 wounded.

Petrograd.

The Russians, having completed a successful offensive South of Lublin, now occupy prepared positions on the heights of the right bank of the Wyuidovka river.

Eiffel Tower.

In spite of the activity shown by the German artillery against the trenches at Carency and on the outskirts of Sauchez, a counter-attack put the French in possession of the part of trenches abandoned on the 11th. The Germans attempted an attack in front of the French positions at the Labyrinth. The attackers were decimated and thrown back in confusion on to their lines. At the Bois le Pretre the Germans delivered two attacks in the neighbourhood of the Croix-des-Carres. The first attack was repulsed with heavy loss by the fire of the French artillery and infantry: the second attack broke before the Germans could even leave their trenches. An attack by the Germans against a bridge head held by the French on the Eastern bank of the Fecht at Sandemesch was easily defeated. A French air squadron, comprising 35 aeroplanes bombarded the station which for strategic purposes has been installed by the Germans at Vigneulbes. Large stocks of munitions and provisions were concentrated there. The French aeroplanes dropped 171 bombs of large size, starting several fires. All the machines returned safely.

(Extracts from Newspapers).

In a letter read at the National Liberal Club, Mr. Asquith said that Lord Haldane more than any other man was responsible for the readiness of the army, and from the first he had strongly advocated the appointment of Lord Kitchener to the War Office.

Lord Haldane, in a speech to the members of the Club, deprecated the pessimistic attitude of a section of the press. The simple fact was that the Allies had a total population of 280,000,000 to organise against the enemies 120,000,000. If the nation had a, concentrated purpose to organise itself for war, we should win. When he (Lord Haldane) was a member of the Government, there was a committee at the War Office in October, presided over by Lord Kitchener and attended by Messrs. Lloyd George, Churchill, McKenna and others, which considered the urgency of enlarging the supply of munitions. They consulted everybody and placed Orders with munition manufacturers, which, if they had been executed, would have placed the country in a tremendous position in regard to munitions; but difficulties arose out of the relations between capital and labour, which confounded the calculations of the manufacturers, who were unable to comply with the demand. The nation had not then awakened.   (Reuter).

The Hon. B. R. Wise, K.C., formerly Attorney-General of New South Wales, who has arrived in London to take up his duties as Agent-General for that State, told a "Morning Post" representative that when he left Australia the men of the commonwealth were responding to the call of the Mother Country with even greater enthusiasm, if that were possible, than in the early days of the war, and that not only the military but the material resources of the whole Australian Continent – men, munitions, food supplies, horses, fodder, everything in fact that the country was capable of supplying – would be placed at the disposal of the Imperial authorities, fully and freely.

"Of even greater significance than numbers," said Mr. Wise, "is the spirit which inspires these volunteers, eighty per cent. of whom were born and educated in Australia. Rich and poor alike have sunk all class distinctions. Both in the Australian and New Zealand Forces men of broad acres and large incomes are serving as privates, while men who were their employees hold Commissions. Indeed, no class has held back. From an official return which was published at the end of April, showing the avocations of the Expeditionary Forces, it appears that the largest percentage of any social class came from the highly-paid Trade Unionists, whose standard of living and minimum wage of 8s a day for eight hours is secured by legal regulation. The next highest percentage of any class was from the countrymen."

"It is thought in many circles that a revolt is about to break out in the Yemen. There is a persistent rumour that the famous Sayed Idris has already gathered his follower's in Assir and has decided to lead an expedition against Sanaa, the capital of the Yemen. The Turkish Vali, it is said, called upon the Imam Yehia to give him help but the latter advised him to apply to the Sherif of Mecca. Sayed Idris evidently thinks that the moment is propitious for the expulsion of the hated Turk, and a rebellion may be expected in the near future."

(Egyptian Gazette).

With reference to the wireless station on Long Island which is reported to have been closed by the United States Government, the New York correspondent of the "Daily Telegraph" writes: It have [sic] been proved to the satisfaction of the United States Government that the wireless station at Sayville (Long Island), communicating with Germany, has committed on various occasions lately gross breaches of neutrality, for which reason officers representing the United States Government, will take possession of Sayville Station and no messages will be sent or received except under their supervision.

It is alleged that, despite the censorship by the Navy Department, Sayville has been communicating with German Submarines, and has also been disclosing the movements of outgoing vessels from American ports. Sayville today is the only means in possession of the Germans for communicating with Germany without recourse to cables through belligerents.

A Chicago newspaper states that the real name of the man who tried to kill Mr. J. P. Morgan, the financier, is not Holt but Erich Muenter and that he was born in Germany, whence he disappeared. After his wife's suspicious death he remarried. (Reuter).

Peninsula Press

No. 57   Friday, JULY 16th. 1915   Official News.

From the Governor General Commonwealth of Australia, To General Sir Ian Hamilton.

14th July, 1915.

"Commonwealth Government would be glad if you would convey message to troops under your command that news of glorious fighting created intense enthusiasm and has resulted in large increase in recruiting particularly in Victoria. During the week ended July 8,550 recruits enlisted in the Commonwealth and every indication numbers still further increasing."

15th July 1915

The Turkish defences on this side of Krithia consisted the day before yesterday of two distinct systems, the first running along the spur just West of the Kereves Dere, through a point about 1,800 yards South-west of Krithia to the Sea, the second running over the spur between the Kereves Dere and the Domuz Dere through a point about 700 yards South-west of Krithia to the sea, West of Krithia. Of the first of these systems part had been taken on the 28th June so that the left of our line was up against the second system in that quarter. In the centre and right the Turks still held their forward line of trenches. Our plan of operations on the 12th July was to seize the right and right-centre sections of the foremost system of Turkish trenches above described from the sea at the mouth of the Kereves Dere over a front of 2,500 yards almost to the main Sedd-el-Bahr-Krithia Road. By this means we hoped to complete the driving back of the Turks to their second system of trenches along the whole front, with the exception of something less than 1,000 yards in the left-centre of our line.

The attack was arranged in two phases, and, after a preliminary bombardment, the French and our 155th Brigade assaulted the first line of Turkish trenches and succeeded in carrying them without great difficulty. Having done this, however as usual, they had to establish themselves and resist the counter-attacks which were at once made from the maze of Turkish trenches in the vicinity. The intricate nature of the ground made it extremely hard to follow the progress of events, and for this reason and, owing to the fact that the telephone and telegraph wires were cut early in the day by shell fire, etc., it was difficult to get back repots from the front lines. Generally speaking, the fighting was confused and trenches were captured and re-captured.

The second phase was then undertaken and the 157th Brigade moved to the attack of the right sector of the enemy's lines. As in the former phase the first line of trenches was easily carried, the preliminary bombardment having been very successful. Following up their success, the Brigade took the second line of trenches capturing some 80 prisoners and by nightfall the line was consolidated some 400 yards in advance of our original position in this part of the field. During the night both the French and the 155th Brigade successfully repulsed two counter-attacks. During the hours of darkness however, it was found that the British right had pressed too far and the Turks made a successful bomb attack recapturing a section of the trenches.

This portion being vital to the safety of the line, a further attack was organised and a brigade of the Royal Naval Division supported by the French artillery was sent forward, and, with the support of the 75's, retook the trenches. In the meantime the French pushed their extreme right down to the mouth of the river Kereves Dere where it runs into the sea. This position was maintained without difficulty. During the night of the 13-14th, as on the previous night, the enemy counter-attacked but without success. Thus the whole of our original objectives is in our hands, except one small portion of about 300 yards.

Our losses have not yet been ascertained, but in the confused and hand-to-hand fighting which took place over that portion of the line in which there is a regular labyrinth of trenches, we fear they may be considerable. The French have not lost heavily but we regret that General Mesnou commanding 1st Division is wounded as well as several of his staff.

We took 422 prisoners, of whom 200 were taken by the French in their first attack when they also took a machine gun.

There are points which are still obscure and which concern the 300 yards of line attacked which still remains in Turkish hands alluded to above. This portion was carried by assault in fine style by a Scots battalion. It constituted a furthest objective. The battalion was seen to continue its advance against a strong trench we had hardly hoped to gain some 500 yards up one of the spurs running down from Achi Baba. There it was seen to charge and carry the trench. But no communication could be secured with this battalion as it was found that the Turks had re-occupied the first trench which had been carried and from which our men had advanced. To enable touch to be gained with the battalion it was necessary again to assault the reoccupied trench. Again the same thing happened as before. The battalion assaulted the trench, took it, passed over it and pressed on to the same objective as the Scots battalion had advanced to earlier on the previous day. The extraordinary fact is that the Turks are still in occupation of this 800 yards of trench line on the French left and no communication can be opened with either of the battalions which have gone forward. A fresh effort to clear up this situation is being made tonight.

Later.

We are most glad to be able to say that both battalions have made their way back in detachments and that their total casualties are not so very serious as might be expected seeing they have been in the midst of the Turkish lines. This makes the battle of the 12-18th an unqualified success and is at the same time as satisfactory and surprising as the reappearance of Jonah out of the whale's belly.

Italian News, 14th July.

The General situation over the whole front is unchanged. A squadron of our aeroplanes bombarded very effectively a large enemy camp at Dintomi-Di-Goriza from a height of about 600 metres.

Rome.

The Austrians, profiting by a storm, attempted a surprise attack on Montenero on the 11th inst., but were repulsed.

Peninsula Press

No. 58   Saturday, JULY 17th. 1915   Official News.

Wireless Messages.

15th July.

Mr. McKenna, Chancellor of the Exchequer, announces that the war loan is now nearly six hundred million Sterling.

Mr. Lloyd George announces in connection with the South Wales dispute that a proclamation has been issued under the Munitions Act making it an offence to participate in a strike without previous arbitration.

Eiffel Tower, Paris, July 15.

After bombarding the French and British lines, the Germans attacked the trenches near Pilken which had been captured by the British. The enemy was repulsed. The Germans bombarded Arras and Saissons with heavy shells. Their offensive in the Argonne was definitely checked.

July 16.

The day has passed relatively quietly. In the Argonne, some fighting took place with bombs and hand grenades near Marie Therese. Two German attacks against La Haute Chevauchee were repulsed. Nothing to report along the rest of the front, with the exception of some artillery engagements notably in the district North of Arras near Quennevieres, on the right bank of the Aisne near Troyn, on the heights of the Meuse around the Sunren Road to Calonne, and in the Vosges near Wissenbach.

German Headquarters, July 15th.

WESTERN FRONT:- In South Flanders yesterday, we exploded a mine West of Wytschaete with good results. Near Sauchez, the French attacked in some places with superior forces. They were repulsed along the whole front. North-west of Beau Sejour Farm, in the Champagne, an enemy attack with handgrenades, which was launched after we had exploded a mine, was stopped. The French made repeated efforts yesterday and well into the night to recapture the positions in the Argonne Forest which we had taken. In spite of a terrific expenditure of ammunition and the arrival of reinforcements their attacks broke against the unwavering German line. In many places there resulted close fighting and grenade throwing. The French paid for their efforts with more than usually heavy losses. The number of French prisoners has risen to 3,688 men. Prisoners agree that this reverse is all the more serious because July 14th was a national French festival and the attack must have been prepared long beforehand. East of the Argonne also yesterday there was heavier fighting than usual.

The "Daily Express" prints a letter from a British Naval officer stating that the Captain of the British warships sent by wireless to the Captain of the German cruiser "Konigsberg," which was recently destroyed, the following message:- "Hope see you soon." The German Captain replied: "Thanks, if you want to see me am always at home."

(German News).

(Extracts from Newspapers).

General Smuts states that the South African Government has offered to the Imperial Government for service in Europe a contingent and a heavy artillery force.

There is a probable intention to form a big training camp in South Africa.

The Imperial Government has accepted the Union of South Africa's offer of a contingent for service overseas.   (Reuter).

Mr. Rudyard Kipling, speaking at Southport said:-
"Turn your mind for a moment to the idea of a conquering Germany. You need not go far to see what it would mean to us. In Belgium at this hour several million Belgians are making war material or fortifications for their conquerors. They are given enough food to support life as the German thinks it should be supported. By the way, I believe the United States of America supplies a large part of that food. In return, they are compelled to work at the point of the bayonet. If they object they are shot. Their factories, their houses, and their public buildings, have long ago been gutted, and everything in them that was valuable or useful has been packed up and sent in to Germany. They have no more property and no more rights than cattle, and they cannot lift a hand to protect the honour of their women. And less than a year ago they were one of the most civilised and prosperous of the nations of the earth."

(Egyptian Gazette).

It is announced in Rome that the cargo of the German liner "Bayern," interned at Naples on the outbreak of war, has been found to consist of half a million revolvers, one hundred thousands rifles, two hundred

169

thousand cases of ammunition, two hangars with four biplanes fitted with wireless and maxims, 1,000 aeroplane bombs, fourteen field guns, hundreds of tons of cement and two complete wireless stations. Important military documents were found hidden in the hold.

(Reuter).

A Board of military supplies has been formed in Russia to be presided over by the Minister for War and comprising members of the Duma, of the Imperial Council, and representatives of industry and commerce. The Board will be empowered to compel manufacturers to give precedence to Government orders and will also have power to requisition public and private supplies. The formation of the Board is hailed as Russia's reply to the German success in Galicia, and is the outcome of a public demand formulated on the arrival of the congress of trade and industry. It is strongly supported in the Duma, and practically all Russia is handed over for the production of munitions to the Board, which is empowered to expend unlimited amounts.

(Reuter).

New York, July 7th.
Holt, the assailant of Mr. J. P. Morgan was found dead in his cell, having apparently shot himself with a revolver.

Washington.
Great mystery surrounds the death of Holt. The doctor certifies the skull to be fractured, but there is no evidence of the existence of the explosion of a bullet. There are conflicting versions as to the cause of death but the most probable is that his cell door being open for a moment Holt rushed out and jumped from a window fifty feet high to the ground.

Portions of Holt's great store of dynamite are cropping up in different places. A trunk containing a hundred and thirty-four sticks with a fuse has arrived at a New York storehouse. Holt confessed to the presence of others at various points in Long Island.

(Reuter).

Peninsula Press

No. 59   Sunday, JULY 18th. 1915   Official News.

(Extracts from Newspapers).

The New York financial correspondent of the "Daily Telegraph" writes:-
Notwithstanding the desperate efforts of the German American bankers here to convince them to the contrary, many authorities in Wall Street persist in the belief that financial exhaustion, if nothing else, will compel Germany to sue for peace much earlier than is generally expected. There are a number of men here who believe that the war will be a long drawn-out affair, but most American financial authorities are convinced that Germany will reach the end of her resources before next winter.

"I believe," said one well known banker who lately returned from Germany, "that this fact finds recognition in German official circles, and that therein may be found the reason for the increased aggressiveness of the Kaiser's forces in the East, where the possibilities are most favourable for an offensive campaign."

"Germany," said this authority, to the "Daily Telegraph" representative, "will fight as long as she is able, and the end will come suddenly, though not immediately. Financially, commercially, and in respect to the number of men available for military service, Germany's strength is failing rapidly."

The belief is gaining ground among the Italian troops that King Victor possesses the gift of ubiquity, as his Majesty seems to be able to be on the same day on every front. He is always where the peril seems to be greatest, and where his encouragement and succour are most needed. He dashes in his grey automobile along the flat roads in the Friuli region, appears on horseback on the hills near Gorizia, climbs on the back of a mule up the Carnic Passes, and gains on foot, helped by an alpenstock, the heights of the peaks from which Rovereto can be seen. Both he and his first aide-de-camp, General Brasati, are great Alpinists. The latter is famous for the skill with which be conducted the retirement of his regiment after the battle of Adowa, along the crests of the Abyssinian hills, and succeeded in saving his soldiers from being enveloped.

On Tuesday evening the King crossed the Isonzo on a pontoon bridge,

South of Monte Nero. After sunset an officer of the General Staff came up to his Majesty, saying that an attack of the enemy was expected during the night, and it would be unsafe to remain on the left bank of the river. The King promptly replied, "If this point is dangerous for my soldiers, it is my place," and remained there the whole night, passing from position to position, encouraging the troops with words and example.

What secures for his Majesty general admiration, is his modesty, simplicity, and calm courage, without affectation. When "lights out" is sounded, the King studies the plans for the next day, or sends his daily report to his family.

To the young Crown Prince, who, in one of his letters, asked when he would return home to his boy, the King replied that he could not leave while thousands of his "boys" were risking their lives.   (Reuter.)

M. Jean Cruppi, the former French Minister for Foreign Affairs, who had the honour of being received by the King at Buckingham Palace, contributes to the "Matin" an account of the impressions which he gained during his visit to England.

Our English friends, he says, are not troubled with an excessive gift of imagination. Hard facts are needed in order to bring them to a sense of realities. In this present war it has taken them some time to realise that the superb effort represented by the British Navy on sea had to be supplemented by a supreme effort on land. Under the impulse of men like Mr. Asquith and Lord Kitchener this effort is being made to the full. After ten months war the visitor to England is surprised less by what remains to be accomplished than by the work already done. Everything had to be created, both the man and the gun.

M. Cruppi expresses admiration at the success of Lord Kitchener's campaign for volunteer recruits. The men are there. As regards their arms, the crusade initiated by Mr. Lloyd George as Minister of Munitions promises to yield immense results at an early date. By whatever means the co-operation of capital and labour to this end may be secured, the work will be done, for it is the will of the nation that it shall be done.

Englishmen of all classes and creeds are one in an inflexible anger in the implacable determination to lavish blood and treasure until Germany has been beaten to her knees. When Englishmen say "The war will be long," that does not mean that they intend to stint their effort, nor that they do not believe that victory is near at hand. It means that, come what may, the British Bulldog will not relax his tenacious grip.

As for what Englishmen think of France and the French, M. Cruppi declares that men of all parties desire that the union between the two countries may emerge stronger and more intimate from the great conflict, in which their sons are shedding their blood together. "In France we know these things; but it is well that they should be said again by a witness who has been able to "experience" them, and to reinforce his impressions by facts."

He concludes:- "Never before have the irresistible forces of the United Kingdom appeared to be so full of energy and so imposing. These forces are in full operation and they are marching forward to their goal."

The "New York Times" commenting on the German debate concerning the answer to be returned to Mr. Wilson's Lusitania Note and the argument that the United States could not harm Germany in the event of war, remarks:-
A nation at war has three arms of service – its army, its navy and its credit. Being a nation of peace we should not be capable of making any very effective military demonstrations but we could use our credit in a way that would certainly be decisive of the conflict. Three billions of money (£600,000,000), not loaned to be repaid but spent on our own account for war purposes in aid of the Allies, would put the issue beyond doubt. The jingoes of the German Press have taken no thought of this factor. We have had it in mind here, but only as a remote contingency, for it has been our sincere desire and purpose to come to an amicable understanding with Germany.

Peninsula Press

No. 60   Monday, JULY 19th. 1915   Official News.

(Extracts from Newspapers).

Eight skilled Clyde workers have just returned from France after spending three days with the troops.

The idea of sending this deputation to the front to see the conditions under which our army fights was Sir William Beardmore's, head of the firm of William Beardmore and Co., Ltd., Glasgow.

"I asked Lord Kitchener if he would allow me to send a number of my men to the front," said Sir William "believing that they would come back determined to work to the utmost and fired with an infectious zeal which would permeate the workshops. Lord Kitcheaner readily acquiesced. The men have been; they have seen Lord Kitchener since and also Mr. Lloyd George, and I think their mission will speedily yield results as far as we are concerned."

The conclusion at which the delegates arrived was expressed by one of the workmen in these words:- "The men at the front are at the mercy of the men at home. We are going to Glasgow to let the men know that, and we want all the workmen of the country to realise it, and if they do we are certain that there will be an end to the shortage of shells and a beginning of the end of the war itself." ("Globe.")

Colonel Robert McCormick, son of a former American Ambassador in Petrograd, who has spent some time at the Russian front, has given to Reuter's Agency an interesting account of the conditions with which the Grand Duke's troops have had to contend.

"In addition to their network of strategic railways," says Colonel McCormick, "the Germans had caused farmers to so construct and locate their buildings as to be of great use for military purposes. Throughout East Prussia, farmhouses all occupy strategic points. They are invariably built with heavy walls and small windows towards the Russian frontier and with thin walls and wide doors towards Berlin. Many of these are connected with secret telephones. Thus, early in the war the Russians were surprised to find their well concealed batteries struck by the first shot of the enemy.

174

"The Russian infantryman is the most splendid physical specimen of the war. If the bayonet is the Russian infantryman's chief reliance, the entrenching tool is his best friend. I have seen a regiment in open order of attack cut a hole for the elbows and build a mound large enough to protect the body from direct rifle fire in a space of five minutes. When it comes to entrenching nothing can be compared to the Russian regiment, except the Roman legions of old. The Russian soldier is a labouring man, accustomed to working in the earth and forest. One night will put him safe underground with a roof to stop the fragments of shells bursting overhead."

It is reported that owing to the persistent defeats of Austrian counter-attacks another high Council of War has been held at Innsbruck, Archduke Eugene presiding, at which there were hot exchanges of criticism between German and Austrian Generals, the former dissenting from the latter's strategic views. The result was the dismissal of the General commanding the Austrian Landstrum and two other Generals.

The capture of Zelienkofel, 7,850 feet high, is one of the most notable Italian feats of arms. It is generally climbed from Plocken, as the ascent on the Italian side, which is devoid of shrubs or any foothold, is considered impossible. But a platoon of Alpinists volunteered to make the ascent. Tied together with ropes, eleven of them, carrying a mitrailleuse, reached the summit at sunset, waited till night when the Austrian company in charge of the signalling station were asleep, then opened with their machine gun and charged with the bayonet. The Austrian commander was the only survivor.

(Reuter)

Under ordinary circumstances the next General Election would take place during the winter of 1915, but to embark upon a great political struggle while a war is in progress would be unthinkable. Postponement has long been agreed to in principle, but the party leaders were to settle details among themselves. The formation of the Coalition Government has rendered such a conference unnecessary, and it is understood that the Cabinet has decided upon the line of action. Mr. Walter Long, as President of the Local Government Board, will bring in a bill putting off the municipal elections due in November, and later on he will deal with the Parliamentary aspect of the question. Should the war continue, the next general election need not take place until 1917, and the change will be wrought by temporarily suspending the clause of the Parliament Act which reduced the duration of the legislature from seven years to five.

(Daily Telegraph).

The "Fremdenblatt," closely connected with the Austrian Foreign Office, has joined in the attempt to persuade Servia that in crushing the Serbians, Austria was actuated by most friendly motives: "Serbia has only one choice," says the Emperor Francis Joseph's favourite newspaper, "to accept the generous hand extended to her, for we wish to prove to her again, for the hundredth time in history, that her only interests are to befriend the Monarchy, and that it is the Monarchy only who can and is willing to save her. We protested for years against her aspirations of an outlet to the Adriatic, now we have brushed that fear aside, and are ready to recognise her rights, for the considerations existing then are no longer existing. She was fighting bravely and honourably; she deserves to be a nation with a future."

When the Norwegian mail steamer "Venus" arrived at Newcastle her master reported that midway on her voyage she was hailed by a German submarine and made to throw overboard the greater portion of her cargo, consisting of provisions destined for this country. The rest of the cargo, consisting of wood, etc., was allowed to remain.

The master was given his choice between jettisoning the foodstuffs and having his ship sunk. Consequently 416 casks of butter and many cases of salmon and tinned fish went overboard. When this had been done the submarine disappeared, and the vessel proceeded on her way.

(Daily Telegraph).

Peninsula Press

No. 61   Tuesday, JULY 20th. 1915   Official News.

Wireless Messages.

Eiffel Tower, Paris, July 18.

In Artois the cannonade is not so intense. Some shells have been fired at Arras. On the right bank of the Aisne, in the district of Troyen, there have been violent bombardments and fighting with mines. Twenty shells were fired at Rheims, killing one civilian and seriously wounding another. In the Argonne the day has been comparatively quiet, without any infantry fighting. On the heights of the Meuse the Germans, after the bombardment of last night, made a violent attack against the French positions from the trench of Calonne to the village of Eparges on the Southern edge of the ravine of Sonvaux. They only managed to reach the portion of the trench which the French had taken from them on the 6th July. Some parties of Germans who had succeeded in getting into the ravine were either killed or taken prisoners. Between the ridge of Sonnaux and the trenches of Calonne the Germans were also repulsed with heavy losses. Bombardment continues in the forest of Arremont.

Italian Press, July 19.

There has been fighting throughout the Trentino and Carnia, which has gone in our favour. On the 16th our artillery bombarded the enemy's works in the Pass of Predil, causing an explosion and a fire which burnt for a long time.

Rome, July 18.

The Austrians, after crossing the Venerocolo and Brizio Passes, attempted to attack the Italian positions but were repulsed. The Italians have solidly occupied the two passes. The Austrians also delivered two determined attacks on the Carnia front. Both were repulsed with heavy loss.

German News, July, 19.

North-east of Kurschang fighting led to the capture of the foremost enemy positions. Between Pisa and the Vistula the Russians continued to retreat, followed closely by the troops under Generals von Scholtlz and von Galliwitz. Wherever the enemy tried to make a stand in a previously prepared position, he was attacked and defeated. The reserves and Landwehr under General von Scholtz stormed the positions of Poremby, Wyk and Prosneyence line. General von Galliwitz broke through the strongly fortified position at Mlodyiano, Karneinz. The number of prisoners taken is rapidly increasing. Four guns were captured. North, as far as the Vistula the Russians have begun to retreat, our troops are in pursuit. In the fighting with the enemy's rear-guard we made 620 prisoners.

South-east front: General von Woynesch's offensive was successful. On the morning of the 17th under a heavy fire our troops stormed a narrow position, one of the enemy's chief and fortified positions, and, breaking through, reached the enemy's trenches over a front of 2,000 metres. In subsequent hand-to-hand fighting, this trench was widened. In the evening our reserve troops forced the enemy to retire behind the Ilyanka section. South of Zwollen the enemy lost heavily. Two-thousand were captured and 5 machines guns were taken. On the upper Vistula and Bug, fighting continues under the control of Field-Marshal von Machensen. German troops drove the Russians from the heights between Pilacy, Korvice, South of Piashi and Krasnostom. Both places were stormed. A fresh Siberian Regiment was thrown in the battle but failed to relieve the situation. We took several thousand prisoners.

England having refused or been unable to supply to Sweden the necessary quantity of coal, Germany has permitted the exportation of 600,000 tons of anthracite coal. Negotiations are pending for the exportation to Sweden of a limited supply of dyes and drugs.

Prince Hohenlohe, temporary German Ambassador at Constantinople, has arrived at Bucharest where he resides in the Royal Castle as the guest of his brother-in-law the King of Roumania.

(Extracts from Newspapers).

Mr. McKenna, Chancellor of the Exchequer, speaking on the need for individual economy, said: We have not only got to learn that in this war, in our present circumstances, extravagance is a crime, and that economy, parsimony even, becomes the highest of national virtues, but that we must look to the individual acting alone in his own home for the foundation of the national resources, by the help of which alone we and our Allies can obtain the triumph to which we look forward.

I do not think we have yet realised what part in the war is going to be played by the financial strength of the United Kingdom. Every month that goes by the strain that is made upon all the combatants becomes greater and greater. Nations can undergo and can suffer the gigantic losses which a great war of the kind entails for a period, but only for a period. The nation which can endure them the longest is the nation which is going to win. If we are to endure, if our resources are to stand the strain, we must not continue to be reckless in our personal and domestic expenditure; we must not go on buying from abroad vast quantities of commodities with which in war time we really could dispense.

We have to buy from abroad; and are buying from abroad, machinery and munitions. If we have to buy and pay for them we cannot pay as readily for much else that we import. Now, the real source of our strength when it is once understood, is the power of the individual to economise, to save, to limit his consumption, and so reduce our demand for foreign goods.

We thereby conserve our resources, we keep high our credit, and, to come to a technical matter, we prevent a fall in the American exchange.

Peninsula Press

No. 62   Wednesday, JULY 21st. 1915   Official News.

Wireless Messages.

The "Idea Nazionale," Rome, states that the Austrian Emperor is dangerously ill.

Telegrams to Paris newspapers say that German prisoners belonging to the Crown Prince's Army declare that the Crown Prince has become unpopular among the troops who openly discuss his tactical errors and severely condemn the cynical indifference with which he sacrificed the lives of his men.

Italian General Headquarters, July, 17.
Our troops successfully continued their offensive, strongly attacking the fortified positions of Falczasigo and Livinal. For three days this position blocked our advance, owing to the difficult nature of the ground and the tenacious resistance of the enemy at the head of Franza Valley and the hills of Col di Lana. Everywhere the action of our infantry was brilliant in winning the Col di Lana, reaching the Andiany Valley, and carrying the enemy's positions at the point of bayonet, especially at one point where the enemy had received reinforcements and had made a small advance.

In the Isonzo zone, the enemy's efforts against our positions have become fiercer, particularly at the bridgehead of Palva. The enemy attacked many times without results.

On the night of the 17th two of our dirigibles dropped bombs on the enemy's works at Gosizia and on the camp on the eastern slope of Mount San Michele with satisfactory results. The airships throughout the attack were continually caught by the enemy's flashlights and fired upon by artillery but they returned to our lines undamaged.

July, 18.
In Carnia the enemy, taking advantage of fog and darkness on the 14th, delivered two determined attacks between Monte Croglisno and Piorzo Arestano. Both attacks were repulsed with losses to the enemy. In the Isonzo zone the situation is almost unchanged. The enemy by small raids especially at night and by artillery of large calibre attempted continually to inflict loses on us, to disturb our advance, and to compel our batteries to fire in order to discover their positions.

In the Artois there has been heavy artillery fire round Souchez, sixty shells being fired on Arras. There was no infantry fighting. In the Argonne there was fighting with bombs and grenades. On the heights of the Meuse, the Germans this afternoon made two heavy attacks against our positions on the ridge South of Sonvoux, both being completely repulsed. The enemy then bombarded our trenches and with weak detachments made a series of attacks on our line and were everywhere defeated with heavy loss. Along the rest of the front the day has been quiet. One of our aeroplanes chased an aviatik and brought it down with machine gun fire. The machine fell burning into the German lines near Soissons and was finished off by our artillery.

(Extracts from Newspapers).

London.

Mr. Bonar Law cabled to Viscount Buxton his congratulations on General Botha's brilliant generalship and the bravery of his troops. Lord Kitchener cabling his congratulations to General Botha says: "We shall warmly welcome you and any South Africans who can join us."

General Botha who attributes the final envelopment of the enemy to incessant marching day and night, to great distances covered at great speed and without water. He pays a fine tribute to his gallant troops.

General Botha's great triumph after immense fatigues and privations has been hailed with the utmost satisfaction. The Germans were completely out-generalled, out-manoeuvred and outwitted.   (Reuter).

M. Julius Szini, writing in the Hungarian "Pesti Naplo" about the new British War Loan, says: "The man of today has the privilege of beholding two groups of belligerents, the one fighting with all its virtues and bravery, the other with all its resources and gold, and one is at a loss to decide which to admire the more, the organisation of the one or the unlimited riches of the other. If the old proverb be still true that three things are needed to carry a war to a successful finish – money, money and money – then England, with the smashing power of her riches, the "silver bullets", as she calls them will ...." (Excision by the Hungarian censor) "The rolling rouble" and its legendary meaning cannot be compared with the power and might of the pound sterling. We see that is the only money in this war stained globe which has grown in value when all other moneys have lost theirs. And if – Gold help us – at the end money and England come out on top, just imagine what an immense amount we and Germany will have to pay to reimburse this waste of milliards, the numbers of which the British Minister of Finance has to calculate with the aid of logarithm tables. Our greatest and mightiest enemy is the English Sovereign and it has appeared again on the war market."

The Inhabitants of the Grand Duchy of Luxemburg have, according to German newspapers, proved themselves inconceivably ungrateful for all the kindness they have received at the hands of the Germans, especially in view of the fact that the fate of Belgium was not visited also on them.

As a proof of this ingratitude the following announcement is quoted from the Luxemburg "Zeitung":- "According to private information that has reached us, 8,678 Luxembourgers have joined the French Army as volunteers. On their journey through France to the front they were everywhere greeted with joyous cheers."

This the Hamburg "Nachrichten" remarks means that 3 percent of the entire population of Luxembourg have offered their services to France, and it considers that this number is so high that it is doubtful if all the offers of service were voluntary.

No Luxembourgers, observes the German Journal have offered to serve the German Army, though it hastens to add that even if they had volunteered they would not have been accepted, for in the first place, only German subjects can serve in the Imperial Army, and in the second place, Germany respects the neutrality of Luxemburg. If the news is really correct, the Hamburg "Nachrichten" remarks in conclusion, Luxemburg is guilty of a gross breach of neutrality, and the German Government is relieved of the obligation to regard that neutrality as still existing.

Peninsula Press

No. 63   Thursday, JULY 22nd. 1915   Official News.

Wireless Messages.

July 20.

Fierce fighting has been general along the whole front, a thousand miles long, from the Baltic to Bessarabia, as the result of a general offensive by von Hindenburg in the North and Mackensen in the South with the object of encircling Warsaw. The Germans claim great successes in both regions while the Russians admit slight withdrawals. A new feature is mentioned in both Russian and German communiques, that great cavalry battles are in progress in the Baltic provinces where General Buelow crossed the river Windau and is advancing North and South of Mitau. The enemy's principal effort is in the region of Prasnyz and between the Vistula and the Bug.

Rome.

The Italians have achieved notable successes. On the 18th we captured 2,000 prisoners, six machine guns, 1,500 rifles and much ammunition. Our offensive is developing favourably at Folsarego. Fort Herinann has been seriously damaged.

Eiffel Tower, Paris, July 20.

In the Artois there has been artillery fighting without any infantry engagements. A violent bombardment of Rheims has caused several casualties among the civil population. Between the Meuse and the Mosselle, at Erarge in the distict of Feye en Haye, and at Bois-le Pretre, there has been considerable artillery fire. On the night of 19-20th one of our airships dropped 23 bombs on the military railway station and ammunition depot at Vigneulles Les Hattonchate. The airship returned to our lines uninjured.

The "Times" is informed from Germany that a deputation of Berlin bankers having insisted on an interview with the Kaiser informed him that if the war were prolonged for another winter the German Empire would he utterly bankrupt. Hence, adds the journal, the Kaiser's prediction that the war will end in October.

Extracts from Newspapers.

There is an extraordinary response to M. Ribot's appeal to the public to exchange their gold for paper money. The whole population is hastening to bring in its gold. At the Bank of France there is an incessant stream at six different entrances. These crowds are formed of all classes of people, from poor women who go to the bank with gold pieces that have been saved for a rainy day, to the rich, who offer gold to the value of tens of thousands of francs.

("Egyptian Gazette").

In the 24 hours ended at eight this Sunday morning two inches of rain were registered at Birmingham. This is the heaviest rainfall in a period of ten years.

It is officially announced that the Archbishop of York has recently been visiting the Grand Fleet at various bases,

In the House of Commons, Commander Bellairs asked if, in view of German attacks on armed merchantmen, the Government would ask neutrals to allow merchantmen to be armed for purposes of defence with only one gun astern, and to trade with their ports despite the carrying of a gun. Lord Robert Cecil replied that merchantmen of belligerent Powers were entitled by established and uninterrupted usage to carry and use armament in self defence.

Several neutral Governments had been communicated with at the outbreak of the war and several more had been approached since as circumstances suggested. The principle of merchantmen carrying arms in self-defence had been generally recognised and British ships so armed had been trading regularly with various countries since the early stage of the war.

(Reuter).

The Press Bureau (London) states that the position of the German cruiser Koenigsberg made the attack most difficult, as only shallow draught ships could get sufficiently close to engage the cruiser ·effectively. Aircraft having accurately located the Koenigsberg, the monitors "Severn" and "Mersey" on July 4, entered the river and opened fire. The Koenigsberg replied immediately with salvoes from five guns and her fire was accurate and rapid. The "Mersey" was twice hit, one shell killing four and wounding four. As the Koenigsburg was surrounded by jungle, the aeroplanes had great difficulty in spotting the fall of shot. She was hit five times early in the action, but after six hours the aeroplanes reported that the masts were still standing. A salvo then burst on her and she became heavily on fire between two masts. She continued to fire one gun intermittently for a while, but during the last part of the engagement the cruiser was silent, either on account of lack of ammunition or the disablement of her guns. Although not totally destroyed as the result of this engagement, she was probably incapacitated. The task of the monitors was extremely difficult owing to the jungle and the difficulties of accurate spotting, but they were assisted by the cruiser "Weymouth" flying the flag of Rear-Admiral King-Hall, which followed them across the bar and engaged the small guns on the banks, whilst the cruiser "Pioneer" engaged the guns at the mouth of the river. In order to complete the destruction of the Koenigsbeug, Rear-Admiral King-Hall ordered a further attack on July 11, when the ship was reduced to a total wreck. Our casualties were only two wounded onboard the "Mersey" in this second engagement.

(Reuter).

The Eton boys who are being employed at ammunition works at Slough are making splendid progress. Very business like they look in their engineering overalls. The boys are keen and enthusiastic, and are doing real good work. They are employed in various shops, and are taking their place side by side with the other workers without any distinction. All of them are senior boys, and cycle to and from Eton to their work. Most of them have already been through a course of training in the School of Mechanics at Eton, and therefore have a good rudimentary knowledge.

At present there are two daily shifts. Ten boys work from seven to twelve in the morning, and ten others from one to six in the afternoon. They are being paid the same wage as other beginners. Some are employed at shaping and drilling machines, and others on the manufacture of munitions.

("Daily Telegraph").

Peninsula Press

No. 64   Friday, JULY 23rd. 1915   Official News.

Wireless Messages.

Petrograd, July 19.

There has been severe fighting at Yjitza. Three battalions of the enemy crossed the river. The Russians furiously counter-attacked and annihilated the enemy in a bayonet charge.

Eiffel Tower, Paris, July 22.

In Artois the cannonade continues. There has been fighting with bombs and grenades around Sauchez but no infantry engagement. At the Eastern boundary of the Argonne the enemy succeeded in retaking a trench which formed a salient in front of our line. Between the Meuse and the Moselle there has been a violent bombardment at Tete de Vache, in the forest of Apremont and in Bois le Pretre. About 20 shells have been fired into Saint Die.

Athens.

M. Venizelos addressing his supporters, said that the dangers of the present situation impelled him to resume the leadership of the party.

In the House of Commons Mr. McKenna stated that the total subscriptions to the War Loan were now nearly £600,000,000. The papers had mentioned £800,000,000, but such a total was neither expected nor desired by the Government. 550,000 subscribers had contributed £570,000,000 through the Bank of England, and 547,000 persons had subscribed £15,000,000 through the Post Office. The Chancellor of the Exchequer emphasised the fact that the £600,000,000 represented new money alone, without conversions. The results were most remarkable as the subscriptions consisted almost exclusively of money immediately available, for at the moment people were unable to sell securities. It was an exhibition of the unrivalled financial resources of the Empire, and a demonstration to our Allies and to our enemies that Great Britain had proved faithful to her trust.   (Reuter).

Extracts from Newspapers.

To the inhabitants the meaning of a German occupation of their country, even in its mildest form, is illustrated by what is going on in Belgium and France. In some places the Germans have articles required by troops manufactured in local factories by the simple method of arresting managers refusing to undertake such work. In one case where employees struck, as a reply to the incarceration of their officials, workmen to the number of some hundreds were themselves sentenced to a term of imprisonment only to terminate when they signed a document that the return to work was voluntary.

In other cases workmen have been shut up in factories and kept without food till they continued working. In one factory a notice was posted that any proprietor of a factory that closes down will be fined 1,000 marks a day during stoppage of work. ("Egyptian Gazette").

News from Capetown says that Botha's total losses throughout the South West African campaign amount to 130 dead and 320 wounded. The financial cost of the campaign is about £15,000,000. (Reuter).

London, July 15.
Reuter is informed that Roumania continues successfully and energetically to prevent arms from Germany and Austria reaching Turkey. Besides stopping double-partitioned wagons, Roumanian officials lately confiscated a consignment labelled Munich beer. The Germans had specially telegraphed to various stations to place ice blocks on the trucks to keep the beer in good condition. Curious officials, however, discovered that the barrels contained ammunition and an examination of large cement blocks disclosed the fact they were filled with shell cases.

The "Frankfurter Zeitung" attacks Roumania for prohibiting the transit of arms and munitions to Turkey. It accuses the government of the country of self seeking unwisdom and ingratitude, and concludes with a veiled threat that the paramount interests of the central powers may overrule those of Roumania. (Reuter).

Reuter's special correspondent with British Headquarters in France says that the news of the arrival of new formations had been kept very secret. There had been rumours of the arrival of certain divisions, but none was aware of their actual presence until one chanced to see them on the road, or to meet them in the trenches. Their sturdiness and discipline have favourably impressed veterans, who have been very keenly interested in the formation and training of the new army. The newcomers were placed in the trenches for short spells, firstly in sections, then gradually in whole battalions. They stood their baptism of fire according to expectation, while one unit exposed to heavy fire showed splendid courage and tenacity. Gunners highly approve the batteries of the new army. The moral effect of the new divisions is undoubtedly great, inspiring those in the trenches with confidence and proving that the country is fully supporting the firing line.

A telegram from Melbourne states that Mr. Fisher, the Premier, is arranging for the reinternment of the body of the late General Bridges in the Federal capital.

Reuter has received information of the remarkable exploit of some Indian troops. One hundred Pathan infantry under a Native officer were Captured by the Germans in Flanders and sent to Constantinople in hope that they would join the Turks. They somehow managed to escape and after a march of four months reached Cabul safely where they were well received. After resting they will rejoin their regiment in India.

188

Peninsula Press

No. 65   Saturday, JULY 24th. 1915   Official News.

Wireless Messages.

Washington, July 23.

The United States Government has decided to inform Germany that further loss of American lives through German submarines will be regarded as unfriendly act.

Petrograd, July 21.

The greatest battle of the war, for the possession of Warsaw, is raging. In the first phase the Germans gained ground but suffered enormous losses, the Russians hurling them back from a favourable point on the line from Wotogeorge and Vikloostrole. South of the Lublin and Cholm railway, the enemy have resumed the offensive and captured Porely village on the Maniven front, but other attacks from the South-west were repulsed. South of the Lublin and Cholm railway the Russians withdrew to their second point, but maintained all points on the Dneister.

Amsterdam, July 23.

The terrific battle near Warsaw still sways indecisively. The Berlin communique shows that the Russians are making important counter attacks from the Narew fortress line and have been reinforced. The Germans made no progress at Blonie, the most vital point on this front, where German reinforcements have arrived.

A most terrific battle is being fought against General Mackensen in another vital sector where the Russians are re-attacking very fiercely. The Germans claim only a slight advance there.

Petrograd, July 23.

There was heavy fighting on the whole front on Tuesday, the Russians repelling the German attacks and attacking successfully. The enemy's offensive in direction of Lublin has been arrested on the Lodel-Peasey front. A desperate battle on both banks of the Vieprez lasted till late at night when the Germans were driven back with heavy losses. The Russians favourably attacked the enemy who crossed the Bug in the Gorkal region. We took 1,000 prisoners.

Petrograd, July 22.

The Germans claim to have captured Windau on the Baltic.

189

The Russians destroyed a convoy Turkish sailing vessels bound for Trebizond with ammunition.

The battle in the Isonzo region is very intense. We have advanced at Plava and capured part of the line of heights commanding the Goriezia and Isonzo bridges from the right bank. We expelled the enemy from a number of trenches on the Carso plateau, after desperate fighting day and night, capturing maxims, rifles, ammunition and many more prisoners.

A suburb of Arras has been bombarded. In the Champagne, near the camp of Chalons, German aviators attempted to drop bombs on the village and supply stations. They were heavily fired upon and their incendiary bombs did no damage. Between the Meuse and the Moselle there has been a violent bombardment with heavy artillery. In Lorraine, to the East of Biancourt on the Seille, the French have driven back a strong German reconnaissance. In the Vosges, North of Munster, the French after obstinate fighting, have occupied the crest of the Linge and South of this point have reached the quarries of Schratzmannel and the woods of Banenkopf.

German Wireless News

South of Leintrey the French attacks collapsed in front of the fortifications of our trenches. In the Vosges, South-east of the Reichsackenhoff, the enemy attacked six times. He was repulsed with great and bloody loss by the Bavarian troops. By a counter-attack we won back a portion of a trench which was in the enemy's hands and took 187 Alpine troops, including three officers, prisoners. Near Sondernach we repulsed an enemy attack in the evening.

An enemy "two decker" (biplane) collapsed under the fire of our guns in Parrey wood. In an air fight above Munster valley, three German aviators overcame three enemy's aviators and in the pursuit; forced two of these to descend.

EASTERN FRONT:- North-east of Sjawle our troops are advancing in an enveloping movement and have captured 4,150 prisoners besides five machine guns, much gear and sappers stores. Having broken through on the lower Dabina the German troops advanced nearly to Grynkisyk-Judjuiny. On the way thither several enemy positions were stormed. The Russians are wavering along the whole front from Rakiewo-lake to the Niemen North of the Mariampol-Kawno Road. We consolidated the various elements of our advance and pressed on Eastward. Four officers, 1,210 men and 4 machine guns were captured. On the Narew, the enemy continued his useless counter-attacks. South of the Vistula, the Russians have been forced back to the broadened bridge-heads of Warsaw, along the line to Blen-Nadaszyuqua-Kalwnyoi-Nadarina.

SOUTH-EAST FRONT:- General von Woyisik's German troops succeeded after heavy fighting in destroying the stand made by the Russians in front of Ivangorod. About midday the great bridge-head of Lagovwola was stormed by our brave Schleswig troops. By a combined movement with the Hungarians the enemy was thrust into the fortress which is now surrounded.

North-west of Ivangorod, the Austro-Hungarian troops are still fighting on the Western bank of the Vistula. Yesterday, more than 8,000 prisoners were taken besides 11 machine guns. Between the Vistula and Bug, fighting continues under the direction of General Von Mackensen.

South-west of Lublin the Austro-Hungarian troops made further progress between Sienicka-Vola, South of Rigorvice and the Bug. Large portions of the enemies positions were stormed

Peninsula Press

No. 66　　Sunday, JULY 25th. 1915　　Official News.

Official Report.

SOUTHERN SECTION:- About 8 o'clock on Friday afternoon, the Turks attacked the Northern trenches on our left flank. Our front trenches in that neighbourhood were shelled rather heavily and under cover of the, bombardment a small force of Turks dashed for our sapheads. Two of our machine guns at once opened fire and the survivors retired. About 40 dead Turks were lying in front of our trenches and more probably out of sight as our shrapnel was effective. Our casualties were about two officers and 28 men, mostly wounded. The whole affair only lasted about twenty minutes.

NORTHERN SECTION:- Inflammatory shell, length about 15 inches by 8 inches, was fired by a, noiseless gun at our lines this afternoon. It burst, making holes one foot in diameter and setting alight the ground eight feet in diameter which was easily extinguished. Last night the Turks threw some liquid into one of the French trenches and then tried to ignite it with bombs but failed. The nature of the liquid is unknown at present. This is the first time on the Peninsula that German tricks have been tried.

Wireless Messages.

German News, July 28.

The "Morning Post" Washington correspondent says that a fire broke out on the Super Dreadnought "Oklahoma" which was about to do her trials. It is believed also that the battleships "Alabama" and "New Jersey" caught fire last week.

Petrograd, July 22.

Austrian prisoners declare that Germans; shot 5 000 Russian prisoners at Rauaruska.

A memorandum from German Headquarters denies the Russian statement that the Germans in Rauaruska, shot 5,000 Russian prisoners.

Mr. Macnamara announced in the House of Commons that it was Commander Max Horton, D.S.O., of submarine E9, who torpedoed the German battleship "Pommern" in the Baltic.

Eiffel Tower, Paris, July 24.

The day was comparatively quiet along the whole front. In Artois there was the usual artillery activity at various points and a few shells were fired at the suburbs of Soissons and Rheims. At Bois-le-Pretre during the night of the 22-23rd, the French regained a line of trenches previously lost, and two German counter-attacks were repulsed with considerable loss. A group of French aeroplanes yesterday evening dropped 28 bombs on the railway station of Conflaus-en-Jarnisy. They compelled two German aviatics to descend in the German lines.

London, July 28.
Field-Marshal Sir John French reports that the British have occupied 150 yards of the enemy's first line of trenches, near Chateau-Hooge.

Berlin, July 23.
Persons of German origin in neutral countries, and especially in North America, are officially warned that to take part in the manufacture of war material is a grave moral crime against the Fatherland and persons so engaged are in danger of legal persecution on their return to Germany.

Extracts from Newspapers.

The Australian is making his Sacrifices and his efforts with renewed energy. The "Sydney Morning Herald" computed that New South Wales alone was, on recent records, after allowing for the rejected, supplying a battalion a week to the contingents in training for Europe.

I have previously noted the universality of this recruiting, and it continues. The great, shearers union, the A.W.U., had some time ago sent in 12,000 of its members. Among the very imperfect records hastily compiled about the end of April one finds 1,000 bank clerks, 164 students from the State Agricultural College, 140 of the State police (and other States are not far behind); from another point of view (the figures being for New South Wales alone) the sports Clubs have sent nearly 1,000 Rugby Union players, nearly as many from the Rugby League, which is making provision for the wives and dependents of footballers killed in action, a smaller but considerable number of Association players, 80 swimmers from two clubs alone, and 40 polo players.

A particularly notable feature is the continuously high quality of the recruits: an experienced officer, viewing yesterday's contingent (which included engineers, blacksmiths, bank clerks, commercial travellers, squatters, tradesmen, farmers, and a schoolmaster), said:- "I never saw a better lot in my life they're simply wonderful." Men turned down for some physical defect merely go off to a doctor to be put straight and then return to the recruiting office, some three or four times, in the hope of being at last accepted.

"Times" Australian Correspondent

The following Imperial Rescript has been addressed to the Russian Premier. M. Goremykin :-

From all parts of the country I have received appeals testifying to the firm determination of the Russian peoples to devote their strength to the work of equipping the Army. I derive from this national unanimity the unshakable assurance of a brilliant future. A prolonged war calls for ever fresh efforts. But, surmounting growing difficulties and parrying the vicissitudes which are inevitable in war, let us strengthen in our hearts the resolution to carry on the struggle, with the help of God, to the complete triumph of the Russian arms. The enemy must be crushed, for without that peace is impossible,

With firm faith in the inexhaustible strength of Russia, I anticipate that the governmental and public institutions, Russian industry and all the faithful sons of the Fatherland, without distinction of ideas and classes, will work together in harmony to satisfy the needs of our valiant Army. This is the only and, henceforth, the national problem to which must be directed all the thoughts of united Russia invincible in her unity.

Having formed, for the discussion of questions of supplying the Army, a Special Commission in which members of the Legislative Chambers and representatives of industry participate, I recognize the necessity in consequence of advancing the date of the re-opening of these Legislative bodies in order to hear the voice of the country. Having decided that the sessions of the Duma and the Council of the Empire shall resume in the month of August at the latest, I rely on the Council of Ministers to draw up according to my indications the Bills necessitated by a time of war.

Reuter.

Peninsula Press

No. 67   Tuesday, JULY 27th. 1915   Official News.

Wireless Messages.

Eiffel Tower, Paris, July 26.

In the Artois and between the Aisne and the Oise there have been the usual artillery duels.

On the right bank of the Aisne, in the district of Troyon, as well as in the Champagne, on the front Perthes-Beau Sejour, the fighting with mines has gone on to the advantage of the French. To the South of Woevre there has been an intermittent artillery duel. In the Vosges the French, in spite of the bombardment, have organised the positions captured yesterday at Ban de Sapt. The number of German prisoners amounts to 11 officers and 825 men of whom only 70 are wounded, and many corpses remain in the trenches. On the French side only two battalions of one infantry regiment were engaged. Six machine guns have already been found in the captured trenches.

Amsterdam, July 24.

The battle at Warsaw continues with unabated energy. The Russians are successfully holding the enemy at vital points on the whole line. The essential railways are hitherto intact.

Before Warsaw itself and on the whole tract of country West of the city, the Russians are offering the stoutest defence. A high bridgehead position is packed with Russian troops.

German Headquarters, July 24.

In Kurland we pursue the Russians who are giving ground Eastward. In the fighting yesterday we took 6,550 prisoners, 85 guns, a large quantity of munitions, waggons and field kitchens. Our enemy drew near Narev and the bridgeheads of Warsaw. In front of Ragan, the village cf Szyzi was stormed with the bayonet, and 290 prisoners were taken. Night sorties from Novo Georgievsk failed.

Italian Press, July 24.

We captured many trenches, a trench mortar, a mitrailleuse, rifles, munitions and other war material. On Caiso plateau, during the night of the 22nd the enemy made several attacks all of which were repulsed. On the following morning, having been greatly reinforced the enemy prepared a great attack with a terrific preliminary bombardment and

195

rushed in dense formation against our front, more especially against our left wing. Our first line sustained and arrested the violence of the attack. The second line counter-attacked with the result that the enemy was routed. We took 1,500 prisoners, among them 76 officers. The battlefield is covered with dead bodies which show how enormous the enemy losses must have been.

Rome.

Our offensive further developed on the whole of Isonzo front yesterday, from Monte Nero to the Caiso plateau. Notwithstanding the enemy's counter-attacks designed to cut off our left from Isonzo bridges, we have everywhere maintained our position and advanced on several points, capturing 500 prisoners, arms and munitions.

Extracts from Newspapers.

The meeting or the Greek Parliament has again been postponed. The elections last month gave M. Venizelos a majority of 68 over all possible combinations. Defeated at the polls, M. Gounaris, the Prime Minister, put off the meeting of parliament until July 20th, on account of the King's health. The reason given for further delay is that His Majesty is still unable to attend to public business.

At the Conference of the General Federation of Trade Unions, held at Derby, Mr. Bramley, of the furnishing trade, moved an amendment calling for a more definite expression of sympathy with the German trade unionists in the peculiar position in which they had been placed by their Government. Mr. Bramley's proposal met with general dissent. Mr. W. A. Appleton described a visit paid to Germany in June last year. They saw with their own eyes the preparations that were being made for this war with the concurrence of the working classes.

Mr. Ben Tillett said that he was amazed at the long rigmarole of his friend Bramley. The German trade unionists openly boasted in their cafes of what they were going to do when the great war came. They were going to crush France and then England. This was a "scrap," and must be fought out in that spirit. Whoever heard of two prize-fighters, in the middle of a prize fight, stopping to kiss each other? Let them have no more or this sentimental "tosh."

("Times").

The Headmaster of Harrow, in his address on Governor's Day, said that the 2,087 Old Harrovians who are, or have been, serving with the colours represent about 90 per cent. of the men of the school between the ages of 17 and 36 – a truly remarkable record. The decorations gained by old boys include, besides three Victoria Crosses, 24 D.S.O.'s and 17 Crosses of the Legion of Honour; 149 men have been killed and 228 are wounded or missing. ("Daily Telegraph").

In a leading article the "Temps" pays a handsome tribute to the work of the British Fleet.

The writer asks what would have happened if Great Britain had remained neutral in the present struggle, and points out the impossibility of the French ships in Indo-China successfully opposing the German cruisers. Cut off from communication with the mother country, the French troops in Africa and Asia would not have been able to continue their defence. This was what was actually happening in German colonial territory, which had virtually all been seized. This was the remarkable part of British Naval work.

Today all the German commerce destroyers had disappeared: distant waters were clear, and the navigation of the Allies could proceed without obstacle. The result, after 11 months of war, was that there was not one German port outside Europe, and, excepting in the Baltic, not one single ship could navigate the seas under the German flag. These results, though not, perhaps, definitive, were due to the naval effort of the Allies. British naval power had imposed its mastery on all the waters of the world except within the radius of action of German submarines, but not a single transport containing troops, munitions, or stores had been sunk by a submarine in the Channel, the Irish Sea, or the North Sea no modern battleship had been torpedoed, and the Battle Squadron remained intact. Thus, from a military point of view the action of the submarines was without result, while the commercial losses were so slight that they could have no influence on the issue of the war.

Peninsula Press

No. 68   Wednesday, JULY 28th. 1915   Official News.

Wireless Messages.

Petrograd, July 27.

Russian counter-attacks brought the enemy's offensive to a standstill between the Vistula and the Bug rivers, except in the region of Grubilszow where the Russian attacks were repulsed on Friday night and Saturday. In the Baltic provinces the enemy continues to advance on the roads from Shavli to Kossiemu in the direction of Ponewiej where the fighting occurred on Saturday. On the Narew front the enemy delivered a series of desperate attacks on Friday night and Saturday along the Eastern bank of the Pissa but suffered enormous losses and achieved no success. Persistent attempts on the part of the enemy to cross the Narew between Ostrolenka and Jojany were also repulsed, though they succeeded in crossing on Friday between Rojoz and Pultusk.

German Headquarters, July 26.

Eastern front:- North of the Niemen, the army of General van Bulow reached the vicinity of Poswol and Poniewitz where the enemy was still entrenched. The enemy was thrown back and over 1,000 Russians were taken prisoners. On the Narew front our troops have compelled the enemy's advanced posts to fall back. Notwithstanding that they are massed and offering fierce resistance they are slowly being driven back over the Bug. Several thousand Russians were taken prisoners with over 40 machine guns.

On the North-west front our troops are advancing towards Novo Georgievsk and Warsaw.

On the South-east and North of the line Wojslawice (South of Cholm)-Hrubieszow (on the Bug), the German troops, in the battles of the last few days, have driven the enemy to near Forden. Yesterday 11 officers, 1,457 men with 11 machine guns were captured. The position, West of the Weichsel with Field-Marshal von Mackensen's army, is unchanged.

London, July 27.

Field-Marshal Sir John French reports that on the 21st inst., our heavy artillery silenced the heavy trench mortars which were assisting the enemy's attack. On the evening of the 23rd we exploded a mine under a salient in the German lines South-east of Zillebike, destroying the enemy's trenches and gaining some ground.

Toulon.

The destroyer "Bisson" destroyed a supply depot of the Austrian submarines and aeroplanes in the island of Fagosta and cut the telegraph.

Eiffel Tower, Paris, July 27.

In the Artois, the cannonade has diminished in intensity. Several heavy calibre shells have been thrown into Arras. In the Champagne, on the front Perthes-Beau Sejour, and at Vauquois, there has been mine fighting in which the French have retained the advantage. Violent cannonade at Bois le Pretre. Pont-a-Mousson has been bombarded. The Germans have also shelled repeatedly the positions which they lost at Bande Sapt.

Extracts from Newspapers.

In opening the session of the Queensland Parliament, the Governor said that Australia had sent her best sons to fight for the Mother Country by land and sea. It was impossible to read without a thrill the gallant deeds of the Queensland lads in the trenches. Much remained to be done if existing civilization was to be speedily saved from a formidable and ruthless foe. The State would co-operate with the Commonwealth in its effort to provide more men, munitions and supplies for the front.

The Government would safeguard the rights of State employees who enlisted. Regarding those not in State employment, they would reserve land for them on their return. The scheme would include ex-service men who had enlisted in the Mother Country for this war.

(Reuter).

The "Times" correspondent with the Russian forces writes on July 14:- "I have been for three days with the Third Army, which has seen the hardest fighting, being that which entered Galicia in the extreme East last year and which fought around Lemberg, Grodez, Przemysl, and thence into the Carpathians, and has now been fighting all the way back with the same determination and stubbornness as enabled it during its advances of 10 months to capture, as its commander informed me, 300,000 prisoners.

I have motored about 100 miles observing the advanced positions and have talked to scores of officers of all ranks of the Army, which during its retirement has inflicted greater loss than it received, and conducted a rearguard action which one general officer assured me was "like a manoeuvre"

An Austrian attack developed on the position which I visited in the afternoon, lasting all night, but it failed to make any impression on our lines, resulting in losses to the enemy which are estimated at 3,000."

Mr. Bonar Law, Colonial Secretary, stated, in answer to a question in the House of Commons, that the German Colonies before the war occupied between 1,100,000 and 1,200,000 square miles. Of that area about 450,000 square miles had been conquered by the Allies. The conquered territory included German South-West Africa, Togoland, Kiau Chan, and German possessions in the Pacific, but excluded that portion of the Cameroons which is in the occupation of the Allies.

("Daily Telegraph").

At the closing sitting of the Prussian Diet Herr Braun (Socialist) said that annexation plans were not and never would be favoured by the majority of people in Germany, and he wished that the Government would not miss any opportunity of an early peace. The speaker also complained that food usurers were sucking the people's blood slowly but surely.

According to a fuller report of the sitting published by the "Berliner Tageblatt," the Progressive deputy Herr Wiemer said he was convinced that the majority of the Socialist party shared Herr Heinemann's views in favour of continuing the war, as against the views of Herr Liebknecht and his friends.

Dr. Liehknecht then shouted: "We have the masses with us. They want peace." Herr Wiemer continued, "We wish to maintain the unity of our people." Dr. Liebknecht again interposed, "The masses want peace."

(Reuter).

Peninsula Press

No. 69   Saturday, JULY 31st. 1915   Official News.

Notice:- The "Peninsula Press" will, for a time, appear only twice a week – on Saturday and Wednesday. We regret that we were unable to make this announcement in the last issue – No. 68, Wednesday, July 28.

It is officially reported from home that on the 24th July, the Turks were heavily routed at Nasiriyah on the Euphrates and fled, leaving in our hands all their guns, stores and many prisoners. The road is now open to Bagdad and the advance continues vigorously. This constitutes a decisive success.

Wireless Messages.

Petrograd, July 28.

The Russians are pushing the Germans back from important points. The German offensive in the Northern regions of the Baltic provinces was repulsed with the assistance of warships. The Russians are now in touch with van Bulow's army on the Niemen front.

The Russians attacked successfully on both banks of the Narew taking 700 prisoners and a number of maxims. East of the Vieprz to the Bug the Germans attacked and took some Russian redoubts. Counter-attacks, however, expelled them. South-west of Knovo the enemy was driven across the Gessia.

Amsterdam, July 27.

The Russians are making a magnificent resistance. All vital sectors are still maintained. The Berlin communique claims that von Bulow has made progress in the Niemen district, taking 1,000 prisoners. The Germans also made a crossing over the Narew above Ostrolenka but on the South the Russians are offering an obstinate resistance. The Germans are tightly held before Warsaw itself.

German Headquarters, July 28.

East Front: A sally from Mitau was driven back by our troops. The Russians yesterday attacked our troops who had crossed the Narew but were driven back. Between Wyrzkow and Serock the Russian counter-attacks were repelled with heavy loss. We have captured 2,319 Russians and 18 machine guns. East and South-east of Rozau our troops have gone forward eastward behind the advanced lines of the enemy. There is no change in the battles on the Vornow, Georgievsk and Warsaw line. South-eastern theatre: Before Ivangorod there is nothing new to report. North of Hrubieszow we have thrown the enemy from more villages and taken 3,941 Russian prisoners. The position of Field-Marshal von Mackensen's army is unchanged.

Petrograd, July, 28.
On Sunday night, Russian Destroyers in the Black Sea bombarded the forts of the Samsun and Trehizond and sank 150 sailing ships near the Anatolian Coast.

Budapest, July 28.
The Hungarian Press disapproves of the stiff tone of the American note to Germany and is unanimous in declaring that it does not meet the most elementary requirements of neutrality, if America is clearly agreed to support the object of the Quadruple Alliance in starving out the population of Germany and her allies by cutting her overseas communications.

The "Pester Journal" writes: It is evident that America is taking sides with the Entente Powers, and bears patiently what is profitable to England and England's allies but finds everything unendurable that Germany does in her desperate struggle for existence.

Rome, July 28.
The official communique says that the Italian troops on the lower Isonzo advanced on Sunday and made appreciable progress. On the left wing they captured a broad stretch of wooded ground in Bosco Cappuccio; in the centre they stormed the trenches of San Martino and the ridge of Carso: on the right wing they won and lost several times Mount Seibuse but finally retained the greater part of it. The enemy is using asphyxiating bombs. We captured 1,600 prisoners.

Eiffel Tower, Paris, July 28.
A bombardment of Ferns and Dunkirk was answered by artillery fire on the German camps at West and Middle Kirke. The five bombs dropped by a German aeroplane on the 26th caused no damage. In the Artois, in the sector of Souchez, there has been considerable artillery fire and fighting with grenades. During the night of the 27th some heavy shells were fired on Arras. In the Champagne, on the front Perches to Beau Sejour, there has been some mine fighting to the advantage of the French. In the Argonne, the Germans attempted two attacks near Binar

Ville la Harazee and were easily repulsed. There has been violent artillery fire at Bois le Pretre. Pont a Mousson has been bombarded. In the Vosges, the French succeeded on the evening of the 26th in extending and consolidating their positions on the crest of Lieskopf and in occupying the small hill situated between the Linge and the Carrieres. The Germans counter-attacked three times unsuccessfully; they have bombarded the Col of Sesrucht.

July 30.

A quiet day from the sea to the Vosges. There has been some activity by the artillery in the sector of Sauchez round Arras and Soissons and in Argonne at Marie Therese and in front of Feyenhaye. In the Vosges, at Band de Sapt, we have seized another group of houses. Saint Dis and Thann have been fired upon. At Baronkopf, the Germans have endeavoured to retake the positions gained by us. Their very violent attack was repulsed and all our gains are maintained. One battery accompanying this attack came under our fire and was destroyed.

Paris, July 28.

The French have occupied Larne in the Cameroons. The German troops mutinied and surrendered. In the Zemen district, the French are vigorously advancing and have joined up with another French column to the North as far as Noangela.

Peninsula Press

No. 70   Wednesday, AUGUST 4th. 1915   Official News.

On Saturday night a successful attack was carried out on the right section of the Anzac position against a network of Turkish trenches which were beginning to threaten the safety of our advanced post – called Tasmanian portion that portion of the line.

The bombardment of the neighbouring works had been arranged and the works themselves were to be occupied after four mines had been exploded under them. The bombardment began up to time and three of the mines were exploded under sections of the trench which were occupied at once. The fourth mine failed, but the section of the trench above it was rushed with the bayonet. The Turks did not counter-attack.

Our casualties were about 12 killed and 75 wounded, while at least 70 Turks were killed in and around the work.

The result of this successful affair has been to give us the crest of the ridge and has materially improved our position in that section of our line.

Wireless Messages.

New York, August 2.

Sir E. Grey sent a message to the American press saying that the reasons which led Great Britain to declare war are fully understood in America. "I am quite contented," says Sir Edward Grey, "to leave the rights or wrongs of the causes and the conduct of the war to the judgement of the American people. The Entire Empire with our gallant Allies, were never more determined than today to prosecute this war to a successful conclusion for liberty and not some burdensome militarism."

Vienna, August 1.

(Official) Austrian cavalry entered Lublin

Amsterdam, August 2.

The German communique says "North west of Lomza and the railway East of Rozhan our attack is progressing. The troops of General Von Wayrsch crossed to the right bank of the Vistula and advanced Eastwards. The heights of the Vistula North of Lublin were occupied yesterday. South of Cholmen the Russians resisted General Mackensen's persuing troops.

Later

The Petrograd communique admits the evacuation of Lublin and the railway between the stations of Novo Aleksandryja and Reioselty. Russian troops between the Vistula and the Bug on Thursday retired successfully into prepared positions at the rear.

German News, July 80.

North of the Nieman, the situation is unchanged. North-east of Suwalki on both sides of the railway running to Olita, our troops gained possession of part of the enemy's positions. By this attack we captured yesterday 2,910 prisoners and two machine guns. South of the Narew and South of Nassielsk, the Russians repeated their attacks last night. These attacks were unsuccessful and we inflicted heavy loss on the enemy. West of Novo Georgievisk, on the South bank of the Vistula, a half company of Germans by a surprise attack took 128 Russian prisoners.

Later.

In the neighbourhood South of Gora-Kalwarija on the night of 27-28th July, the Russians attempted to press forward to the East. They were attacked yesterday and thrown back.

Eastern Front: North of the Niemen there has been no advance. North-east of Rozan we repulsed a Russian attack. During the month of July, between the Ostsi and the Pilica we have captured 95,028 Russian prisoners, 41 field guns and 230 machine guns.

Eiffel Tower, Paris, August 1.

The day (July 31st) has passed without any infantry engagement. German aviators dropped some bombs on Dunkirk doing only slight damage. Near Arras there has been the usual activity. A long range German gun fired nine shells on Compiegne causing some damage and also a fire which was quickly extinguished. In the Argonne, in the district of Fontaine Aux Charnes and at Four de Paris, the bombardment of the trenches at one point or another has been constant. At Bois le Pretre there has been a violent cannonade. In the Vosages the Germans have bombarded the French positions on Hill 627 from Fontenelle and from the village of Metzeral. Seven French aeroplanes have bombarded the railway station and the aviation factory at Fribourg in Brisgau. One of our machines was forced to come down during its return in the German lines owing to a failure of the motor.

August 2.

Artillery engagements of moderate intensity between the sea and the Oise and the valley of the Aisne, and more violent to the North-west of Rheims, near the farm of Luxembourg (between Canroy and Loiure) and in the Western Argonne, in the district of Fontaine aux Charmes and Hill 213. Between the Meuse and the Moselle, in the district of La Haye, a German battalion was caught in close order in the village of Vilcey on Trey and came under rapid and effective fire from several of our batteries. Pont a Mousson and the village Maidieres have been bombarded but the damage was trifling. German aeroplanes dropped about 20 bombs on the plateau of Milzerville near Nancy causing neither loss nor damage.

August 3.

There has been less artillery activity in Artois and in the valley of the Aisne. Arras and Soissons have received a few shells. In the Argonne there has been considerable infantry fighting and late in the night, of 2nd on Hill 213 the Germans captured one of our trenches which a counter attack partially retook. During the day, after using liquid fire the enemy made a violent attack against our trenches in the district of Marie Therese and succeeded in gaining one of them but we immediately counter attacked and re-occupied most of the lost ground. On the heights of the Meuse in Woevre there has been the usual artillery duel chiefly round Champlon. In the Vosges there has been a series of fights since the evening of August 1st in front of the positions captured by us on the high ground at Schlatz Mannel and Banonkoff. We have captured several German trenches, inflicting heavy losses and taking fifty prisoners belonging to two different regiments.

Peninsula Press

No. 71   Saturday, AUGUST 7th. 1915   Official News.

Wireless Messages.

Amsterdam August 4.

Germans admit losses in the Vosages

A very significant passage in the Berlin communique says that along the Narew front and before Warsaw there was minor fighting. Germans claim progress in the Northern region, but the army of General von Woyisch is at a standstill North of Ivangorod. The communique mentions General von Koever's success before the West front of Ivangorod and claims success after a day's fighting. The Russians, it is added, have taken up positions.

August 3.

The German communique reports the occupation of Mitau. The situation before Warsaw is unchanged. The ring round Ivangorod is drawing closer. The Russians are still engaging Field-Marshal von Mackensen's army.

London, August 3.

The Admiralty announces that a British submarine sank a German destroyer on the German coast on 26th July.

Petrograd, August 3.

A British submarine sank a large German transport in the Baltic.

The "London Gazette" announces that the exportation of cotton is prohibited, except to British possessions and protectorates.

Rome, August 2.

The Italians took the offensive in the Carnic region, capturing trenches and prisoners. In the second phase of the battles for the Carso hills, the Italians successfully attacked the Austrians and captured 100 prisoners and some guns and war material.

August 3.

The Italians have already captured 380 officers and 17,000 men on the Bronzo front.

The Italians in the Carnia district have captured Mount Medetta, Northeast of Cima Cristallo.

Eiffel Tower, Paris August 6.
Moderate artillery activity on the Western portion of the front. In the Argonne fighting with artillery and bombs has continued but with less activity on the part of the enemy. There has been a violent bombardment in the forest of Aprement. In the Vosges there has been very heavy fighting on the heights North of the Fecht, particularly on the hill of Schratzrmaennelle where the enemy, after taking one of our blockhouses, was immediately driven out by a counter-attack and our artillery barrage inflicted very heavy losses. One of our aeroplanes, owing to a motor failure, was compelled to come down near Moulin-sous-Touvent in our lines and close to those of the enemy. On reaching the ground the machine caught fire. Both aviators were saved.

London, August 2.
A submarine shelled the Leyland liner "Iberian," killing five crew. The "Iberian" was afterwards torpedoed and sank. Sixty three of the crew took to the boats, two died on board the rescuing steamer.

Washington, August 4.
The Argentine, Brazil, Chili, Guatinala [sic], Bolivia and Uruguay have accepted the invitation of President Wilson to a conference with a view to settling the Mexican troubles.

Extracts from Newspapers.

In a remarkable speech delivered at Cape Town, General Botha made interesting revelations concerning German designs on South Africa. He said that one of the most interesting discoveries in German South West Africa was a map showing the redistribution of the world after the peace of Rome 1916. The whole of Africa below the equator was put as the German Empire except a small portion segregated as a Boer reserve. This and other indications showed designs on the Union. It was now established that Maritz had sent a delegate to German South West Africa in 1913 and had received an encouraging reply. Before the war, rebellion had been growing and Maritz was enquiring how far help in artillery arms and ammunition would be sent. Correspondence then took place between the Government and the Kaiser, the latter replying: "I will not only acknowledge the independence of South Africa but will guarantee it, provided the rebellion starts immediately."

General Botha proceeded to emphasise the value of the territory won and gave details of the terrible atrocities committed by the Germans. He announced his intention to hold an enquiry into the circumstances of the Herroro rebellion when 2,100 natives were killed in reprisal for the alleged murder of Germans, now proved never to have occurred.

General Smuts followed in the same strain, saying that it was clear to him now that if German South West Africa did not belong to the Union, the Union would have ultimately belonged to German South West Africa.

A curious coincidence is that of the Union casualties. Among the dead are 126 English names and 126 Dutch names, among the wounded 278 English, and 275 Dutch showing how the two races realised the duty of supporting the principles of free Government against the curse of militarism.

(Issued from the Residency, Cairo)

In moving the adjournment of Parliament till September 14th, Mr. Asquith emphasised the fact that the war for some time was likely to be a contest of endurance. "We should be ungrateful and insensitive indeed." he said, "if we did not recognise the indescribably gallant efforts of our Russian Allies" (loud cheers).

"I do not think" said Mr. Asquith, "that in the whole of military history has there been a more magnificent example of discipline and endurance than that displayed by the Russians during the last seven weeks" (renewed cheers).

"Our new Allies with carefully prepared movements are steadily gaining ground, and it is believed they will very shortly reach their objective" (cheers).

"Our fleet is stronger than at the beginning of the war. Submarines are not going to inflict substantial injury to our trade. Recruiting is highly satisfactory, the latest returns being the best that we have had for a long time."

(Reuter).

Peninsula Press

No. 72   Wednesday, AUGUST 11th. 1915   Official News.

Wireless Messages

Petrograd, August 1.

The Russian Foreign Minister, M. Sasonoff, speaking at the opening of the Duma, said: The unequalled valour of the Allied troops fighting in Gallipoli provokes our unanimous admiration. Despite the almost unsurmountable obstacles which nature has created, our valiant Allies, with unflinching tenacity, bring nearer the longed for moment when closer and direct communication will be established between us. The Turks, scenting the coming storm, pounce upon the Christians still in their power. Armenians have to submit to persecution which, none the less, do not break their spirit, for many Armenian volunteers fight courageously with us against their oppressors. At Van they withstood the pressure of the Turks for months, until the town was relieved by our troops.

August 4.

Desperate fighting round Warsaw. The Germans are progressing only at enormous cost. They crossed the Vistula on Sunday, August 1st, after tremendous losses and captured a portion of the great forest, North of Matzoditzo.

Our seaplanes attacked a gunboat near Windau and forced it to run ashore. They also put to flight a Zeppelin.

Wellington (New Zealand), August 5.

A National Ministry has been formed which includes five members of the opposition. Sir Joseph Ward is Minister for Finance and Mr. Allen Minister for Defence.

Extracts from Newspapers

Eiffel Tower, Paris, August 8.

In the Artois there have been artillery duels round Souchez and Rocincourt and between the Oise and the Aisne. On the heights of Nourons in the Argonne, the Germans twice renewed their attacks round height 215 and were repulsed. By exploding two mines they succeeded in setting foot in one of our trenches from which they were driven by immediate counter-attack. In the forest of Apremont the bombardment continued with the same intensity as on the previous day. In the Vosges the enemy several times shelled our positions on the Linge and the

Schratzmannengele. At about two o'clock delivered an attack on Schratzmannengele along the Honnac road but was stopped by the defensive fire of our artillery. Towards evening a fresh German attack was repulsed by bayonet and bomb.

August 9.

On the Western front there have been a few artillery duels in Belgium on the Steen-Straete-Hetsas sector and in the Artois on the Santerre front and in the Aisne valley. Soissons has been bombarded. From the Argonne only trench fighting with bombs and hand grenades is reported. In the Woevre artillery activity has been pronounced particularly in the Fliroy district and in the Bois le Pretre. In the Vosges the Germans again attacked during the evening our positions on the Linge and were completely repulsed. Lhilsenfurst has been violently bombarded by the enemy.

August 10.

Along the whole front there have been artillery actions in the Artois between the Somme and Oise and in the Aisne valley. Rheims has been bombarded. In the Argonne near the Fontaine-aux-Charmes the enemy tried to take our listening posts but was everywhere repulsed. In the Vosges there was a cannonade only. This morning a squadron of 32 bomb dropping aviators escorted by other aviators to engage those of the enemy set out to bombard the railway station and the works at Saarbrueck. The atmospheric conditions were unfavourable, the valleys being covered with mist and the sky clouded. In spite of the difficulties of orientation 28 aviators reached their objective and dropped on their targets 164 bombs of different sizes. The aviators forming the escort put to flight the enemy's aviators who attempted to bar the way of the squadron. The smoke of numerous conflagrations was observed rising from the points aimed at.

There is a significant change in American opinion. The speeches of Mr. Roosevelt which previously bad been confined to the back sheets have now suddenly been given prominence in the front columns of the newspapers. In a stirring address delivered at San Francisco entitled "Peace or War." Mr Roosevelt declared that the real title should be "Damn the Mollycoddles." He affirmed that if the fate of Belgium overtook America it would arouse derision and contempt. (Reuter)

In the House of Commons, on the occasion of the Colonial debate, Mr. Bonar Law emphasised the failure of the German raid on the Uganda railway, and said that the reason we were able more than to hold our own was due to the fact that colonists not only volunteered, but were of a class whose services happened to be specially valuable. The situation in Nyassaland at the outbreak of the war was most precarious and its safety was largely owing to acts of great enterprise on the part of the steamer Lady Gwendolen.

Turning to general considerations Mr. Bonar Law pointed out that in Africa, as in Europe, we had the superiority in men. Our Colonial fellow subjects had splendidly supported the Empire. As one instance of this he stated that 95 per cent. of the unofficial Europeans in Togoland took up arms on our behalf. "We are surely entitled to say," added Mr. Bonar Law "that the spirit of our forefathers animates the Colonies today." He paid a tribute to the work that had been carried out on the West African frontier. The force of African Rifles had shown the greatest courage in the face of modern weapons. There had been no excess, and no want of discipline. The natives had shown that they appreciated British rule: throughout they have been thoroughly loyal and helped in every way. Perhaps nothing had done more to make the African native appreciate British rule than the natives' experiences of German rule. Mr. Bonar Law concluded by referring to the soldiers from our Dominions fighting in France and at Gallipoli: he could say nothing which could possibly raise the estimate of the House and the Empire as to the quality of these troops.

Mr Steel Maitland, Under Secretary for the Colonies, winding up the debate, declared that it was intended to take the responsible Ministers of the Dominions into the confidence of the Imperial Government in every matter concerning the war; as well as all matters arising out of the peace settlement. The wish of the cabinet was to consider all things freely with them. That was why Sir R. Borden had attended the Cabinet meeting,

(Reuter)

Peninsula Press

No. 73   Saturday, AUGUST 14th. 1915   Official News.

Wireless Messages

Eiffel Tower, Paris, August 11.
Only artillery actions reported in Artois in the Aisne valley (Troyon district) on the borders of the Argonne and in the forest of Apremont. Four of the aviators who took part in the bombardment of Saarebruck have not returned to our lines. One of them is reported to have descended in Switzerland at Paverne, in the Canton of Vaud.

Extracts from Newspapers.

The Petrograd Correspondent of the "Morning Post" telegraphs:
The Russian naval forces have again been active both in the Baltic and in the Black Sea, but only in subsidiary operations. In the Black Sea on Sunday some destroyers caught and destroyed another forty coal transports which were sailing fully laden for Constantinople. As the cargoes of these vessels indicated the restoration, to some extent at least, of the mining machinery of the enemy the destroyers proceeded to the source of the coal supply and destroyed the pit-head machinery of a new shaft. A suspension bridge was also destroyed by bombardment from the destroyers. Russia has thus not only crippled the business of coal-getting at the pit-mouth, but during the past fortnight has sunk over a hundred laden transports, thereby very seriously incommoding if not causing an entire cessation of work at the Constantinople factories, upon which a continuance of the defence of the Dardanelles largely depends.

Mr. Lloyd George, speaking in the House of Commons before the adjournment, said that during the past month the number of munition workers had been increased by 40,000, nearly half of whom were skilled workmen. One hundred thousand voluntary munition workers had been enrolled, the bulk of whom belonged to the engineering and shipbuilding trades. Sixteen national factories had been established in different parts of the country under national control, and these would lead to an enormous increase in the output of shells; but, in consequence of the conferences in France where he had met the French Minister of Munitions, and where distinguished French and British artillery officers had compared notes regarding the lessons to be learnt by this campaign, it had been decided to embark upon a. new programme, which would very considerably tax Great Britain's engineering resources for some months. It had been decided, in order to meet the gigantic demands, to establish an additional ten large Government arsenals. He hoped equipment would be ready in a few weeks to enable Great Britain to equip her armies in such a way that even the best armies in Europe would be unable to claim superiority in the slightest respect.

Despite difficulties due to the unwillingness of men to leave the front, thousands of skilled workmen in the last month had been released from the colours to work at the output of munitions, and thousands more would be available in the next few weeks. Mr. Lloyd George mentioned that an Inventions Branch of the Ministry of Munitions had been established, similar to that controlled by Admiral Fisher in the Admiralty. (Reuter).

The New York "Sun's" correspondent at Washington says: it is considered significant that the announcement of the President's interest in National Defence was made the day after the presentation of the American Note to Berlin.

The plans of the War Department anticipate the development of a reserve army of a half a million men, exclusive of militia.

The Navy Department will request thirty or probably fifty submarines, several battle cruisers, four dreadnoughts, and many auxiliary vessels. The Department already is experimenting with aeroplanes and submarines and is spending one hundred thousand dollars on devising means of enabling battleships to fight submarines.

It is believed that the Navy Department will ask for an appropriation of 250 million dollars and the War Department 200 millions, both double of last year. (Reuter).

Sydney, July 23rd.
Australians welcome the Colonial Secretary's assurance that the Dominion Ministers will be taken into the confidence of the Imperial Ministers regarding the settlement of the war. (Reuter).

Melbourne, July 22.
The £20,000,000 local loan for war purposes has been passed by the House of Representatives, and the War Census Bill by the Senate.

The Commonwealth has decided to double the Australian General Hospital in England by providing an additional 1,040 beds. (Reuter).

At a large and representative meeting of agricultural delegates.M. Krivocheine, Russian Minister of Agriculture, said: "The agricultural resources of Russia are in no way shaken by a year of war. Our soil, as formerly, abounds in reserves of foodstuffs. Thanks to God, who has given us almost everywhere magnificent harvest, Russia is ready to continue the struggle for years yet without the slightest danger of any weakening whatever. Moreover, Russia can provide in abundance the necessary reserves, not only for her own armies, but also for the armies of all her Allies." He could say definitely that even if the war lasted a long time the last word would be said by the country capable with its own resources of feeding its armies and its population for an indefinite period.

By the capture of German South West Africa Germany has lost the whole of her colonies with the exception of her possessions in East Africa, which she is not likely to retain for long. Togo was in the hands of the Allies within the first week of the war, and the Cameroons, Tsing-Tan, the Samoan Islands, Kaiser Wilhelmsland, the Carolines, the Marschall and Soloman Islands and the Bismarck Archipelago have in turn abandoned their allegiance to Berlin. The loss of her Colonial Empire is to Germany a matter more of prestige than of profit, since, with possibly one exception, her colonial outgoings have exceeded the incomings. That is in great part due to Germany's lack of genius for colonisation, to the fact that, while hordes of soldiers and officials were exported, the average German would emigrate anywhere but under his own flag, and to the Germans treatment of native races. But it is also fair to bear in mind that one reason why the German colonies have hitherto not been profitable is because of the large sums spent in developing them. It is not the least of Germany's tragedies that others will reap the fruits of this development.   (Egyptian Gazette).

Peninsula Press

No. 74   Wednesday, AUGUST 18th. 1915   Official News.

Wireless Messages.

London, August, 11.

The Turkish battleship "Barbarossa" has been sunk by a submarine.

Field-Marshal Sir John French reports that we attacked and retook all the trenches at Lorge which were recently captured by the enemy.

The Admiralty announces that the small patrol boat "Ransey" was sunk by the German auxiliary cruiser "Metor" in the North sea. Four officers and nine men were saved. The "Metor" was subsequently sighted by a British squadron of cruisers whereupon the crew abandoned the vessel and blew her up.

The "Times" correspondent learns from a, competent Vatican source that Germany is engaged in preliminary overtures to obtain the mediation of the Pope for the discussion of peace on the basis of the restitution of Belgium. Germany and Austria in their overtures manifested great unwillingness to face another winter campaign.

August 15.

The Press Bureau reports that two Zeppelins visited the East coast yesterday and dropped bombs. Two women were killed and three men, and eleven women and children were injured. Fourteen houses were seriously damaged. The Zeppelins were chased by British aviators but succeeding in evading our aircraft patrol zone. They were probably damaged by the anti-aircraft sections.

Petrograd, August 11.

We repulsed persistent attacks by the German Fleet of nine battleships, twelve cruisers and numerous destroyers at the entrance to the Gulf of Riga on 9th inst. One of the enemy's cruisers and two destroyers were damaged by Russian mines. The enemy on Saturday renewed the attacks on the fortifications of Kovno and severely bombarded our positions all day on Sunday. Between Divina and Niemen the Russians pressed the enemy in the direction of Friedrich-Stadt and dislodged the German advance guards, North-east of Vilkoir. There were isolated actions on Sunday on the left of Narew, particularly in the direction of Smonza and North of the Lomze and Ostrow road.

August 18.

The Germans made a desperate assault on the Western fortifications of Kovno. The Germans attacking the South fortress of Novo Yeorgievisk were repulsed. The enemy made a stubborn offensive in the direction South of Astrolenka Rozan and Pullusk. The Russians are resisting vigorously on the whole Bug line. They drove back the Germans from the South Lemberg district.

August 14.

The Russian victory in Caucasus is reaching big dimensions; one column has captured 19 officers and 1,172 men, hundreds of loaded waggons, arms, ammunition and tools.

Petrograd, August 15.

The Russians near Kovno continue to repulse German attacks. The enemy on the Narew front is persistently attacking on the roads from Lomza to Suiadovakossewo but to the South on both sides of the Keiff-Walkal railway the Russians have assumed a counter offensive. Desperate fighting continues between the Vieprz and Bug rivers and along the Cholin-Lodova roads. Here the enemy's attacks in the high district were repulsed.

A German squadron on Tuesday bombarded the lighthouses at the entrance of Ovafofoighand Island but fled from the fire of the Russian warships and shore batteries.

Rome, August 14.

An Italian submarine in the upper Adriatic torpedoed and sank an Austrian submarine, the crew of which were lost.

The Austrians on Tuesday night crossed the Furva river and attacked the Italians at Mount Vioz, 1,100 feet high. Other Austrian forces simultaneously crossed the Cevedale Pass 12,000 feet high, and attacked Cedeb. The Italian Alpine troops discovered the approaching Austrians and drove them back in disorder.

Paris, August 11.

The French have scored a success in the Southern and Eastern Cameroons. The Germans evacuated Gadi.

British and French troops in the North Cameroons, have occupied Singeereen.

217

On the Oise there has been some artillery fighting in front of Lombaerteyde St. Georges Bonsinghe and Woesten. In Artois, East of the Lille road, the French have destroyed the advanced works of the enemy by means of a mine. An ammunition depot blew up in the German lines between Nouchy and Ransart. North of Lassigny the French have bombarded the German positions of La Tour Roland.

August 16.
A quiet day along the entire front. In the Argonne the intervention of our artillery checked the bombardment of Courtes Chausses and of Fontaine-aux-Charmes. In the sector of Bagetelle the explosion of a mine brought about a fight in which we were successful. The enemy has fired with long range artillery on the open town of Montdidir. Our counter batteries checked the enemy's fire. West of Lingkorpf we have bombarded the railway station of Sainte Marie-aux-Maines and the German camp of Barkenstall.

August 17.
There have been considerable artillery actions throughout the day at a number of points on the front. The French batteries inflicted noteworthy losses on the enemy in the Quenne-veres district and silenced an enemy bombardment on the Nouvron plateau. They also seriously damaged the German works to the North of Godat (between Berry-au-Aoc and Loivre). The enemy again shelled Saint Die. We fired on the gasometers at Sainte Marie-aux-Maines which exploded. Another fire of reprisals caused the burning of a German factory East of Munster.

Peninsula Press

No. 75   Saturday, AUGUST 21st. 1915   Official News.

Wireless Messages.

London, August 16.

The Turkish communique indicates that the British are progressing since the recent landing at Ari Burnu.

August 17.

The Victoria Cross has been awarded to Commander Eric Robinson.

The "Gazette" also announces that the V.C. has been awarded to Commander E. Unwin, Midshipmen G. L. Drewry, H.M.S. "Hussar" and W. S. Malleson, H.M.S. "Cornwallis," and Leading-Seaman Williams and G. M. Samson, H.M.S. "Hussar."

August 19.

A German submarine fired several shells at Harington and Whitehaven. No material damage was done.

Washington, August 18.

The United States Government has been advised that the Allies intend to declare cotton contraband of war.

Athens, August 19.

The Greek Government has resigned. The King has sent for
M. Venizelos.

Sofia, August 17.

Important signs are manifest that the Turkish-Bulgarian negotiations have failed.

Government circles announce that they have been provisionally adjourned.

Petrograd, August 16.

No change in the Riga region, but severe fighting in the Dwinsk (Dunaburg) district. German attacks between the Narew and the Bug were repulsed. Attacks on the Novo Georgievsk fortress were generally repulsed.

August 18.

The Germans in the Bransk district have been driven back towards the river. The bombardment at Koufm(?) continues furiously between the Narew and the Bug, in repulse of German attacks.

Rome, August 16.

The enemy's armoured trains attacked the railway station at Serravalle but were repulsed.

The Italians have advanced considerably along the valley and at Sexten, Piazza and in the Monte Nero district.

Eiffel Tower, Paris, August 19.

Heavy artillery duels in Artois, in Champagne, in the forest of Apremont at La Louviere and at Vaux-Fery, as well as in Bois-le-Pretre and in the region of the Croix-des-Carmes. Mine fighting still continues at a large number of points and near Beuvraignes, South of Roye the explosion of one of our mines destroyed the German saps. In the Argonne attempted counter attacks made by the Germans near Marie-Therese were all repulsed. In the Vosges the positions captured by our troops on the ridge of Soudernach have been held in spite of very violent bombardment.

Amsterdam, August 16.

Information from good sources says that the relations between the Kaiser and the Imperial Chancellor Dr. von Bethmann-Hollweg are less cordial. The resignation of the Imperial Chancellor is imminent. His probable successor is General von Biasing ex-Governor of Belgium.

Extracts from Newspapers.

Mr. Bonar Law, speaking at Folkestone, said there was no more striking example of the reality of the strength of the moral force in the world today than the part played by the British Dominions. The Germans lost in Africa territory as large as the German Empire to the force of a self-Governing Dominion led by its Premier. The feeling of pride in that victory was increased enormously by the knowledge that the man who fought England only fifteen years ago was the man who gave his word to stand by the Empire and was standing by it nobly today. Mr. Bonar Law paid a tribute to the deeds of the Canadians, Australians and New Zealanders. Things, he said, would not be the same after the war.

(Reuter).

All accounts agree that the deliberation of the Russian withdrawal is owing to the gravity of the losses inflicted on the enemy by the Russians, whose use of the bayonet has been very effective. The attacks of both sides often coincide. That the retirement is not begotten of panic, but is the result of far sighted strategy is apparent, from the comments of the German papers, which grudgingly admit that the Grand Duke has done much more than was expected.

A semi-official statement at Petrograd says: "The Russian front is generally unshaken, but there are deep reasons demanding our withdrawal from the advanced Polish theatre; the abandonment of the territory, however, will not be prolonged. The fact that the enemy is not obstructing our withdrawal shows how his strength is being reduced to impotence through exhaustion. The initiative remains on our side.'

Unofficial accounts ascribe the staleness of General Mackensen's best troops, who are unable to harrass the retiring Russians, to Mackensen's pitiless pressure, sending them forward in light order with only one reserve of rations and allowing them little sleep. What the Russians had to confront during the past month is evident from the fact that the Germans had 300(?) machine-guns per one thousand men. When the Russians drove the Germans from three quarters of their lines of trenches they found in the rear another army with field guns, besides hundreds of guns concealed among the trees. (Reuter).

American papers in articles on the anniversary of the war recognise that the victory of Germany would mean that the United States, as the representative of freedom of Government, would have to confront her.

The "New York World" pays a tribute to the British Navy and says that but for it Germany would now be master of the world. The "New York Times" says that Germany's material losses in the war are nothing when compared with her moral losses. She is now without a friend in the world. "Hohenzollern Germany is damned for ever" says the journal.
(Reuter).

Peninsula Press

No. 76   Wednesday, AUGUST 25th. 1915   Official News.

Wireless Messages.

Petrograd August 23.

The enemy's fleet has left the Gulf of Riga. Our land front remains firm in the region of Riga and the direction of Jacobstadt and Dvinsk (Dunaburg).

The announcement that the German fleet had left the Gulf of Riga, was the first intimation of a great Russian naval victory. Details were subsequently announced to the Duma by President Rotdzianko who said that the super Dreadnought "Moltke," three cruisers and seven torpedo boats bad been sunk, whereupon the remains of the German fleet quitted the gulf.

The Germans attempted to land at Pernau four big barges filled with troops. The Russian militia exterminated the invaders and captured the barges.

The Russians are still holding the Germans in the Baltic provinces and have checked the enemy's offensive in the region of Kovno.

Torpedo boats sank a hundred Turkish sailing ships in the Black Sea.

A Russian submarine sank a Turkish steamer, laden with, 8,000 tons for Constantinople, off the Anatolian coast.

(The "Moltke" was a battle-cruiser of 22,640 tons, built in 1910 with a trial speed of 27.25 knots. She carried ten 11-in. and twelve 5.9-in guns, two of her turrets being en echelon, so that there was a full broadside of heavy guns. The "Goeben" which the Germans sold to the Turks, is the sister ship of the "Moltke.")

Rome, August 23.

Italy has declared war against Turkey. The grounds for this declaration are:- (1) The support which the Turks gave to the new revolt in Libya; (2) Preventing the departure of Italian residents in Turkey, Symrna[sic] and elsewhere.

The news has caused the deepest impression in Berlin; Amsterdam asserts that it is feared in Germany that the entry of Italy will seal the fate of the Dardanelles.

Athens, August, 23.

A momentous move is expected in the Balkan situation today.

M. Venezelos has accepted the Premiership and has had audience of the King. Athens is en fete.

August 20.

The Balkan situation is exciting self-absorbing interest in view of the possibility of the re-establishment of the Balkan League on the side of the Entente Powers. Importance is attached to the audience granted today to the British Minister by King Constantine.

Sofia, August 21.

The Bulgarian War Minister, General Fitcheff has resigned owing to bad health. General Jerkoff who succeeds him was military expert in the abortive negotiation with Turkey. He is essentially a soldier and not a politician.

London, August 22.

The White Star liner "Arabic" has been torpedoed off Fastnett. She floated only eleven minutes. Five passengers and twenty-five of the crew are missing. The "Arabic" had a gross tonnage of 15,800 and was built in 1908.

Of the missing passengers some are American.

Rome, August, 28.

Steady progress is reported especially at Carno. A squadron of Italian aeroplanes attacked the enemy's aerodrome near Gorizia, bombarding it for half an hour, and returned absolutely unharmed. Austrian aviators replied by bombing the citizens at Udine and murdering five.

Eiffel Tower, Paris, August 22.

In Artois there has been considerable activity in the region of Noulette and in the sector of Neuville and also in the district of Roye and Lassigny, in the valley of the Aisne and in Champagne. The enemy have fired about forty shells at Rheims wounding one person. There has been fighting along the front Perthes to Beausejour. In the Argonne the enemy, after bombarding Vauquois, brought heavy artillery fire to bear on our trenches. In Alsace, in the district of Hammerswiller, our trench mortars have seriously damaged the enemy's trenches and blown up several ammunition depots.

August 23.

In Artois and particularly in the district of Neuville and at Roclaincourt there has been great activity on the part of the German artillery heavily replied to by the French. There has been considerable fighting in the district of Roye on the plateau of Quennevieres near Rheims. In the Argonne it is reported that there has been particularly violent bomb fighting especially at Courtes-Chaussees. In the Woevre there has been bomb fighting North of Flirey and in the Vosges near the river Fecht there have been some artillery duels.

August 24.

In Artois, North of Souchez, and in the sector Neuville-Roclaincourt there has been constant artillery activity and the enemy. The shelled Arras, Montidier and Rheims have effectiveness [*sic*] of our artillery on the enemy's trenches and batteries was very noticeable. In Champagne, along the front Pertbes-Beausejour there has been sharp fighting with grenades and bombs. In front of Ville-sur-Tourhe an advanced German trench has been destroyed by one of our mines.

Peninsula Press

No. 77   Saturday, AUGUST 28th. 1915   Official News.

Notice:- Arrangements have been made with the War Office for a daily service of news telegrams. These messages will be printed in a separate news sheet called "War Office Telegrams" and will be circulated among the troops daily.

The "Peninsula Press" will continue to appear weekly as a Sunday newspaper.

Press News by Cable from London.

August 26.

Russia is still retiring before German forces; rate of advance however now much slower.

According to Vienna, resistance of Grand Duke's troops to South-west of Brestlitowsk has been broken; they have now retired within fortress zone. Both North and South of fortress, enemy claim to be driving Russians into forests and marshes. According to Berlin, von Scholtz has crossed the Narew East of Tykocin, von Vallwitz further South. Leopold of Bavaria holds Byelostok in the hollow of his hand if he has not already occupied it.

Only artillery actions reported from Western front.

Italians have captured height of Tonale zone, Western Trentino.

Turkish Ambassador and staff have left Rome.

Concentration Austro-German troops reported North-east of Serbia and Roumania frontier.

German march on Constantinople through corner of Serbia said to have been announced at Sofia and definition of Bulgarian attitude demanded by Germany.

British reconnaissance at Aden killed twenty Turks and captured sixteen yesterday.

Squadron Commander Bigsworth this morning destroyed single-handed German submarine by bombs from aeroplane off Ostend.

Bernstorff, German Ambassador, has asked President of the United States to take no action until he receives report of German Government on sinking of "Arabic." There is disposition in United States to take this as sign of grace on part of Germans. Others scout it as mere device to gain time.

Wireless Messages.

Petrograd, August 22.

M. Sazonoff, Russian Foreign Minister, informed a deputation of press representatives that the attempt of the enemy to invite a discussion on a separate peace between Germany and Russia had entirely failed. The confidence of the Allies in the ultimate result of the struggle is in nowise shaken.

August 24.

The naval communique confirms the announcement that the Russians sank in the Gulf of Riga two German cruisers and eight destroyers, while a British submarine sank one of Germany's latest Dreadnoughts, the "Moltke."

Paris, August 24.

Two French destroyers torpedoed a German destroyer off Ostend and sank her. The French suffered only insignificant damage.

Eiffel Tower, August 26.

In the sector North of Arras there has been considerable artillery fighting, particularly around Souchez and South of Neuville near the Lille road. Some artillery duels are also reported from the district of Roye and in the valley of the Aisne where we have bombarded the German positions North of Soissoins. The enemy has bombarded Rheims with some violence and we replied with very effective fire against the trenches in front of Seinay-les-Rheims. In the Argonne constant bomb fighting is going along the whole front and we are employing some artillery. In Woevre, North of Flirey, in the Vosges at Fontenelle and in the region of Luise, as well as in Alsace, in the valley of the Doller, there has been some artillery activity. During the day of the 25th our aviators in Woevre have bombarded the German camps of Pannes and Banssant causing some fires. The German railway stations and bivouacs at Grand-Pre, Chateau-Gornay, and Feville in Armonte, the railway station of Tergnier, the aviation park at Vitny in Artois, and the railway station of Boisleux have also been bombarded by our aviators. A joint operation with artillery and aeroplanes by the French, British and Belgian army and the French and British fleets, a total of 60 aeroplanes, was carried out against the forest of Houthulst, causing several fires. All the machines returned safely. During the nights of the

25th and 26th one of our air squadrons dropped 127 shells on the railway station of Noyon.

Comrades of the men mentioned below will be glad to hear that letters, signed by these men, have been received at General Head-quarters, stating that they are in hospital at Yalova:-

-	Pte L. Moore, 6th Bn. E. Yorks. Regt.
No. 1849	Pte R. Royds, 7th Bn. Lancs. Fus.
-	Pte Andrew Cannon, 7th Bn Gloucester Regt
No. 21202	Pte H. Davies, 4th Bn. Worcs. Regt.
No. 22082	Pte Alfred Lee, 4th Bn. Worcs. Regt.
-	Pte Chas. Reddington, 4th Bn. Worcs. Regt.
No. 14578	Pte R. Whitcombe, 4th Bn. Worcs. Regt.

Peninsula Press

No. 78   Sunday, SEPTEMBER 5th. 1915   Official News.

Washington, Sept. 2.

Count Bernstorff, German Ambassador to the United States, acting on instructions from Berlin states that Germany accepts the American proposal that "all passenger boats are to be warned before being attacked by submarines!"

A Washington message of August 28th says: "It is understood that Germany will announce the suspension of warfare against passenger vessels."

Sept. 4.

Cardinal Gibbons has handed to President Wilson a message from the Pope regarding peace.

London, Sept. 2.

A conference between the Government and representatives of the miners has settled the South Wales coal crisis. Forty-two thousand men had stopped working.

August 27.

The Admiralty announces that Squadron Commander Arthur W. Bigsworth destroyed single handed a German submarine which he observed to have been completely wrecked and sunk off Ostend.

During the week ended August 25th nineteen merchant ships were sunk out of the 1,369 which arrived at and left British ports.

The Government of Nigeria reports the occupation of Gaschaaka in the German African Colony, Cameroon. The enemy was forced to retire to the Eastern frontier. Cameroon, which has an area of 295,000 square miles and a population of 3,500,000, and a portion of German East Africa, are the only German colonies that have not been occupied by the Allies.

Petrograd, Sept. 1.

The recent victory of Russian troops in the Caucasus resulted in the capture of vast booty. Five thousand, two hundred and thirteen prisoners were taken. The Cossacks in pursuit killed 2,000 of the enemy.

The week's wireless messages make clear the fact that the Austro-German offensive against the Russians has spent its force and that in some districts the Russians are more than holding their own. Yesterday's report from Petrograd states that there is no important change on the Riga and Divna front and that the Russians are making successful progress between the river Sventa and the Vilna. Russian cavalry carried two villages near Scherventy at the point of the bayonet, the Germans fleeing in disorder. The Russians are progressing along the right bank of the Vilna, between which river and the Niemen the situation is unchanged. After fierce combats on the banks of the Styr in the region of Lusk, the Russians retreated from the front at Olyka, capturing never the less several hundred prisoners and some machine guns.

On Thursday the Russians were holding defensive positions on the river Missa and repulsed the enemy's attempt to cross the Dvina North of Friedrichstadt. The Germans had crossed to the right bank of the river but were driven back. The Russians assumed the offensive on the right bank of the river Vilna and continued to hold defensive positions between Vilna and Nieman. They also repulsed attacks in the Lipsksidra and Gorodee regions.

In Galicia the Austro-German troops began a series of attacks on the 29th and 30th ult., along the whole front. The attacks were particularly fierce North of Zloczow (East of Lemburg). Eight attacks were repulsed in the Pomorzany-Zborov districts and along Strypa front, the enemy being forced to retreat. The Russians counter attacked, capturing 30 guns, 24 machine guns and 3000 prisoners.

The week's news from the Italian front shows that – in the Western zone of Trentino where the Italians, having secured good positions on both sides of the frontier, are merely guarding the passes, the Austrians have been trying in vain to attack some of the Italian positions. In one of these attempts in the Strino Valley, near the Tonale Pass, the Austrians suffered very heavily, abandoning five strongly entrenched positions and some machine guns and ammunition.

In the zone North-east of the Trentino (Cadorine Alps) where the Italians, having already occupied Cortina D'Ampezzo and other positions beyond the frontier, are dominating the strategical Dolomites Road from Toblach to the heart of the Trentino and are threatening to cut in the Willach-Toblach zone the main strategical Austrian road from Vienna to North Trentino, some new progress has been made, by the Italian occupation of strong positions on Innichriechel Knoten (Sexten Valley) and lately of another dominating position on Mount Maronia.

In the Northern Isonzo district where the Italians are acting against the forts of Malborghetto to protect the left of the Isonzo front, nothing new has been signalled.

In the middle Isonzo district new progress has been made in Plezzo region, where the recent occupation of Mount Rombon (North of Plezzo), of Mount Polounik and the ridge North of Mount Vrsik (the two latter belonging to the Nero group), is threatening Plezzo from every side.

The Austrian garrison of Tolmino itself is in a critical situation after the recent Italian occupation of the ridge South-east of Mount Nero and of the South Lucia hills dominating the town from the South-west.

Gorizia, which General Cadorna seems to intend taking not by direct attack but by indirect action from Plawa and from the Carso plateau, has been lately more severely pressed by the new progress the Italians have made on the latter fronts.

At Plawa some strong Austrian positions East of the Isonzo river were lately attacked and conquered by the Italians. At the same time, pressed by the Italian advance the Austrians evacuated on the Carso plateau some very strong positions on their actual line of defence, to the South of Corlia.

French official reports received by wireless during the week show that there has been unusual artillery and aerial activity along the whole front. Yesterday's report states that violent mutual bombardments have taken place in the sector of Lorette and Neuville, North of Arras; in the neighbourhood of Fouquescourt, Laucourt and Tilleloy near Montdidier, between the Somme and the Oise; near Souain, East of Rheims, in the Champagne; in the Argonne, where the Crown Prince's Army is stationed, and on the Lorraine front.

French aviators dropped bombs on the railway station at Ostend and the enemy's camps in the vicinity. German aviators bombed Luneville and killed a few civilians.

At six o'clock on the morning of August 29th six German aeroplanes tried to reach Paris but got no further than Nogent-Sur-Marne, Montmorency, Ribecourt and Compiegne. There were no casualties except at Compiegne where two hospital nurses and a child were killed. The enemy's aeroplanes were fired at from several points and were chased by French machines. The commander of a French air squadron pursued one of the German aeroplanes to a height of 3,600 metres and brought it down North of Senlis. The German aviator and pilot were found burnt to ashes.

PENI.ULA PRESS.

No. 78   SUNDAY SEPTEMBER 5th, 1915.   Official News.

Washington, Sept. 2.
Count Bernstorff, German Ambassador to the United States, acting on instructions from Berlin, states that Germany accepts the American proposal that " all passenger boats are to be warned before being attacked by submarines!"

A Washington message of August 28th says : " It is understood that Germany will announce the suspension of warfare against passenger vessels."

Sept. 4.
Cardinal Gibbons has handed to President Wilson a message from the Pope regarding peace.

London, Sept. 2.
A conference between the Government and representatives of the miners has settled the South Wales coal crisis. Forty-two thousand men had stopped working.

August 27.
The Admiralty announces that Squadron Commander Arthur W. Bigsworth destroyed single-handed a German submarine which he observed to have been completely wrecked and sunk off Ostend.

During the week ended August 25th nineteen merchant ships were sunk out of the 1,369 which arrived at and left British ports.

The Government of Nigeria reports the occupation of Gasconika in the German African Colony, Cameroon. The enemy was forced to retire to the Eastern frontier. Cameroon, which has an area of 205,000 square miles and a population of 3,500,000, and a portion of German East Africa, are the only German colonies that have not been occupied by the Allies.

Petrograd, Sept. 1.
The recent victory of Russian troops in the Caucasus resulted in the capture of vast booty. Five thousand, two hundred and thirteen prisoners were taken. The Cossacks in pursuit killed 2,000 of the enemy.

The week's wireless messages make clear the fact that the Austro-German offensive against the Russians has spent its force and that in some districts the Russians are more than holding their own. Yesterday's report from Petrograd states that there is no important change on the Riga and Dvina front and that the Russians are making successful progress between the river Sventa and the Vilna. Russian cavalry carried two villages near Schervinty at the point of the bayonet, the Germans fleeing in disorder. The Russians are progressing along the right bank of the Vilna, between which river and the Niemen the situation is unchanged. After fierce combats on the banks of the Styr in the region of Lusk, the Russians retreated from the front at Olyka, capturing nevertheless several hundred prisoners and some machine guns.

On Thursday the Russians were holding defensive positions on the river Missa and repulsed the enemy's attempt to cross the Dvina North of Friedrichstadt. The Germans had crossed to the right bank of the river but were driven back. The Russians assumed the offensive on the right bank of the river Vilna and continued to hold defensive positions between the Vilna and the Niemen. They also repulsed attacks in the Lipaksidra and Gorodee regions.

In Galicia the Austro-German troops began a series of attacks on the 29th and 30th ult., along the whole front. The attacks were particularly fierce North of Zloczow (East of Lemberg). Eight attacks were repulsed in the Pomorzany-Zborov districts and along Strypa front, the enemy being forced to retreat. The Russians counter-attacked, capturing 80 guns, 24 machine guns and 8,000 prisoners.

The week's news from the Italian front shows that—in the Western zone of Trentino where the Italians, having secured good positions on both sides of the frontier, are merely guarding the passes, the Austrians have been trying in vain to attack some of the Italian positions. In one of these attempts in the Sterino Valley, near the Tonale Pass, the Austrians suffered very heavily, abandoning five strongly entrenched positions and some machine guns and ammunition.

In the zone North-east of the Trentino (Cadorine Alps) where the Italians, having already occupied Cortina D'Ampezzo and other positions beyond the frontier, are dominating the strategical Dolomites Road from Toblach to the heart of the Trentino and are threatening to cut in the Willach-Toblach zone the main strategical Austrian road from Vienna to North Trentino, some new progress has been made, by the Italian occupation of strong positions on Innichriechel Knoten (Sexten Valley) and lately of another dominating position on Mount Maronia.

In the Northern Isonzo district where the Italians are acting against the forts of Malborghetto to protect the left of the Isonzo front, nothing new has been signalled.

In the middle Isonzo district new progress has been made in Plezzo region, where the recent occupation of Mount Rombon (North of Plezzo), of Mount Polounik and the ridge North of Mount Vrsik (the two latter belonging to the Nero group), is threatening Plezzo from every side.

The Austrian garrison of Tolmino itself is in a critical situation after the recent Italian occupation of the ridge South-east of Mount Nero and of the South Lucia hills dominating the town from the South-west.

Gorizia, which General Cadorna seems to intend taking not by direct attack but by indirect action from Plawa and from the Carso plateau, has been lately more severely pressed by the new progress the Italians have made on the latter fronts.

At Plawa some strong Austrian positions East of the Isonzo river were lately attacked and conquered by the Italians. At the same time, pressed by the Italian advance the Austrians evacuated on the Carso plateau some very strong positions on their actual line of defence, to the South of Corlia.

French official reports received by wireless during the week show that there has been unusual artillery and aerial activity along the whole front. Yesterday's report states that violent mutual bombardments have taken place in the sector of Lorette and Neuville, North of Arras ; in the neighbourhood of Fouquescourt, Laucourt and Tilleloy, near Montdidier, between the Somme and the Oise ; near Souain, East of Rheims, in the Champagne ; in the Argonne, where the Crown Prince's Army is stationed, and on the Lorraine front.

French aviators dropped bombs on the railway station at Ostend and the enemy's camps in the vicinity. German aviators bombed Luneville and killed a few civilians.

At six o'clock on the morning of August 29th six German aeroplanes tried to reach Paris but got no farther than Nogent-sur-Marne, Montmorency, Ribecourt and Compiegne. There were no casualties except at Compiegne where two hospital nurses and a child were killed. The enemy's aeroplanes were fired at from several points and were chased by French machines. The commander of a French air squadron pursued one of the German aeroplanes to a height of 8,600 metres and brought it down North of Senlis. The German aviator and pilot were found burnt to ashes.

231

Peninsula Press

No. 79   Monday, SEPTEMBER 13th. 1915   Official News.

Wireless Messages

Petrograd.

The Czar is taking supreme command of the Army and Navy and has appointed the Grand Duke Nicholas Viceroy and Commander-in-Chief of the Caucasus.

The vast German losses in Russia may be inferred from the fact that the Guards Corps alone lost 539 officers and 23,692 men.

German brutality in Poland is causing the bitterest discontent among the people.

Volkovisk, 45 miles South-east of Grodno, is apparently the centre of a great battle which began in Poland on a front of 110 miles between the rivers Nieman and Pripiati. Berlin report admits that the Russians are stubbornly resisting on a thirty mile front between Skideley and Volkovisk, while the Petrograd communique says that on Sunday and Monday the enemy continued to develop operations East and South-east of Grodno. The Russian rear-guard on Monday was engaged in particularly fierce action near Volkovisk and southward on the whole front as far as the Pruzany-Slonim road. The Russians in a series of fights continue to hold the enemy's offensive eastward.

Near Vilna the Germans maintain their old positions. In the Riga district the Russians re-crossed the Dvina on Thursday and surprised and drove the Germans back from the river.

Fierce fighting was resumed near Grodno on Thursday when the Russians re-entered the town and captured eight maxim guns and 150 prisoners. This enabled the divisions whose positions found a salient to retire unmolested. Altogether, the Russians took 3,560 prisoners.

Bucharest.

The Roumanian Minister of Commerce who has recently returned to Bucharest after visiting Petrograd, speaks enthusiastically of the way Russia is developing her vast resources for dealing with the Teutonic invaders who will be utterly unable to maintain themselves during the winter.

The Russians, says the Minister are more determined than ever to continue the struggle until victory is theirs.

London, Sept. 11.
During the night of Wednesday-Thursday a Zeppelin raid killed 12 men, 2 women and six children, seriously injured 8 men, 42 women and 2 children, and slightly injured 38 men, 23 women and 11 children. All were civilians except one among the killed and three among the injured.

The German account states that among the places bombed were Holborn Viaduct, a big factory in Norwich, big iron works near Midlesboro and the railway between Southbank and Redcar.

Paris.
Artillery duels have been continuous along the whole Western front and the Germans are showing anxiety as to the meaning of this activity which has lasted nearly fourteen days. Infantry engagements have been rare. In the Vosges the Germans have attacked with asphyxiating bombs and liquid fire, but with one unimportant exception the French have maintained their front. In the Argonne, where the German Crown Prince's army made two attacks with asphyxiating gas the struggle continues. The French communique of Saturday says that the German despatch announcing the capture of a large number of prisoners is a "fantastic lie." The German losses have been very heavy and without compensating gains. During the year that the Crown Prince's army has fought in the Argonne it has lost over 100,000 men and has won nothing.

On Tuesday the French artillery in the neighbourhood of Nieuport in Flanders co-operated with the British Fleet in bombarding the coast at Westende. On Sunday, the 5th, the Germans fired one hundred shells on Rheims but no loss of life was reported.

Aeroplanes have been active on both sides. The four German aviators who bombed Lunaville on the 1st inst., deliberately aimed at the populous quarters of the town and selected the hour when the people were in the streets. Their victims were mostly women and children. By way of reprisal four French aeroplanes dropped bombs on the railway station and military establishments of Sanrbrucken and did considerable damage. On Tuesday, a German aeroplane was forced to come down at Calais and its occupants were made prisoners. In reply to the German bombardment of the open towers of St. Die and Gerardmer, in the Vosges, a French air squadron dropped bombs on the railway stations and military works at Freiburg, causing an outbreak of fire. French aviators have also bombed the railway stations of Saarbourg, Pont-Faverger (North-east of Rheims), Tergnier (North-east Compiegne) and Lens (South-east of Lille). Following the bombardment of Nancy by German aeroplanes, a French squadron dropped bombs on the military establishments at Frascati (?) and on the stations at Metz.

According to the French official report, the number of German officers killed, wounded and missing from the beginning of the war to June 1st was 43,972. These losses had increased to 52,041 by July 15th, showing an increase of 9,069 in 45 days or 360 officers per day.

Wireless news from the Italian front during the week:-·
Tonale district (West frontier of Trentino).- On the 5th September the Italians attacked and took from the Austrians two strong positions at Colle Lagoscnro and Corno Debole (South of Tonale Pass). These positions as well as those already taken on Mount Palu group (North-east of Tonale Pass) threaten the flank of the Austrian forts in Vermiglia Valley, namely Sacarano, Pozzi, Alti and Strino. Already the two former have been severely damaged by the Italian heavy artillery.

Cardorine Alps district.- The Italians dislodged the Austrians from their positions on Mount Chaidemo and Avara.

Carnia district.- An Austrian attack against the strong Italian position at Mount Croce Carnico Pass, was easily repulsed. The numerous attempts the Austrians are making here are justified by the strategical importance of this pass the only one followed by a carriage road between Pontebba pass and the Cardorine alps. An Austrian advance through it, along the But river (Tagliamento Valley) would threaten the communications of both Cadore and Pontebba. The pass is however strongly guarded by troops and fortifications.

Isonzo front:- In the Plezzo district the Italians had already taken Mount Rombon (North of Plezzo), Pluzna (West of Plezzo) and Ceszoca (South of Plezzo). At the end of August the Italian troops passed to the East of Plezzo, cutting its communications along Coritenza and Isonzo rivers. On the 8th of September the Italians attacked Plezzo, routing the Austrians and taking a big booty. On the lower Isonzo the Italians destroyed the electric station of Lensumo and attacked twice with aeroplanes and severely damaged the Austrian aerodrome at Aisoviza (East of Gorizia).

Peninsula Press

Wireless Messages

The Admiralty announces that the enemy claims to have sunk submarine E.7 (Lieut. Commander A. Cochrane) in the Dardanelles and to have taken 3 officers and 25 men prisoners. As no news of this submarine has been received since the 4th September, it must be presumed that the report is correct.

The Russian Successes in Galicia are making their effect felt all along the line.

Lord Kitchener made a speech yesterday in which he referred to the recruiting question. The War Minister's remarks have led many to believe that we are on the verge of conscription, but there is a strong body of opinion, which believes that this interpretation is incorrect. Other important points of this speech were Lord Kitchener's reference to the French line as almost impregnable. He eulogised our new divisions as worthy of the best traditions of the Army, refered to the Italians as occupying positions of first rate strategic importance and dismissed Germany's achievements against Russia, as a strategic failure with nothing more than barren territory and evacuated fortresses as tangible results. Regarding the advance into Russia he added that the Germans appeared to have almost shot their bolt.

Rinella Press 17th

Mr Asquith announced that a despatch from the Dardanelles will be published shortly. The negotiations between the Anglo-French Commission and American financiers progress satisfactorily in spite of attempts by pro-Germans to hamper them. The loan will possibly be divided into 4 series of 5% bonds payable in dollars. It is understood that the Commission has assured the representatives of American cotton growers that cotton as well as other trade with France and Great Britain will be cared for. A supplementary vote of 250 millions was announced in the House of Commons today. Mr Asquith explained certain abnormal items for financing the necessary operations, the particulars of which it would not be in the public interest to disclose. The average daily expenditure was over three and a half millions sterling. The future weekly average will exceed 35 millions. The total expenditure of the financial year hitherto is 510 millions. Advances of 30 millions to

Foreign Governments and 28 millions to the Dominions had been made. Since the outbreak of war not far short of three million men had enlisted in the Army and navy. Mr Asquith concluded by paying tribute to the gallantry of Russia saying:- "It is a war of mechanics, organisation and endurance. Victory will incline to the side which can arm itself best and most steadily. That is what we want to do." (Great cheering)

Field Marshal Sir John French reports considerable artillery activity on both sides particularly North-east of Armentieres and in the neighbourhood of Ypres. Three hostile aeroplanes (were bought down?), two of which were hit by our anti-aircraft guns. During the week there have been altogether 21 flights over the German lines and in every case the Germans were driven to the ground.

Rome

On the 16th the Italians captured new positions at Mount Valpiana and Mount Fossernica, North-east of Trento.

In the Plezzo zone they took position on Mount Javorcek, taking 500 prisoners.

Paris

A French communique states that the Russian war Minister is satisfied with the improvement in the provision of munitions of war. The enormous increase in the output has been fully maintained in the last fortnight.

The Eastern Front

Wireless messages received during the week from sources show that the German offensive is still being pressed in the North. On the other hand a vigorous Russian offensive in Galicia has achieved important successes. The following are some of the most important messages received from the front:-

Operations in the North:- Petrograd, 14th September. – The enemy attacking West and South-west of Dvinsk succeeded in cutting the railway between Dvinsk and Wilna near the station of Novo Svetziany. As a result of the enemy's pressure between the station and Wilna the Russians are retiring. The enemy greatly reinforced is attacking East of Skidel. (Skidel is about 20 miles East of Grouno)

Petrograd September 17th.

South-east of Dvinsk the Russians repulsed repeated German attacks. North-east of Wilna the enemy succeeded in crossing the Wilna river. In the direction of Pirsk the Russians are retiring.

236

Operations in the South:- London, Sept. 12th – A Petrograd communique issued last night states that General Sanoff's[?] earlier victory at Tarnopol has been repeated. The Tsar's troops broke down the German resistance capturing more than 2000 men and several quickfiring guns.

Paris, September 17th
Fierce fighting continues on the Eastern front resulting in further successes for the Russians. Prisoners have been taken amounting to 4,078. A Petrograd Communique says the Russians captured two villages and many prisoners and drove the enemy back Westwards. South-west of Tarnopol the Russians are vigorously attacking and have captured a village and driven the enemy headlong across the Strypa. In the evening the Russians broke the wire entanglements and hurled the enemy from their trenches with the bayonet, captured a village close by, and crossed the river closely persuing the enemy. This engagement resulted in the capture of 500 more prisoners.

THE WESTERN FRONT

Throughout the past week, artillery duels have continued along the western front, attaining great intensity in certain localities. Numerous air raids into hostile territory have been carried out by the French airmen. The following extracts are of interest:-

Paris, September 12th.
North of Arras there was incessant bomb and grenade fighting. Fresh attempts by the enemy against our positions at Sapigny completely failed. We successfully bombarded with heavey shells the enemy's aircraft hangers at Biseville.

Paris, September 14th.
A squadron of 19 airmen flew over the town of Treves on which about 100 bombs were dropped. The railway station and the Imperial German Bank were clearly hit. The same squadron after returning to our lines and descending on the same afternoon dropped 58 more bombs on the station of Bommary-Barroncourt, while other airmen flying low bombarded the station at Donaueschin on the Danube and at Morlado. Our bombs were seen to hit their targets.

Paris, September 17th.
There has been incessant grenade fighting in the region of Arras. Fierce artillery fighting around Roye and in the Champagne. The enemy attempted to attack in the Argonne, but was completely repulsed. The French guns in Lorraine proved their superiority against the German

237

positions and concentrations of troops. The Germans attempting to debouch were enveloped in a curtain of fire by our guns and infantry.
German airmen threw bombs on Compigne, our airmen replied by attacking hangers at Ernyelle[?] with heavy bombs.

Paris, September 19th.
East of St Mihiel a German captive balloon was brought down. In front of St. Mihiel our artillery destroyed the main bridge, a bridge of boats and three foot bridges.

BRITISH CASUALTIES
London, September 16th.
Mr Tennant stated in the House of Commons, that the total British casualties for the first year of war were: officers killed 4,965, wounded 9,973, missing 1,500; men killed 70,992, wounded 241,086, missing 23,466

Peninsula Press

No. 81   Tuesday, SEPTEMBER 28th. 1915   Official News.

The following leading article appeared in the "Times" of September 4th:-

HEROISM IN GALLIPOLI.

We may all have our opinion about the strategy that dictated the enterprise in the Dardenelles. But about the behaviour of the men who have been sent to carry it through there can only be one opinion. Mr Ashmead Bartlett sent us yesterday, and sends us again today an account of attacks by these men many of them tasting battle for the first time – against the Turkish positions around Suvla bay and in the "Anzac" zone. These accounts should serve to make the least imaginative realize the conditions that an army in Gallipoli has to face. The Turks are well entrenched, well supplied with machine guns, well served by artillery that has proved itself a worthy rival to ours. Our ships and the batteries that we have been able to land, do their best to make the Turkish trenches untenable. They plaster them with shells, spread a screen of fire before each advance, and lift – as the line goes forward – to make the bringing up of enemy reserves difficult and costly. But the hills of Gallipoli rising in tiers from the coast, broken by rocky ravines, clothed in stubborn scrub – are ideal for defence. They are held by men who have an old name for the dogged bravery in defence – men who fight with the knowledge that failure means the loss of Constantinople, expulsion from Europe, disgrace to the Crescent. Mr Ashmead Bartlett has shown what the results are, and we, who have never failed to honour a worthy foe, may give the Turk the praise that is his due. But if we praise him, what shall we say of our own men? Seldom have British soldiers been called upon – with so complete a knowledge of the difficulties confronting them – to face emergencies calling for such sustained endeavour, endurance so long drawn out, faith so unconquerable in the certainty of ultimate victory. Landed on bare beaches under a storm of fire, knowing nothing of the country over which they have to advance, they have gone forward again and again with stern bravery that has yielded ground only when it was swept by fire that no living thing could remain. Several times they have actually carried commanding positions, only to be forced to give them up by a hail of destruction that made of stubbornness but a useless sacrifice of life. We speak of them all – Australians, New Zealanders, Indians – as our men. These are ours as much as those who have gone out from among us – as conscious of the call of the race, as proud of our traditions, as resolute to maintain the honour of their country. When we think how all have risen to the height of so arduous an enterprise we find no words that can express our pride in them. *Feret ad astra virtus.*

Wireless Messages

Athens, September 26.

Greece has mobilised twenty classes. The King signed the mobilisation decree. Great enthusiasm prevails. The Chamber meets on Wednesday to proclaim martial law. The Government has ordered the requisitioning of steamers and railways and prohibited the transport of good.

London, September 24th.

The fact that a General Mobilization had been ordered in Bulgaria was known in London yesterday when the diplomatic representative of that country explained that Bulgaria will maintain "an armed neutrality".

The "Times" correspondent in Sofia reports that on Monday the 20th, the Bulgarian Prime Minister informed his supporters that a convention had been signed with Turkey for the maintenance of "an armed neutrality" by Bulgaria.

A Berlin telegram says that the Bulgarian Legation warns all Bulgarians to leave Germany immediately for their own country.

In Greece, this new Balken crisis is causing considerable emotion. The British, French and Russian Ministers in Athens conferred with M. Venizelos, the Prime Minister, yesterday.

An associated Press message from Sofia to Berlin gives some details of the audience granted by King Ferdinand to the leaders of the parliamentary Opposition. The delegation was headed by the ex-Premier, M. Guechoff, M. Malinoff and Dr Daneff. Their mission was to lay before his Majesty arguments showing that the Government of Dr. Radoslavoff does not represent the sentiment of the majority of the people in its dealings with the international situation which, according to the Russophile Opposition, had been treated with a decided tendency towards the Central Powers. The action of the delegation was taken hurriedly, application for an audience being made only on the previous day. King Ferdinand granted the request without delay. It was known in Sofia that the Opposition decided to approach his Majesty after it became certain that the Government was about to publish a manifesto on the relations between Bulgaria and Turkey. Insistent reports of a general mobilisation on Tuesday also accelerated action by the opposition. What result was achieved by the delegation was not known when the message was despatched. Less Radical Russophiles were however, of opinion that the Government's course could not now be changed, seeing that the army stood unconditionally behind the king and his Prime Minister

Petrograd, September 26.

The great battle in the Baltic provinces is still intense. The Russians have defeated the enemy West of Riga and Friedrichstadt, especially in the region of Eckan. The Germans fled abandoning quantities of grenades and ammunition. The Russians continue to follow them up. Before Dvinsk (Dunaburg) everything is stationary. The Russians are successful also among the lakes of Novo-Alexandrovisk, taking many prisoners and machine guns. Fighting around Smorgon is very intense, while further South and in the Upper Nieman region the Russians have engaged the Germans in hand-to-hand fighting. The Russians have resumed the offensive in the Southern theatre and are progressing in the region of Dubno, where they captured 26 officers and 1,400 men.

The Russians have scored successes against the Austrians in the South, capturing 1,600 prisoners. The Austrians entered the Russian trenches cheering. Desperate bayonet fighting followed and the enemy was expelled with great loss. The Russians counter-attacked and pursued the Austrians to their trenches whence all who were not bayonetted or made prisoner fled.

Washington.

The United States Administration refuses to accept the so-called "explanation" offered by Dr. Dumba, the Austrian Ambassador to Washington, whose despatches, together with dispatches from the German Embassy, were found on Mr. Archibald an American journalist who was conveying them from America to Berlin and Vienna. No order for Dr. Dumba's recall having been received from Vienna, the Ambassador will be handed his passports.

London, September 20.

Mr. Byran reports that the United States loan to Great Britain and France will be between L120,000,000 and L140,000,000. It will be underwritten by a large syndicate of financiers and bankers who will receive a small commission, possibly one half or one per cent. The security will be British and French Government bonds, and the price to investors will be par.

241

Peninsula Press

No. 82   Monday, OCTOBER 4th. 1915   Official News.

Wireless Messages

More than 23,000 German prisoners have been taken on the Western front since September 25. The French have captured in Artois and Champagne alone 121 heavy and field guns with many more abandoned between us and the enemy, as well as 40 machine guns, in addition to many more destroyed by the bombardment.

The Eiffel Tower (Paris) report of October 3rd states that in Belgium the French heavy artillery co-operated with British fleet in bombarding the German batteries at Westende. In Artois the Germans directed on the whole of the French front between Neuville-St-Vaast and the wood to the North of ----- a violent cannonade to which the French replied briskly. There has been heavy shelling on both sides North of Berry-au-Bac, towards Cholern farm, and South towards Sapigneul. On the Champagne front there was a mutual cannonade in which the Germans again made use of asphyxiating shells. Between the Meuse and the Moselle, to the North of Fleurey the Germans fired some rifles on the French trenches, but were silenced by the French batteries.

In Lorraine a strong German reconnaissance was repulsed and scattered to the South of the Fort Paroche. A squadron of 64 aeroplanes bombarded today the station of Vouziers, the aerodrome near the town and the station of Challerange. More than 300 bombs were dropped and the targets were hit.

Sept 29.

The German Crown Prince's attack in the Argonne resulted in a serious defeat for the Germans.

Petrograd, Oct. 1st

The struggle for Dvinsk (Dunaburg) continues with unabated fierceness. The Russians are keeping the enemy in check. Supported by a hurricane of artillery fire the Germans attacked repeatedly and desperately. All their assaults were beaten off and their losses were enormous. It is reported that the Germans are bringing up reinforcements but they are being stopped.

Near Tarnapol the Russians captured the enemy's trenches at several points.

Russian warships bombarded the German positions in the Gulf of Riga silencing all the enemy's batteries.

The enemy is making fierce assaults in the districts of Vileika and Ossmiana, East of Vilna.

On this front on Monday, no fewer than 10,000 heavy shells were rained on a single Russian regiment. The enemy has brought up large forces from the river Pripet and on the Galician frontier their attacks are leading to severe actions, especially in the Kolki region.

Numerous German attacks in the direction of Novo-Alexandrovsk were repulsed. Russian cavalry are vigorously attacking the fords of the upper Villea river and charged the German cavalry capturing 68 and sabring 100. To the West of Viln Kofour the German attacks were repulsed. Though the Russians were pressed, fighting never slackened. One of their armies captured 13 guns including five heavy and 33 machine guns and over 1,000 prisoners. Stubborn fighting continues on the whole front from the South to the Pripet river.

A telegram despatched from Sofia on Sept. 23rd says that it is officially announced that Bulgaria in ordering mobilisation of her forces has no aggressive intentions but is resolved to be fully armed to defend her rights and her independence, thus following the example of Holland and Switzerland at the beginning of the war. In view of the movement of troops by her neighbours and the Austro-German offensive against Serbia, Bulgaria is obliged to proclaim an armed neutrality while she continues her pourparler with the two belligerent groups.

A telegram from Athens on September 26th states that at an interview between King Constantine and M. Venizelos, the Prime Minister, complete agreement was reached as to the measures to be taken for dealing with the situation and as to Greece's duty and obligations.

M. Venezelos has since (Oct. 2) announced the decision of Greece to stand by Serbia if she is attacked by Bulgaria.

Sir Edward Grey speaking in the House of Commons on Sept. 29th said: "It is officially announced in Sofia that Bulgaria has no aggressive intentions whatever against her neighbours."

Nish (Serbia) Sept 25.
On the river Save front the Serbian artillery interfered with the enemy's

243

fortifications on the heights opposite Ostrovitza (Bosnia). The attempts of the enemy to cross the Save and the Drina rivers towards Ratcha on Wednesday were repulsed.

Rome Oct. 1st

The Italian artillery has bombarded the railway station at Tarvis, east of Malorgheto causing huge fires. Italian troops defeated another attack in the Cividale zone east of Udine, on Sept. 29th, and also succeded in driving back the enemy's advance on the river Chiarso, north of Tolmezzo.

Further small succeses are reported on October 1st, the most important being the throwing back of the enemy in places on the outer works of Monte Nero and on the slopes above Tolmino.

A New York telegram of Oct. 1st states that all the morning newspapers predict the greatest success for the Anglo-French loan of L100,000,000 at five percent. Three hundred million dollars worth of issue will be taken by New York alone, while Chicago will probably subscribe 100,000,000 dollars.

A powerful syndicate which includes some of the strongest banks and most influential business firms in the United States has been formed to float the loan.

Wellington (New Zealand), Sept. 26th

The New Zealand Registration Bill was passed by Parliament through all its stages. The Prime Minister said it was absolutely necessary to ascertain the country's resources and it was the Governments duty to place every available man in the field. He was in favour of compulsory national training but in emergency would not hesitate to adopt compulsory service.

The Czar has telegraphed his congratulations on the successes of the Allies on the western front.

Genaral Marchand of Fashoda fame has been seriously wounded in the spine.

Mr Keir Hardie, M.P., Leader of the Independent Labour Party, is dead.

Peninsula Press

No. 83   Monday, OCTOBER 11th. 1915   Official News.

Wireless Messages

Petrograd, Oct. 4.

The Russian Minister at Sofia has been ordered to hand to Dr. Radoslavoff, President of the Council, the following note:-

"Events are happening in Bulgaria which show the final resolve of the Government of King Ferdinand to place the fate of the country in the hands of the Germans. The presence of German and Austrian officers in the Ministry of War and on the Headquarter Staff, the concentration of troops in the zone abutting on Servia, the substantial financial assistance accepted by the Bulgarian Cabinet from our enemies: all these admit of no further doubt as to the object of the present military preparations of the Bulgarian Government. The Entente Powers, who have at heart the realization of the aspirations of the Bulgarian people, have many times warned Dr. Radoslavoff that any hostile act against Servia would be considered to be hostile to the Entente Power. The prodigal assurances given by the Bulgarian Minister in reply to these warnings are contradicted by the facts. The representative of Russia, tied to Bulgaria by imperishable memory of the latter's liberation from the Turkish yoke, cannot sanction by his presence aggressive fratricidal perparations against an allied Slav people. Consequently the Russian Minister has received orders to leave Bulgaria with all his Staff and Consuls, if within 24 hours the Bulgarian Government does not openly break with the enemies of the Slav cause and of Russia and does not take immediate steps to remove officers belonging to the armies of States which are at war with the Entente Powers."

Oct. 8.

The Bulgarians reply to the Russian note not being considered satisfactory, diplomatic relations have been broken off. The British, French, Italian and Servian Ministers in Sofia have demanded their passports.

Oct. 9

The Russian minister who is suffering from appendicitis remains in Sofia. The representatives of the other Entente Powers have left.

Rome, Oct. 9.

Baron Sonnino, Minister of Foreign Affairs, has handed the Bulgarian Minister his passport.

News from Bucharest shows that Roumania is taking extraordinary military measures. Troops have gone to the Bulgarian frontier and officers of Bulgarian origin are being transferred to the interior. Giurgevo, on the Danube, South of Bucharest is being fortified.

Athens, Oct 9

The new Government formed after the resignations of M. Venizelos, owing to King Constantine's opposition, has decided to observe an attitude of "benevolent neutrality." M. Venizelos majority support the new government in order to avoid "complications at this critical juncture."

London, Oct 9

The Austro-German attack on Serbia has begun with an attempt to cross three frontier rivers, the Danube, the Savo and the Drina. The enemy claim to have effected a crossing at many places, and to have obtained a firm footing on the Serbian banks.

Petrograd, Oct 8.

The Russians are attacking vigorously on an eighty mile front extending from South of lake Drysviaty to a point South of Vileika. Around Dwinsk (Duneburg), where the Germans have been making great preparations for attack, the artillery duel continues without intermission.

Oct. 5

Further successes are reported from the Russian front. German attacks have been beaten back and the enemy has fled in disorder. Trenches and villages have been captured by brilliant bayonet assaults. In the fighting in the lake region, several instances are reported of German inability to withstand the Russian artillery fire. Cavalry has played an important part in these operations. The Russians stormed a village and farm and captured eight howitzers and six guns.

Oct. 5.

The Russian Headquarters Staff claims that the German plan of thrusting an army between Dwinsk (Dunburg) and Vilna has been defeated, and the initiative has been won by the Russians. The threatened advance on Minsk with the object of breaking through the Russian centre has failed and, after 20 days fighting, the German Army entrusted with the task has been checked, shaken and finally thrown back.

The vigour of the Russian offensive is increasing. The Austrian communique states that a Russian force used great quantities of ammunition and crossed the river Styr at several points North-east of Kollki, North-east of Lusk.

London, Oct. 5.

The King has sent a message to Sir John French congratulating the Army under his command on the gallant efforts in the combined attack. His Majesty recognises that the operations are but the prelude to greater deeds and further victories.

Rome, Oct. 5.

The Italians are fighting successfully in the high mountain regions where storms are raging and heavy snow is falling. Austrian attacks on positions recently won by the Italians have failed. On the Isonzo front the enemy's firing was so bad that many shells fell into their own first line trenches.

Paris, Oct. 9.

Two fresh French divisions have succeeded in penetrating one point in the direction of Saint Marie, North-west of Navarin. Saint Marie is on the Northward railway which is the Germans vital line of communications with the Crown Prince's Army in the Argonne.

Washington, Oct. 8.

The United States Ambassador has been instructed to inform the Porte that unless the massacre of Armenians ceases, friendly relations between the United States and Turkey will be endangered.

Peninsula Press

No. 84   Monday, OCTOBER 18th. 1915   Official News.

The following notes on the climate of the Dardanelles are taken from the 'Westminster Gazette' and are based upon the results of observations made by a close observer of nature during a period of over thirty years: "From October 10 to 14 there is a period of uncertainty; sometimes a south-westerly wind, which veers round to the north-west, and a good rainstorm. The first distinct drop in temperature now takes place (about the 10th to the 14th), one feels autumn in the air, the nights continue fairly warm and this period continues fine and generally calm up to about the 20th – sometimes the 18th or 19th – when a well-defined and most absolutely regular period is entered upon. This spell begins with three or four days of very heavy northerly or north-westerly winds, sometimes a gale, accompanied by rain for several days, and it is this period – from October 20 to October 25 – which is intensely interesting to naturalists owing to the passage of all kinds of birds, the sweeping past of the last of the quails, the arrival of the first woodcock, the clockwork precision of the passage of stock doves (pigeons); in fact it is the moment of the big migration, when the night air and day is full of birds on the move. Towards the end of October, and in the way of a counter coup or re-action to the northerly gales, there is generally experienced a fierce three or four days of southerly winds, sometimes gales. It is to be noted that these gales or changes in the weather are usually of three or seven days' duration, the first day being generally the strongest, and for some of these regular winds the natives have special names. November generally, almost always, comes in fine with a lovely first ten days or so. It, however, becomes rather sharp at night and there is to be expected a very marked period now of cold weather – a cold snap in fact."

"This snap is generally in the second or third week of the month, and only lasts a few days, the weather going back to fine and warm, and calm about the end of the month. Barring such a cold snap, the month is marked by fine weather and the absence of wind, and many people consider it the most glorious month of the year, the sunsets being especially fine."

"In the last days of November or the first days of December another period is entered upon. This is generally a heavy south wind lasting from three to seven days, which is succeeded by a lovely spell of fine weather, perfectly calm and warm, which brings one well through

December. Onward for such a time in December, say a little before Christmas or just after, the weather varies greatly. The marked periods are past – the weather may be anything, sometimes calm and mild, varied by rain, with strong north winds, but no seriously bad weather; in one word, no real winter weather need be looked for until, as natives put it, the Old Year – otherwise the New Year, old style, which is January 14, our style comes in.

After January 14, or a few days later, the weather is invariably bad; there is always a snow blizzard or two, generally between January 20 and 25. These are really bad blizzards, which sometimes last from three to seven days; and after, anything in the way of weather may happen in the next six weeks or two months. The snow has been known to lie six weeks. Strong southerly gales succeed, as a rule, the northerly gales, but one thing is to be noted, that the south and west winds no longer bring rain; it is the north and northeast which bring snow and rain.

"To those who have relations or friends at the Dardanelles (and I quote from a letter from a friend), let them send good warm stockings for the men besides the usual waistcoats and mufflers; and as for creature comforts, sweets, chocolate, and tobacco, especially cigarettes.It is the Turk who will suffer the cold; they cannot stand it long, and being fed generally mainly on bread, they have no stamina to meet cold weather. Most of their troops come from warmer climes.

Wireless Messages

London, Oct. 13

Sir Edward Grey speaking in the House of Commons this afternoon said that if Turkey had remained neutral the Allies would have seen that Turkey and Turkish territory did not suffer at the close of the war. The Allies were ready to do all in their power to obtain concessions for Bulgaria but an essential preliminary was that Bulgaria should take the side of the Allies. It was too much to ask them to believe that Bulgaria was influenced to enter into war without the promise of considerable territory. Our relations with Romania are of friendly character: and she was favourable to the policy of promoting agreement between her neighbours in the Balkans and had shown her readiness to persue the same policy as they persued. Servians were meeting the new crisis with some splendid courage, but the entry of Bulgaria made a difference in the situation. It was obvious that the interests of Greece and Servia were one: they stood and fell together. It was only through Greek territory that assistance could be given by the allies to Servia and they deserved to have that help. The cooperation of Russian troops was promised.

The Greek Government has formally informed Servia "that the Bulgarian attack arises out of an extension of area of European war and is not a Balkan war, consequently Greece declines to abide by the Treaty concluded with Serbia."

PENINSULA PRESS.

| No. 84 | MONDAY, OCTOBER 18th, 1915. | Official News |

The following notes on the climate of the Dardanelles are taken from the "Westminster Gazette" and are based upon the results of observations made by a close observer of nature during a period of over thirty years : "From October 10 to 14 there is a period of uncertainty ; sometimes a south-westerly wind, which veers round to the north-west, and a good rainstorm. The first distinct drop in temperature now takes place (about the 10th to the 14th) one feels autumn in the air, the nights continue fairly warm, and this period continues fine and generally calm up to about the 20th—sometimes the 18th or 19th—when a well-defined and most absolutely regular period is entered upon. This spell begins with three or four days of very heavy northerly or north-westerly winds, sometimes a gale, generally accompanied by rain from October 20 to October 25—which is intensely interesting to naturalists owing to the passage of all kinds of birds, the sweeping past of the last of the quails, the arrival of the first woodcock, the clockwork precision of the passage of stockdoves (pigeons) ; in fact it is the moment of the big migration, when the air night and day is full of birds on the move. Towards the end of October, and in the way of a counter coup or re-action to the northerly gales, there is generally experienced a fierce three or four days of southerly winds, sometimes gales. It is to be noted that these gales or changes in the weather are usually of three or seven days' duration, the first day generally being the strongest, and for some of these regular winds the natives have special names. November generally, almost always, comes in fine with a lovely first ten days or so. It, however, becomes rather sharp at night, and there is to be expected a very marked period now of cold weather—a cold snap in fact."

"This snap is generally in the second or third week of the month, and only lasts a few days, the weather going back to fine, warm, and calm until about the end of the month. Barring such cold snap, the month is marked by fine weather and the absence of wind, and many people consider it the most glorious month of the year, the sunsets being especially fine."

"In the last days of November or the first days of December another period is entered upon. There is generally a heavy south wind lasting from three to seven days, which is succeeded by a lovely spell of fine weather, generally perfectly calm and warm, which brings one well through December. Onward from such time in December, say a little before Christmas or just after, the weather varies greatly. The marked periods are past—the weather may be anything, sometimes calm and mild, varied by rain, with strong north winds, but no seriously bad weather ; in one word, no real winter weather need be looked for until, as the natives put it, the old New Year—otherwise the New Year, old style, which is January 14, our style—comes in.

After January 14, or a few days later, the weather is almost invariably bad ; there is always a snow blizzard or two, generally between January 20 and 25. These are real bad blizzards, which sometimes last from three to seven days; and after, anything in the way of weather may happen for the next six weeks or two months. The snow has been known to lie six weeks. Strong southerly gales succeed, as a rule, the northerly gales, but one thing is to be noted, that the south and west winds no longer bring rain ; it is the north and north-east which bring snow and rain."

"To those who have relations or friends at the Dardanelles (and I quote from a letter from a friend), let them send good strong warm stockings for the men besides the usual waistcoats and mufflers ; and as for creature comforts, sweets, chocolate, and tobacco, especially cigarettes. It is the Turks who will suffer from the cold ; they cannot stand it long, and being fed generally mainly on bread, they have no stamina to meet cold weather. Most of their troops come from warm climes.

Wireless Messages.

London, Oct. 13.

Sir Edward Grey speaking in the House of Commons this afternoon said that if Turkey had remained neutral the Allies would have seen that Turkey and Turkish territory did not suffer at the close of the war. The Allies were ready to do all in their power to obtain concessions for Bulgaria but an essential preliminary was that Bulgaria should take the side of the Allies. It was too much to ask them to believe that Bulgaria was influenced to enter into war without promise of considerable territory. Our relations with Roumania are of friendly character; and she was favourable to the policy of promoting agreement between her neighbours in the Balkans and had shown her readiness to pursue the same policy as they pursued. Servians were meeting the new crisis with some splendid courage, but the entry of Bulgaria made a difference in the situation. It was obvious that the interests of Greece and Servia were one : they stood and fell together. It was only through Greek territory that assistance could be given by the Allies to Servia and they deserved to have that help. The co-operation of Russian troops was promised.

Athens, Oct. 14.

The Greek Government has formally informed Serbia "that the Bulgarian attack arises out of an extension of area of European war and is not a Balkan war, consequently Greece declines to abide by the Treaty concluded with Serbia."

R.E. Printing Section, G.H.Q., M.E.F.

Peninsula Press

No. 85   Tuesday, OCTOBER 26th. 1915   Official News.

Wireless Messages

The French official report of the 24th states that the French troops that crossed the Greek frontier have got into touch with the Serbian troops. The landing of French troops at Salonica continues regularly under the best conditions.

Paris, Oct. 25

On the 21st inst. French troops were engaged with the Bulgarians at Slabrovo fourteen kilometres from Strumitza. The village remained in our hands. Our losses are very slight.

Athens, Oct. 21

Twenty four hours have elapsed since the British and Russian Ministers conferred with M. Zaimis, the Prime Minister, and informed him that their Governments do not agree with the Greek interpretation of the Serbian treaty. Hitherto nothing has happened.

(The Greeks were bound by treaty to come to the aid of Servia [sic] when she was attacked by Bulgaria but refused on the ground "that the attack on Bulgaria arises out of an extension of the area of the European war and is not a Balkan War!")

Miss Carell [sic], an English nurse in Brussels, who was tried by Court-Martial for aiding British, French and Belgium prisoners of war escape from Belgium, has been brutally murdered by order of the German authorities. A full account of this atrocity is given in the papers issued by the Press Bureau in London on 20th inst. Miss Carell was not allowed to see her counsel before trial, and was not permitted to inspect the documents for the prosecution. She was found guilty at a second Court-Martial and was condemned to death. Desperate protests by the United States and the Spanish Ministers in Brussels were ignored. Both ministers pleaded for delay in order that an appeal might be lodged, but the Germans were unmoved. The execution took place at an early date after sentence had been passed. On seeing the firing party Miss Carell collapsed and was shot by a German officer while she lay on the ground. Intense indignation has been roused all over the world by this tragic example of German inhumanity.

Artillery duels and bombing on the Western front have been followed by attacks in which the Germans have suffered heavily.

Paris, Oct. 26th

The Germans again attempted yesterday evening to advance and attack the fortifications Givenchy wood and the French advanced posts round hill 140. When scarcely out of their trenches they were decimated and compelled to retire. This is the eighth check inflicted on the Germans in five days in this one sector of the front. The artillery duel continues with great violence being almost incessant south of the Somme in the Lihons Caney and Beurraegnes district. Elsewhere the French batteries have been used with destructive effect on the German trenches and field works in Champagne South-east of Tahure between the Meuse and the Moselle, North of Regneville and in Lorraine in the neighbourhood of Embcrmesnil and Domevre.

The operations on the Italian front are described in general Cadorne's despatch of October 22nd:-

The offensive so successfully began along the Tyrol-Trentino front now extends as far as the sea. We have taken many positions and large quantities of war material. The Alpine troops have occupied positions in the valley of Iagarina, east of lake Garda. Supported by heavy batteries on the evening of 22nd inst., the enemy attempted to counter-attack our new positions on the Crocano but were repulsed with heavy losses. At the head of the Rienz our troops advanced against the armed works on the massif of Monte Cristallo and gained the crest of Rauch Kofl. Towards Schlendderbach we took some trenches and prisoners. In the valley of Fella a dashing assault by our troops inflicted serious damage on the enemy and secured some arms and munitions. Leopolds-Hoehe was destroyed by fire. In the valley of Schesima a strong force of the enemy was attacked and put to flight leaving many killed. Along the whole front of the Isonzo, from Caporetto to the sea after intense artillery preparation, on the morning of 21st inst., our troops attacked the enemy's positions which were strengthened by mines, barbed wire, etc., and defended by numerous forts. Under a violent and concentrated fire from the enemy's artillery, machine guns, infantry and bombs our infantry advanced impetuously, taking at the point of the bayonet important positions in the Monte Nero zone, carrying numerous well armed trenches in the sector of Tolmino, on the hill of Santa Lucia, to the North of Gorizia, as well as a very solid redoubt on the slopes of Monte Sabatino, and also piercing in many places the strong advanced lines of the enemy on the Carso front. Dispersed groups of the enemy to the number of 1184 men and 25 officers were taken prisoner.

Mr. Asquith, the Prime Minister, is suffering from gastro-intestinal cataarh.

It is understood that Sir Edward Carson resigned his office as Attorney-General in the Coalition Government on the question not of conscription but the position in the near east.

PENINSULA PRESS.

No. 85   TUESDAY, OCTOBER 26th, 1915.   Official News.

Wireless Messages.

The French official report of the 24th states that the French troops that crossed the Greek frontier have got into touch with the Serbian troops. The landing of French troops at Salonica continues regularly under the best conditions.

Paris, Oct. 25.

On the 21st inst. French troops were engaged with the Bulgarians at Slabrovo, fourteen kilometres from Stramitza. The village remained in our hands. Our losses are very slight.

Athens, Oct. 21.

Twenty-four hours have elapsed since the British and Russian Ministers conferred with M. Zaimis, the Prime Minister, and informed him that their Governments do not agree with the Greek interpretation of the Serbian treaty. Hitherto nothing has happened.

[The Greeks were bound by treaty to come to the aid of Servia when she was attacked by Bulgaria but refused on the ground "that the attack on Bulgaria arises out of an extension of the area of the European war and is not a Balkan War!"]

Miss Carell, an English nurse in Brussels, who was tried by Court-Martial for aiding British, French and Belgium prisoners of war to escape from Belgium, has been brutally murdered by order of the German authorities. A full account of this atrocity is given in papers issued by the Press Bureau in London on the 20th inst. Miss Carell was not allowed to see her counsel before trial, and was not permitted to inspect the documents for the prosecution. She was found guilty at a second Court-Martial and was condemned to death. Desperate protests by the United States and the Spanish Ministers in Brussels were ignored. Both Ministers pleaded for delay in order than an appeal might be lodged, but the Germans were unmoved. The execution took place at an early date after sentence had been passed. On seeing the firing party Miss Carell collapsed and was shot by a German officer while she lay on the ground. Intense indignation has been roused all over the world by this tragic example of German inhumanity.

Artillery duels and bombing on the Western front have been followed by attacks in which the Germans have suffered heavily.

Paris, Oct. 26th.

The Germans again attempted yesterday evening to advance and attack the fortications Givenchy wood and the French advanced posts round hill 140. When scarcely out of their trenches they were decimated and compelled to retire. This is the eighth check inflicted on the Germans in five days in this one sector of the front. The artillery duel continues with great violence being almost incessant south of the Somme in the Lihons Cancy and Beurraegnes district. Elsewhere the French batteries have been used with destructive effect on the German trenches and field works in Champagne South-east of Tahure between the Meuse and the Moselle, North of Regneville and in Lorraine in the neighbourhood of Embermesnil and Domevre.

The operations on the Italian front are described in General Cadorne's despatch of October 22nd :—

The offensive so successfully began along the Tyrol-Trentino front now extends as far as the sea. We have taken many positions and large quantities of war material. The Alpine troops have occupied positions in the valley of Lagarina, East of lake Garda. Supported by heavy batteries on the evening of the 22nd inst., the enemy attempted to counter-attack our new positions on the Crozzno but were repulsed with heavy losses. At the head of the Rienz our troops advanced against the armed works on the massif of Monte Cristallo and gained the crest of the Rauch Kofl. Towards Schlenderbach we took some trenches and prisoners. In the valley of the Felix a dashing assault by our troops inflicted serious damage on the enemy and secured some arms and munitions. Leopolds Hoehe was destroyed by fire. In the valley of the Scheslina a strong force of the enemy was attacked and put to flight, leaving many killed. Along the whole front of the Isonzo, from Caporetto to the sea, after intense artillery preparation, on the morning of the 21st inst., our troops attacked the enemy's positions which are strengthened by mines, barbed wire, etc., and defended by numerous forts. Under a violent and concentrated fire from the enemy's artillery, machine guns, infantry and bombs our infantry advanced impetuously, taking at the point of the bayonet important positions in the Monte Nero zone, carrying numerous well armed trenches in the sector of Tolmino, on the hill of Santa Lucia, to the North of Gorizia, as well as a very solid redoubt on the slopes of Monte Sabatino, and also piercing in many places the strong advanced lines of the enemy on the Carso front. Dispersed groups of the enemy to the number of 1184 men and 25 officers were taken prisoner.

Mr. Asquith, the Prime Minister, is suffering from gastro-intestinal cataarh.

It is understood that Sir Edward Carson resigned his office as Attorney-General in the Coalition Government on the question not of conscription but of the position in the near East.

R.E. Printing Section, G.H.Q., M.E.F.

Peninsula Press

No. 86   Monday, November 1st. 1915   Official News.

Wireless Messages

London, Oct. 29: A message from Salonica states: "There is news to hand which, however contested, permits us to state with precision that very serious internal difficulties have arisen in Bulgaria and that Bulgarian troops have broken out at various points."

The "Matin" (Paris) states that when Mr. Asquith speaks on Tuesday be will "put a different complexion on the Balkan situation, and will announce that at the proper time help will come to the Serbians from several points at once."

London, Oct. 29: Lord Loreburn asked in the House of Lords whether the naval and military advisers of the Government were satisfied with the despatch of troops to Salonica. Lord Lansdowne replied that he was afraid it was highly improbable that the Serbians would long be able to withstand the German attack, especially with the Bulgarians at their back. He dwelt on the difficulty of making public statements on military matters. Referring to the impression in some peoples' minds that civilian members of the Cabinet are in the habit of devising great strategic plans and imposing them on their military advisers, Lord Lansdowne vehemently denied that such a thing happened, seeing that Lord Kitchener is invariably a party to the Governments decisions.

London, Oct. 28. Sir Edward Grey announced in the House of Commons that the offer of Cyprus to Greece was conditional on the Greeks giving immediate aid to the Serbians. The offer has now lapsed. (Cyprus was until Oct,. 1914 when it was annexed to the British Empire still nominally pat of the Ottoman Empire, though occupied by Great Britain under the treaty of 1878. The island has an area of 3,600 square miles and a population of 275,000 of whom 20 per cent are Moslems and the remainder mostly Greeks.)

London, Oct. 29. British submarines have sunk in the Baltic four German steamers, and in the Sea of Marmora a munition laden Turkish transport. These are in addition to the cruiser "Prinz Adalbert" which the Germans acknowledge was sunk off Liban. (The "Prinz Adalbart" (1901-2) was an armoured cruiser of 8,856 tons, with a speed of 21 knots and an armament of four 8.2in and ten 5.9in guns.)

254

Bucharest, Oct. 30. The Russian fleet again bombarded Varna and Burgas, the Bulgarian ports in the Black Sea, causing important damage. Russian aviators dropped bombs in the harbours. The enemy's submarines unsuccessfully attacked the fleet.

Wireless messages received during the week show that at several points on the Eastern front the Germans are making desperate efforts to break down the Russian resistance. In the Riga district a series of attacks South of the Drina have been repulsed. On the Dvinsk front furious fighting is incessant. The Germans attempted to advance from Illukst but had to withdraw again across the river. In the Stry district, North west of Rafalovka, the Russians captured a village with prisoners and machine guns. In an attack North of Violki, on the Styr, the Germans were out-flanked and lost over 2,000 prisoners. The enemy was enveloped in a village and suffered enormous losses. Three German attacks North of Nevolisinatz were beaten off and heaps of the enemy's dead were left on the ground.

The following comment on the moral of the Russian and German troops is made in a recent official report from Petrograd:- "The spirit of our troops, which has been demonstrated in the most striking fashion in innumerable rearguard actions, has received a fresh impulse from the successes gained by us over the Germans recently in desperate hand-to-hand encounters, and in our successful assumption of the offensive against the Germans.

"The depression which has been observed in the ranks of the Germans has not been without its influence on the moral of our men. This depression manifests itself in more and more frequent instances of the abandonment by the Germans on the battlefield of slightly wounded soldiers, of wagons on the line of their retreat, of the throwing away of arms and projectiles, and of disorder and nervousness in their firing."

Paris, Oct. 31 (Official Report): Heavy fighting reported in the course of the day at several points on the front of Artois. In the Bois-en-Hache the French have made marked progress bombing their way inch by inch. North-east of Neuville-St-Waast the Germans have succeeded in re-occupying by a surprise attack some portions of the trenches they recently lost and in which the French had established their advanced line. Their progress was at once stopped by the fire of the French trenches in immediate support. East of the "Labyrinth" the German's exploded a mine near one of the French barricades. Those of the enemy who attempted to occupy the crater were thrown back into their trenches by the French fusillade. In Champagne, the Germans shelled with great violence the French positions on the Tahure knoll and the ground Southeast of it. The French replied with fire from the counter batteries and with rafales on the German trenches and field works.

Pretoria, Oct. 27. It is understood that General Botha, Prime Minister of the Union of South Africa, has decided to continue in office with his present colleagues.

Lord Derby's new recruiting scheme continues to be a striking success. Lord Derby was recently put in charge of recruiting in the United Kingdom.

Peninsula Press

No. 87   Monday, November 8th. 1915   Official News.

Wireless Messages

The resignation of the Greek Government, after the refusal of the Chamber to pass a vote of confidence in the Zaimis Cabinet, raises once more the constitutional issue between King Constantine and Parliament. At the general election in June, M. Venizelos was returned with a majority of 63 over all possible combinations. The illness of the King was made the excuse for postponing the meeting of the new Parliament until late in August when M. Venizelos again accepted the Premiership. The Greek Army was mobilised on Sept. 26 and on Oct. 2. M. Venizelos announced that Greece would stand by her treaty with Serbia if the Bulgarians attacked the Serbians. King Constantine refused to recognise this treaty as binding. M. Venizelos thereupon resigned, and a new Cabinet pledged to neutrality was formed on Oct. 8, under the leadership of M. Zaimis. The Chamber rejected the vote of Confidence by a majority of 33 and a dissolution of Parliament was expected. A telegram from Athens on Nov. 5 states that the King of Greece has summoned the party leaders to a conference on the political situation.

A later telegram announces the formation of a new Cabinet with M. Skonldoudi as Prime Minister in place of M. Zaimis who ceases to hold any portfolio. The other Ministers of the old Cabinet remain with the addition of M. Michaeldaki, late President of the Cretan Chamber.

Serbia, through her representative in London, has issued an appeal to her friends in Great Britain begging that help will be sent to her quickly. "Serbia has been condemned to death by Germans, Austrians and Bulgarians," says the Serbian Minister. "For twenty days our common enemies have been trying to annihilate us. In spite of the spirit of our soldiers our resistance cannot be expected to be maintained indefinitely. Franco-British Forces have said to have reached a point 90 miles North of Salonica, but it is doubtful if they can join the Serbians in time to prevent them from being surrounded."

A French communique issued on Nov. 2nd, states that detachments of Bulgarians who occupied Istip on Oct. 27th sent reconnoitring parties South-east toward Krivolaka who fell back before our outposts without fighting. It is unofficially reported that British troops moving Northwards from Salonica have joined hands with the Serbians and that a Russian Army of 250,000 men is on its way to Bulgaria.

An Athens message dated Nov. 5th reports the complete success of the Serbians between Prilep and Monastir. Important British contingents have arrived at Strumitza to reinforce the French troops operating in Macedonia.

Stockholm, Nov. 1st:- Negotiations between Great Britain and Sweden with a view to agreement on commercial questions have been broken off.

According to the "Daily News" the Government has created a new General Staff in London to supervise the prosecution of the war in various fields. The new War Cabinet will confer with the General Staff.

The "Times" states that General Joffre came to London to discuss the Balkan situation and to arrive at a complete understanding with regard to the military policy on all fronts, and the necessity of giving rapid help to Serbia.

A German submarine flying signals of distress has been towed by a Dutch lifeboat to Terseilling where it is guarded by two Dutch destroyers.

We have to thank the Eastern Telegraph Company for the following cable giving the result of the racing for the Melbourne Cup:-
(1) Patrobus, (2) Westcourt, (3) Carlita, (4) Garlin. Patrobus won by half a neck: the betting was 8 to 1. Westcourt (betting 50 to 1) was second by a length: Carlita (betting 7 to 1) was third by a length. The betting on Garlin was 25 to 1.

New York, Nov. 5th:- Bases for submarines are reported to have been established in Mexico and the West Indies by ships plying in the name of German Americans. They are ordered to send supplies via Scandinavia and to tranship through neutral countries chemicals which a corner has been made in New York.

A message from Wellington (New Zealand) states that Parliament has been prorogued. During the final sitting of the House of Representatives, Colonel Allen, the Minister for Defence, stated that the total number of men who had gone to the war was 28,000 and 10,000 more were in training. It had been decided to increase reinforcements by 15 to 20 per cent. According to the 1911 census there were 198,000 men of military age. The Minister did not doubt that an appeal to their patriotism would secure the full number.

A Reuter telegram from Copenhagen states that: Bremen, Hamburg, Kiel and Dantzig newspapers describe the preparations of the German coastal towns against aerial raids. People have been elaborately warned that in the event of a raid guns would be fired and church bells would be rung. The authorities decided on a rehearsal. When the firing and bell ringing began the people in every town, instead of obeying instructions, became panic stricken and rushed en masse to the military headquarters. The newspapers appeal to the public to show greater self-possession next time.

PENINSULA PRESS.

No. 87   MONDAY, NOVEMBER 8th, 1915.   Official News

Wireless Messages.

The resignation of the Greek Government, after the refusal of the Chamber to pass a vote of confidence in the Zaimis Cabinet, raises once more the constitutional issue between King Constantine and Parliament. At the general election in June, M. Venizelos was returned with a majority of 63 over all possible combinations. The illness of the King was made the excuse for postponing the meeting of the new Parliament until late in August when M. Venizelos again accepted the Premiership. The Greek Army was mobilised on Sept. 26 and on Oct. 2, M. Venizelos announced that Greece would stand by her treaty with Serbia if the Bulgarians attacked the Serbians. King Constantine refused to recognise this treaty as binding. M. Venizelos thereupon resigned, and a new Cabinet pledged to neutrality was formed on Oct. 8, under the leadership of M. Zaimis. The Chamber rejected the vote of Confidence by a majority of 33 and a dissolution of Parliament was expected. A telegram from Athens on Nov. 5 states that the King of Greece has summoned the party leaders to a conference on the political situation.

A later telegram announces the formation of a new Cabinet with M. Skouloudi as Prime Minister in place of M. Zaimis who ceases to hold any portfolio. The other Ministers of the old Cabinet remain with the addition of M. Michaeldaki, late President of the Cretan Chamber.

Serbia, through her representative in London, has issued an appeal to her friends in Great Britain begging that help will be sent to her quickly. "Serbia has been condemned to death by Germans, Austrians and Bulgarians," says the Serbian Minister. "For twenty days our common enemies have been trying to annihilate us. In spite of the spirit of our soldiers our resistance cannot be expected to be maintained indefinitely. Franco-British Forces have said to have reached a point 90 miles North of Salonica, but it is doubtful if they can join the Serbians in time to prevent them from being surrounded."

A French communiqué issued on Nov. 2nd, states that detachments of Bulgarians who occupied Istip on Oct. 27th sent reconnoitring parties South-east toward Krivolaka who fell back before our outposts without fighting. It is unofficially reported that British troops moving Northwards from Salonica have joined hands with the Serbians and that a Russian Army of 250,000 men is on its way to Bulgaria. An Athens message dated Nov. 5th reports the complete success of the Serbians between Prilep and Monastir. Important British contingents have arrived at Strumitza to reinforce the French troops operating in Macedonia.

Stockholm, Nov 1st:—Negotiations between Great Britain and Sweden with a view to agreement on commercial questions have been broken off.

According to the "Daily News" the Government has created a new General Staff in London to supervise the prosecution of the war in various fields. The new War Cabinet will confer with the General Staff.

The "Times" states that General Joffre came to London to discuss the Balkan situation and to arrive at a complete understanding with regard to the military policy on all fronts, and the necessity of giving rapid help to Serbia.

A German submarine flying signals of distress has been towed by a Dutch lifeboat to Terschilling where it is guarded by two Dutch destroyers.

We have to thank the Eastern Telegraph Company for the following cable giving the result of the racing for the Melbourne Cup:—(1) Patrobas, (2) Westcourt, (3) Carlita, (4) Garlin. Patrobas won by half a neck; the betting was 8 to 1. Westcourt (betting 50 to 1) was second by a length; Carlita (betting 7 to 1) was third by a length. The betting on Garlin was 25 to 1.

New York, Nov. 5th:—Bases for submarines are reported to have been established in Mexico and the West Indies by ships plying in the name of German Americans. They are ordered to send supplies via Scandinavia and to tranship through neutral countries chemicals of which a corner has been made in New York.

A message from Wellington (New Zealand) states that Parliament has been prorogued. During the final sitting of the House of Representatives, Colonel Allen, the Minister for Defence, stated that the total number of men who had gone to the war was 28,000 and 10,000 more were in training. It had been decided to increase reinforcements by 15 to 20 per cent. According to the 1911 census there were 103,000 men of military age. The Minister did not doubt that an appeal to their patriotism would secure the full number.

A Reuter telegram from Copenhagen states that: Bremen, Hamburg, Kiel and Dantzig newspapers describe the preparations of the German coastal towns against aerial raids. People have been elaborately warned that in the event of a raid guns would be fired and church bells would be rung. The authorities decided on a rehearsal. When the firing and bell ringing began the people in every town, instead of obeying instructions, became panic stricken and rushed en masse to the military headquarters. The newspapers appeal to the public to show greater self-possession next time.

R.E. Printing Section, G.H.Q., M.E.F.

259

Peninsula Press

No. 88   Monday, November 15th. 1915   Official News.

Summary of Wireless Messages

French Front – The Germans have been making a great effort to repair their reverses. Their attacks have been particularly violent and sustained in the Champagne region about the Tahure Hill and the trench of La Courtine, also in the Loos sector. The whole of their costly efforts have been repulsed, with the solitary exception of one point, where they were able to gain a little ground which placed in their possession the summit of the Hill of Tahure. The offensive has now collapsed and the latest messages report the methodical progress of mine, bomb and artillery warfare on the part of the British and French.

Russian Front – The offensive has been resumed by the Russians with excellent results, particularly in the extreme North and South of the front. Hindenburg has now been obliged to abandon the offensive, which had been desperately pressed for 11 days in the Riga-Dvinsk region, and to retire as the German Press states, "according to plans." In the South the Russians have gained a new victory on the much contested battlefield of Chartorysk and have advanced 20 kilometres in depth on a width of 48 kilometres.

Extracts from latest messages – Riga-Dvinsk region. The Russian offensive is being maintained successfully with assistance of a powerful artillery. To the West of Riga the Russian attacks are being supported by the fire of warships in the Gulf. The Russians have captured Kemmern and Anting and inflicted serious losses on the enemy.

Styr region – At Rudko on the middle Styr the Russians broke the enemy's line and captured over 2,000 prisoners and 20 machine guns. At Kolki the Russians captured 3,500 men and 71 officers. At Chartorysk the Russians captured 6,000 prisoners of whom 1,000 were Germans.

Italian Front – The Italian offensive continues. Fighting has taken place in the Trentino, in the mountain zone of the Upper Isonzo and on the Carso Plateau.

Extracts from Italian communiques:-

7th Nov. – We captured enemy positions at Marga and Stapene. Near San Michele we took some enemy trenches, 153 prisoners and much material.

13th Nov. – On the middle Isonzo in the Plava sector, we advanced beyond Zagora, capturing 260 prisoners. We progressed also North-west of Gorizia, also to the South-west of San Martino del Carso, capturing prisoners in both sectors.

The Balkan Theatre – The Serbian forces are withdrawing towards the South-west of the country before the superior combination of Austro-German and Bulgarian forces. It is still difficult to form a clear picture of the situation, but on the whole it may be said that the Serbian efforts have been devoted to the preservation of their forces, so as to be able to join hands with the Franco-British reinforcements now arriving in Salonica, with a view to menacing the flank of the German advance eastwards. At the same time the Serbs have inflicted very severe losses both on the Germans and Bulgarians. The French and British troops have repulsed several Bulgarian attacks in the neighbourhood of Babuna and Stumnitza.

America – After the Germans had openly surrendered to the American view on the submarine question and practically abandoned their submarine campaign in the Atlantic, the American Government forwarded their note to Great Britain on the interruption of American trade. Developments in America showed signs of taking a turn favourable to German interests. However, there are now four distinct issues which have re-awakened American indignation against German methods. These are, firstly the brutal execution of Miss Cavell, secondly the plots to destroy American munition factories, thirdly the breach of their parole by eight German naval officers interned in America and lastly the torpedoing of the Italian steamer "Ancona" in the Mediterranean, which carried 25 American passengers. With regard to the German officers breach of their word of honour, the following from the "New York Times" is typical of many similar articles in the American Press: "The breaking of their parole by German officers proves that the German is so lost to all sense of shame and decency that the word of a German or of the German Government means nothing, that a lie is meritorious if it will serve a German's purpose and any nation that would trust Germany shows its folly."

British submarines in the Baltic – latest success are the torpedoing of the German light cruiser "Undine" and of two destroyers, besides the sinking of a large number of vessels engaged in the metal trade from

Sweden to Germany. According to the Swedish Press the British submarines now dominate the Baltic and German seaborne trade is at a standstill. The Swedish sympathy for Germany has been profoundly modified by the action of the Germans shelling the Swedish submarine "Hvalen" without previously ascertaining her nationality.

Germany – In spite of Germany's strenuous efforts to represent internal conditions in a favourable light, it is becoming increasingly evident that the strain of the war combined with the British blockade is telling. Many industries especially the cotton spinning and weaving mills are short of supplies, food prices are rising in spite of Government measures. A food monopoly is demanded, and food riots have taken place in Cologne.

A certain change is also noticeable in the tone of the Press towards the British army. Thus a War Correspondent writing to the "Berlin Tageblatt" about some British Prisoners who fell into German hands near Loos, speaks of their devoted patriotism, cleanliness and self-respect. He says that none of them expressed sentiments of hatred to Germans, they fought for their country's cause and that was all that concerned them. It is certain that no German paper would have written in this strain of the "contemptible little army" a year ago.

Greece – The Chamber has been dissolved and new elections have been fixed to take place on December 19th.

The Cabinet – Mr Winston Churchill has resigned.

Peninsula Press

No. 89   Monday, November 22nd. 1915   Official News.

Wireless Messages

WESTERN FRONT.- At the beginning of the week, the Germans were still continuing their efforts to shake the French in their possession of the ground captured by them during the great advance of September. Later, a surprise attack was attempted by them in the region of the Labyrinth. All the German efforts have been unavailing and on the rest of the front there has been only the usual give and take of trench warfare. The mutual cannonade forms its usual the chief feature of the daily communiques, but latest messages point to an increased intensity in the French fire on certain sectors of the line. The only incident of note on the British front appears to have been a very successful little affair South-west of Messines, when a patrol broke into the enemy trenches, bayonetted 30 Germans and brought twelve prisoners into our lines with a loss of only one man killed and one wounded. This was described by the Germans as "The repulse of a British attempt to attack." Latest messages:- Paris 18th. Artillery duels were continuous especially in the region of the Navarin Farm, Champagne and Tahure.

19th.- The French artillery bombarded the German positions with visible effect. A German work was completely demolished and the enemy batteries silenced. In the Eastern Argonne a German field-work was destroyed by one of our mines.

EASTERN FRONT.- The Russian offensive has continued both in the Riga-Dvinsk region and further South in the Volhynian and Galician areas. A resumption of the offensive by the enemy won him a temporary success on the River Styra but later advices state that Von Linsingen advance has been checked and heavy fighting is now in progress at the crossings of the river. Latest messages:-

Petrograd, 16th.- In the course of the Russian month of October (i.e. 14th Oct. to 13th Nov.), we have captured on the Austro-German front, 674 officers, 49,200 men, 21 guns, 118 machine guns, 18 bomb throwers and 3 projectors.

19-11-15.- The Russians have secured a substantial success at Kimmern. The German left flank was bombarded by the Russian fleet and a large number of prisoners were taken. The Germans evacuated Kimmern, destroying the pump rooms at this Spa and burning the books in the Public Library. A German Zeppelin visited the Dvinsk region but dropped its bombs on the German trenches, creating a panic.

20-11-15.- The Germans attempted to renew their offensive on the left bank of the Styr, but were checked.

DENMARK.- Lieut.-Commander Layton recently in command of the submarine E13 which was set on fire by German destroyers, while lying helpless in Danish waters, has escaped from the barracks in which he was interned. It was stated in German official wireless messages that he had broken his parole. This is of course false.

SWEDEN.- A German destroyer attempted to attack a British steamer in Swedish waters, and was only prevented from doing so by a Swedish torpedo boat, which threatened to fire on the German.

PERSIA.- German and Turkish emissaries have recently been conducting an active propaganda in Persia. They have been raising bands of irregulars, attacking the consulates of the Allied Powers and attempting in various ways to induce the population and Government of Persia to throw in their lot with the Central Powers. The Persian Government and the Shah have now emphatically declared themselves the friends of the Entente, the Turkish, German and Austrian Ministers have been obliged to leave the country, and the pro-German bands have sustained a decided reverse at the hands of the Russians on the Turko-Persian border. A band of 500 under Turkish and German Commanders were routed and pursued.

"s.s. ANCONA".- Out of a total of 507 passengers and crew, 208 were saved. Of ten Americans on board, nine were drowned. The survivors state that the submarine was unmistakeably German, and that no warning was given before opening fire. The Austro-German official statement is that the submarine was Austrian and that 45 minutes were given in which to lower the boats.

Local News.

The 52nd Division carried out a very successful attack on the 5th inst. for which careful preparations had been in progress. At 8 p.m. mines were fired at three different points under the enemy's trenches; at the same moment the assaulting and bombing parties dashed forward, and our guns by sea and land opened supporting fire. The enemy was taken completely by surprise, and our infantry captured the objectives selected, namely about 160 yards of trench on the East and about 120 yards on the West of the Krithia Nullah. The position captured was at once consolidated and parties pushed up the communication trenches leading to the Turkish support trenches and erected barricades. The enemy in the captured position appeared demoralised by the explosions and offered little resistance, but the Turks in neighbouring and support trenches opened a heavy fire. They were caught by prearranged fire from rifles, machine guns and bombs and suffered heavily, causing them after a time to keep below their parapets and fire wildly in the air. Our artillery fire was maintained until the position was reported consolidated. The enemy's artillery fire, though heavy, was very erratic owing to our supporting fire and in particular to the very effective fire of our ships' guns. About 70 dead were counted in the captured position, and a wounded prisoner states that 80 of his own company were buried by one of our explosions, Our own losses were under 50. The units taking part were the 4th and 7th Royal Scots, the 7th and 8th Scottish Rifles and the Ayrshire Yeomanry.

The Navy with aeroplanes spotting has carried out some most effective long range bombardments during the week.

The R.N.A.S. has made several long distance reconnaissances as far as Rodosto on the Sea of Marmora and to Uzun Keupri and Ferejik on the Turco-Bulgarian railway. The aerial offensive in Southern Turkey has been continued and various large camps have been bombarded with good effect.

Considerable damage has been done at Ferejik junction where one of the main buildings was set on fire by a 100 lb. bomb and completely destroyed. In this connection a dramatic incident occurred on the 19th inst. One of five aeroplanes engaged in a bomb attack on Ferejik railway junction and a bridge in the vicinity, was hit by fire from a machine gun, and the pilot was forced to descend. In the course of his descent he dropped several bombs on the junction and then glided down and landed in a marsh about a mile from the station. He set fire to his machine and ran towards the coast hoping to escape capture. As he ran he saw another aeroplane preparing to land near his own, evidently with the intention of picking him up. It occurred to him that one bomb which was still in his burning aeroplane might explode. Just as the other machine approached, he therefore ran back and exploded the bomb at close quarters by firing at it with his revolver. The pilot of the descending aeroplane sheered off on seeing the explosion and landed further on. He picked up the other pilot and both got away just as a number of Turks appeared on the scene.

Peninsula Press

No. 90   Monday, November 29th. 1915   Official News.

Wireless Messages.

WESTERN FRONT.- No actions of special importance have occurred. The daily bulletins record bombardments of varying intensity first in one sector, then in another with occasional references to bombing and mining activity.

Latest Messages:-
EIFFEL TOWER, 25-11-15.- Quiet all along the front except in the Woevre, and at the Bois Brulé where the Germans threw some asphyxiating shells without effect. Artillery fire rather violent in Artois, where about fifty shells fell on the station at Arras, and in the neighbourhood of Loos and Souchez, weaker in the Soissons district and the Champagne, fairly lively in the Vosges at the Tete-de-Vaux and Hartmannsweilerkopf. Everywhere our batteries replied successfully and kept the upper hand.

24-11-15.- Yesterday our aircraft were engaged in encounters with the enemy. Two German machines were forced down in the Champagne. On the borders of the Argonne five aerial duels took place. In the result three German Aviatiks were forced to descend hurriedly in their own lines, the fourth fell disabled and the fifth in flames.

26-11-15.- A despatch from Sir John French announces that during the past few days our artillery has successfully bombarded many positions of the enemy. Mining has been constant. On the 25th a squadron of 23 of our aeroplanes successfully bombed the German camp at Achiet Legrand. The enemy replied with one aeroplane which dropped six bombs near Bray doing no damage.

EASTERN FRONT.- During the week the Russians have continued to make progress in the Northern sector. In the centre, on the line of the Styr, heavy fighting with varying success has continued. Czartorysk appears to have been taken by the Austro-Germans, retaken by the Russians and then to have again passed into the hands of the Germans, who have since tried unsuccessfully to establish themselves on the right bank of the river, while the Russians have pushed across the river somewhat further to the North and inflicted a reverse on the enemy. Further South again, in Galicia, a new attempt to assume the offensive has been repulsed with very heavy losses, by the Russians on the Strypa. Latest Telegrams:-

NORTHERN SECTOR, 25-11-15.- The Russians captured a line of trenches South-west of Dvinsk. The enemy assumed the offensive along the river Lavkaska, but were repulsed with heavy losses.

26-11-15.- The Germans have been obliged to fall back before the Russians on the Riga front, where the new Russian troops from. Lithuania have shown great bravery and skill. Heavy fighting is still in progress on the Dvina.

27-11-15.- Fighting still continues for the crossing of the Dvina at Bersemude a few miles from Riga, but the Russians have made further progress near Lake Sventen and Hindenburg is said to be preparing to evacuate Mitau, one of his principal bases in Courland.

CENTRAL SECTOR (Volhynia), 23-11-15.- The Russians re-captured Czartorysk and another important village.

24-11 15.- Petrograd reports that advanced guards of the enemy succeeded in crossing the Styr and fighting is now going on the right bank.

25-11-15.- The Russians attacked the enemy on the left bank of the middle Styr. The enemy fled leaving two officers and 177 prisoners, and abandoning large quantities of ammunition.

SOUTHERN SECTOR (Galicia), 25–27-11-15. - An enemy attempt to resume the offensive was repulsed with very heavy losses. The Russians attacked near the village of Simikowice and drove the Austro-Germans back to the Strypa. Those of the enemy who escaped the Russian fire were drowned in the river. It is reported that a whole battalion were drowned by the ice of the river breaking owing to the Russian artillery fire.

ITALIAN FRONT.- Events of great importance have taken place on this front. The Italian offensive has been pushed and positions of very great value have been gained. The Italians are steadily closing in on the fortress of Gorizia, and the fall of this important Austrian stronghold is described as imminent.

Latest messages:-

21-11-l5.- The official bulletin describes the renewed attack by the

267

Italians on the Austrian positions on the Carso as a marked success. Seven furious counter-attacks by the enemy failed to regain the ground they had lost along the ridge in Monte San Michele zone, which fell to the Italian troops.

ROME, 23-11-15.- A series of important successes are recorded. The Italians captured the village of Oslavia, (N.W. of Gorizia). Here the Austrians abandoned their trenches which were full of dead. 450 prisoners were captured. Further to the South the Italians captured two lines of trenches at Podgora on the Calvaria heights. On the slopes of Monte San Michele, the Italian advance continued and 137 prisoners were captured. 100 bombs were dropped on the Austrian aircraft park at Aisovizza.

26 and 27-11-15.- Still further progress near Gorizia. On the Carso a long line of trenches on the fourth summit of Monte San Michele was carried by storm.

SERBIA.- The Serbians continue to make a heroic resistance against overwhelming odds. The Northern army is withdrawing fighting towards the West. It is reported that the seat of Government is to be located at Scutari. The Southern army has apparently extricated itself from a dangerous position and turned the tables on the Bulgarians, who had pushed forward as far as Prilep. A message dated 24th inst. states it is officially announced that the Serbians have reoccupied their front on the Kuprulu-Veles-Prilep line and are advancing to reinforce the troops defending the Babuna Pass. The Anglo-French troops have repulsed repeated Bulgarian attacks. For the present the main object in this theatre is to preserve the integrity of the Serbian army, pending the arrival of reinforcements. Troops continue to pour into Salonica at a steady rate.

GREECE.- Has officially accepted the Note presented by the Allied Governments. She clings to her attitude of non-intervention, combined with an attitude benevolent to the Allies, and has guaranteed all the points considered essential to secure to the Allied forces complete liberty of action on Greek territory.

MESOPOTAMIA.- The British forces in Mesopotamia have now arrived before the city of Bagdad, and captured the Turkish position at Ctesiphon, 18 miles South of the city. The following telegrams contain all that has so far come to hand regarding the action:-

25-11-15.- After a night march from Zeur, which was occupied on the 19th, General Townshend's Division attacked the Turkish position at Ctesiphon. The position was captured on the 22nd after severe fighting which lasted all day. About 800 prisoners and a large quantity of arms and equipment were taken. Our force bivouacked on the captured position. Heavy Turkish counter-attacks were repulsed on the two following days, but the lack of water made it necessary for our troops to fall back to the river about 3 miles below the position.

27-11-15.- The India Office announces that a telegram from General Nixon reports the Turks to be retiring to Diala, about ten miles from Bagdad. General Townshend is engaged in clearing the wounded and prisoners. It now appears that 1,300 prisoners have already been sent back by march route. The wounded were to leave that day by steamer to Basra. General Nixon writes in terms of the highest praise of the handling of the troops by General Townshend and of the splendid spirit shown by them after their severe losses and hardships from want of food and water.

Peninsula Press

No. 91   Monday, December 6th. 1915   Official News.

Wireless Messages.

WESTERN FRONT.- There have been no events of outstanding importance during the past week. The telegrams record the usual incidents of trench warfare, bombardments, hand-grenade encounters, and aerial attacks by both sides. A gas attack by the Germans was repulsed with great ease, showing that this method has lost its effectiveness. The following items of interest are extracted from the daily bulletins.

30th Nov.- A German aeroplane was forced down into the sea at Westende. A German torpedo boat and some launches from Ostende attempted to salve the machine, but were also attacked by our aeroplanes, and had to retire. One of the boats was sunk.

3rd Dec.- Sir John French reports that during the past four days successful bombardments of enemy trenches, posts and gun positions have been carried out. The enemy's reply to our fire was weak. We sprang two mines opposite Givenchy, and consolidated the craters. While this was in progress the enemy sprang a mine burying ten of our men. Two enemy aeroplanes were brought down on the 30th.

EASTERN FRONT.- Here also there have been no actions on any very important scale. The German efforts to secure the passage of the Dvina have now continued for more than two months, and have so far only resulted in a prodigious expenditure of German men and material. The only events of any importance recorded during the week are contained in the following telegram:-

1-12-15. A German offensive N.W. of Dvinsk was repelled with the result that the retiring Germans came under their own artillery fire. The Russians following up their advantage entered Illukst, and extended their capture to the South of the village. To the S.W. of Pinsk (Central Sector) a surprise attack resulted in the annihilation of the guard of the Headquarters of the 82nd German Division and the capture of two German generals.

CAUCASUS FRONT.- Russian activity on this front has been renewed with satisfactory results:-

8-12-15.-South of Lake Van, after two days fighting near the village of Varkonis, the Turks were driven out of two fortified positions. The Turks are in full flight westwards pursued by Russian troops.

ITALY.- On his way back to England Lord Kitchener visited the Italian front and conferred with the King and General Cadorna. The enemy has lately been industriously spreading reports that Italy was anxious to secure a separate peace. These attempts to sow distrust between the Allies have been countered by the Italian Prime Minister, who has announced Italy's adherence to the compact to conduct the war and conclude peace in common, and has further promised all the assistance to Serbia which it is possible for Italy to render.

GERMANY.- Two incidents throw light on the growing uneasiness in Germany as the result of the incessant drain on her manhood and the dislocation of all commerce and industry. The first is the publication of a scheme for enforcing military service in the German Army on all Belgians in the occupied territory capable of bearing arms. The second is the publication of a bombastic rescript on the economic situation in Germany, in which it is pretended that the war has had such beneficial remits on the situation that all poverty and destitution in Germany has ceased. For the impressment of neutrals and the encouragement of the population Germany's enemys are represented to be in the last stages of breakdown, and for the truth of the whole statement the Bulgarian Minister of Finance, who has been personally conducted on a tour through Germany, is cited as a witness.

The German Emperor has paid a visit to Vienna. It is significant that this visit has come at a time when the German Empire is putting pressure upon Austria-Hungary to enter into a, customs union with Germany, and when public opinion in Austria is becoming increasingly exercised as to the possibility for Austria of continuing the struggle. Three of the Austrian Ministers have resigned.

NAVAL EVENTS- A British aeroplane has destroyed a German submarine near Middelkerke on the Belgian coast, by smashing it with a bomb.

A British submarine in the Baltic ordered a German steamer to heave to. The steamer shaped a course for the Swedish coast pursued by the submarine, which fired across its bows both to enforce the order and to warn the steamer that it was heading for a sandbank. The German ship held on and ran aground. The British submarine thereupon entered Swedish waters, which the steamer had now reached, in ordered to save

271

life, should this become necessary, but later on abandoned the ship. It appears that the German ship, which carried a cargo of nearly 8,000 tons of iron for Stettin, later blew up, presumably as a result of the sea reaching the boilers. The German Government has published a characteristic statement that the steamer was blown up by a dynamite bomb placed on board by the British submarine while in Swedish territorial waters.

Local News

The Navy have continued their attacks on the enemy's works, camps and communications. Among the most effective naval bombardments may be instanced that of the forts and barracks at Kalid Bahr and of two camps to the North of the town, where much damage was caused. The very important road bridge at Kavek, on the principal line of communication with the Peninsula, was attacked by ship's guns on the 2nd and completely wrecked.

The R.N.A.S. have been active in spotting for ship's and shore guns, also in reconnaissances and bomb attacks on the enemy's communications, aerodromes, etc. Another successful bomb attack was made on Ferejik railway station. Two bombs were dropped on to a. large steamer lying in Ak Bashi Liman. This ship was later seen being removed under escort and in tow.

One of our aeroplanes while spotting for ships guns, attacked and drove off a Taube, which appeared and attempted to drop bombs on the ship. The enemy was forced down over his own lines, our aeroplane following him down to a height of only 1,000 feet and coming under very heavy machine gun and rifle fire at close range. Though the planes were pierced by numerous bullets, the machine returned in safety.

From statements made by numerous prisoners and our own observations it is evident that the enemy suffered severely during the recent inclement weather. In many places the enemy were forced out of their trenches by the floods and as a result suffered numerous casualties from our fire. Prisoner's statements that many of their troops are not equipped with winter clothing are confirmed by the state in which prisoners were found when captured, some being practically in a state of collapse from cold, being without boots or great-coats. Following are extracts from statements by different prisoners:-
(a) In his regiment the men have one blanket each and a waterproof sheet for every ten men.

(b) (Prisoner very badly clothed and half frozen). His company were forced out of the trenches by the floods, four men were drowned. Some ran back to the higher ground leaving their rifles and machine guns. Others took refuge behind the parapet.

(c) 90 men of his battalion had been washed away in the flood. Trenches were still kneedeep in mud. His regiment had no winter clothing and most of the men only old sandals as footgear. They had only some biscuits fished out of the mud to eat on the day before his capture. In his company two men died of exposure.

The above are representative of many similar reports.

Peninsula Press

No. 92   Monday, December 13th. 1915   Official News.

Summary of Wireless Messages

WESTERN FRONT.- The daily bulletins record only the usual incidents of trench warfare. One of the French messages records a brilliant exploit by a French airman, who attacked and chased a fast German machine at a height of 10,000 feet, and succeeded on overhauling him. The French airman opened fire from a distance of only 25 yards with a machine gun. The German machine immediately caught fire and collapsed into the French lines

EASTERN FRONT.- Here also there are no events of special importance to record. At the commencement of the week a Geneva telegram of doubtful reliability recorded a Russian success near Tukkum in the Northern sector. It was stated that the Russians had captured enemy trenches on a front of 20 kilometres, with 700 prisoners. As no Russian communique reports so large a capture of trenches, the report is probably merely an exaggeration of one of the numerous local successes gained by the Russians. Taking the official messages of the week together it may be said that the Germans have sought to maintain their positions by local and weak offensive movements, which have been easily repulsed by the Russians, who have inflicted severe punishment. The enemy is now faced with the prospect of maintaining an enormous front through the Russian winter, while he has altogether failed to achieve his objectives. Not only has he failed to reach Riga and other points which were to be the goal of his autumn campaign, but above all he has entirely failed to cut off or annihilate any mass of the Russian army. He has now to spend the Russian winter faced by an active and growing army, with ever increasing supplies of munitions. Even at this early stage the state of parts of the German army, notably in the Pinsk region, is said to be deplorable. A German airship was forced to descend by Russian gunfire and appears to have exploded in the German lines.

PERSIA.- Telegrams of the 11th inst. announce that the Russians have· occupied the Sultan Bulak Pass defeating a mixed force of about 2,000 composed of Germans, Turks and Persian insurgents. The road to Hamadan is now open. The enemy fled in complete disorder persued by the Russians.

ITALY.- At the commencement of the week the Austrians made counter-attacks on the positions recently captured by the Italians on the Monte Nero. The enemy were repulsed leaving 500 dead on the ground and 180 prisoners in the hands of the Italians. Since then the Italian bulletins record daily progress and the capture of about 100 prisoners a day. The bombardment of the fortress of Gorizia continues.

AMERICA.- American diplomatic relations with the Germanic Empire have again entered upon an acute stage, the disputes being over the sinking of the liner "Ancona" and the various plots against American Industries instigated by the officials of the German Embassy. The ingenuous Count von Bernstorff has now enquired the reason for America's demand that the German Naval and Military Attaché's should be recalled. Of the criminals actually convicted of outrages three were sentenced to 16 months and one to a year's imprisonment. The officials of the Embassy are of course not subject to American Law. Telegrams dated the 11th announce that German conspirators have practically destroyed the American town of Hopewell, while an American oil steamer was shelled by a submarine of unknown nationality in the Mediterranean. These incidents will still further increase the bitterness felt in America against the German methods.

THE BALKANS.- For the present the overwhelming masses of the Austro-Germans combined with the Bulgarians have been achieving successes in this theatre, which recall the early successes of the German campaigns in France and Russia. In face of three fold superiority the Serbian forces have had to retire on the Montenegrin, Albanian and Greek frontiers. Practically the whole of Servia is in the enemy's hands, the points announced to have been captured being Ypek and Jakova in North-east Montenegro, Prisrend and Ochrida near the Albanian, and Monastir near the Greek frontiers. Further East the Anglo-French forces have met repeated attacks by superior Bulgarian forces and have fallen back to new positions nearer to the Greek frontier. Everywhere the Serbian and Anglo-French troops have inflicted heavy losses on the enemy. Meanwhile reinforcements continue to arrive at Salonica, and the Serbian forces in Albania are being supported by Italian supplies.

As before it will be found that sea power will deprive the enemy of the opportunity of reaping the fruits of his initial successes. Meanwhile signs are not wanting that dissensions may at any moment break out between such unnatural allies as the Bulgarians and Turks. It appears that the latter would now like to rest content with the conquest of Macedonia, and are anxious to see the Turks depart from Bulgarian territory, in particular from the part recently ceded by Turkey. The question of Greek neutrality appears now to be in a fair way to friendly settlement between Greece and the Allies. A joint railway commission is being appointed to settle the question of the railways, so far as they are required for the operations of the Anglo-French troops.

GERMANY.- A German ammunition factory at Halle has been blown up with a loss of several hundred lives. An attempt to blow up another factory was only averted at the eleventh hour. Both eases are reported to be due to disaffection amongst workmen.

Local News.

The latest successes to the credit of British submarines in the Sea of Marmora are the sinking of the Turkish destroyer "Yar Hissar," of the supply ship "Bosphorus" and of four sailing ships. After torpedoing the "Yar Hissar" the submarines succeeded in rescuing 2 officers and 40 men of the crew of 80, and placed them on board a sailing ship. The supply ship "Bosphorus," like the "Carmen" and "Bithynia" recently sunk, had been active as a transport for munitions and foodstuffs from Constantinople. Submarines have also attacked and hampered railway traffic on the railway near the Gulf of Ismid

On the 10th inst. the enemy's gun positions and groups of dug-outs in the neighbourhood of Gaba Tepe and the Olive Grove were subjected to concentrated bombardment by naval guns. Several hundred shells of calibres from 6" upwards were fired at these targets and very material damage was done.

The work of our aircraft has been much hampered by low clouds and poor visibility. Even in days when to observers on the ground the sky has appeared clear, the refraction of the slanting rays of the sun on the moisture rising from the ground has rendered observation from any height practically impossible. Nevertheless our aircraft have continued their reconnaissance and spotting flights, by flying at low altitudes. We have however to record two machines damaged through forced descents into the sea, the pilots having been unable to plane down to safe landing places from these reduced altitudes.

Peninsula Press

No. 93   Monday, December 20th. 1915   Official News.

Summary of Wireless Messages

WESTERN FRONT.- Only the usual incidents of trench warfare are recorded from day to day. French aircraft have been very active, and have bombed important railway stations, airparks, etc. far back in the enemy's country, notably in the fortress of Metz, at Muelheim, and at Muelhausen in the Rhine valley. The allied superiority in the air has been very marked, all the German attempts to retaliation having been feeble and easily repulsed. The Germans have lost a number of machines, some bombed in their hangers, others shot down in the air.

Field-Marshal Sir John French has vacated the command of the British Army in France and has been appointed to command the forces in the United Kingdom. The King has conferred upon him the dignity of Viscount. General Sir Douglas Haig has been appointed to command the British Army in France and Flanders.

A British naval aeroplane encountered and chased a large German seaplane off the Belgian coast. Several exchanges of fire took place. The British machine was severely damaged but kept the air long enough to enable Flight Sub-Lieut. Graham's passenger to disable the German machine, which fell, exploded on striking the water and disappeared leaving no trace of machine or occupants. The British officers executed a forced "landing" in the sea and were rescued.

RUSSIAN FRONT.- On the Russo-German front no events of importance are recorded. It is evident that the German offensive has come to a complete standstill. Fragments of a German wireless message were intercepted, in which it is mentioned that "the Russians succeeded in [*word missing*? *Capturing?*] weak German posts." This refers to Von Hindenburg's army on the Riga front. Here the Germans have fallen back considerably and are evidently well held along the whole rest of the front. In Persia the Russians have occupied Hamadan, in the Black Sea Russian torpedo boats have sunk two Turkish gunboats, and in the Caucasus they are following up their recent success near Lake Van.

A British officer, who has just arrived at the Dardanelles from a mission in Russia during which he visited the Galician front, states that he was very greatly impressed by the improvement in the situation there. He was particularly struck by the air of confidence in ultimate victory, which animates all ranks of the Russian army. They feel that Germany has shot her bolt and done her worst, and that now that the terrible disparity in artillery, which forced the great retreat upon them has been largely rectified, they can wear down the enemy during the Russian winter, secure in the knowledge that when their forces are augmented by the millions in training, they can turn the tables on him.

ITALY.- All reports speak of the steady and methodical progress of the Italian offensive, and of the operations for the reduction of Gorizia. It is now reported officially that the Italian military expedition has been safely landed in Albania despite attacks of enemy destroyers. Whether this expedition actually consists of a fighting force, or chiefly of arms and supplies for the Serbian Army is not stated.

SERBIAN FRONT.- After the retirement of the Serbian Army into Albania, and the hostile occupation of Monastir, it was now clear that the positions of the Allies in Serbia must become untenable in view of the strength, which the Bulgarians would be able to concentrate against them. The Bulgarians attacks appear to have culminated about the 10th or 11th. The retirement was carried out deliberately, the railway bridges and tunnels were blown up as they were left behind, and the Allied Force has now for several days not been molested by the Bulgarians. A War Office communique contains the following:-
"After violent attacks of the enemy in overwhelming numbers the 10th Division with the help of reinforcements, succeeded in retiring to a strong position from Lake Doiran Westwards towards the Varder Valley in connection with Allied Divisions. It is reported that they fought well against the heaviest odds and it was largely due to the gallantry of the troops, especially the Munsters, Dublins and Connaughts that the withdrawal was successfully accomplished. Owing to the mountainous nature of the country it was necessary to place eight field guns in a position from which it was impossible to withdraw them when the retirement was effected. Our casualties numbered about 1,300."

AMERICA.- Has sent an ultimatum to Austria-Hungary and insisted upon compliance with her demands within a week. In this document the sinking of the "Ancona" is described as "the assassination of defenceless non-combatants." America demands Austria shall not only declare the act committed to be illegal and unjustifiable, but shall also punish the commander of the submarine besides indemnifying the American Survivors and the families of the drowned. The terms of the ultimatum are said to have given great offence in Vienna and a complete rupture of diplomatic relations is thought probable.

GERMANY & AUSTRIA-HUNGARY.- The difficulties of the internal situation becomes increasingly apparent as time progresses. The preoccupation of the German Government appears to be to exploit the situation created by the temporary success of German arms and diplomacy in the Balkans, in such a fashion as to induce one or other of the great belligerents to conclude peace on easy terms, thus leaving Germany at liberty to deal with the others. With this in view the German chancellor recently made a speech in the Reichstag in which he made the usual exaggerated statements of Germany's military position and painted the economic situation in glowing colours. At the same time he threw out certain hints as to Germany's willingness to make peace and stated that she did not wish to make a war of conquest. The German official wireless messages now complain that certain parts of the speech were not reproduced in the English and French Press, as they fear that the Chancellor's hints may therefore fail to reach their proper addresses. It is really rather naïve of the German Government to expect the British and French Press to act as their advertising agencies, but what makes the matter still more comic is that at the very moment that the Chancellor was thus describing how peace and plenty reigned in the interior of Germany, food riots were taking place in the streets of Berlin. These assumed such proportions that the troops had to be called out, and a number of casualties in killed and wounded occurred. A French telegram commenting on this remarks:

"The scene is characteristic of the true situation in Germany. The Germans have speculated on dissension among their opponents. But, were this necessary, in order to acquire the certitude that the Allies have only to wait with calm assurance unmoved by this or that incident in the gigantic struggle, you have but to compare events in the Germanic capitals with those in the capitals of the Allies."

While the object of the German Government is thus to pave the way for a premature peace, which should be half a victory for Germany, large and growing sections of the population in the Germanic Empires are beginning to clamour for peace at any price. This may be seen from incidents such as that mentioned above, and from a petition signed by more than a million persons presented to the Hungarian Government concerning the lack of food. It is stated herein that the Government has "piled blunder upon blunder," that "the present winter will be even more disastrous than the last," and begs for the prohibition of the export of food, since Germany is drawing the last ounce of bread from her allies in order to be able to boast that she wants for nothing.

279

Speeches made in the Hungarian Parliament demand peace and articles in the Austrian Press are now permitted by the censorship to describe peace as "necessary."

It is reported in Copenhagen that the newly constructed "Super" Zeppelin airship LZ22, when leaving her shed in Schleswig for her maiden trip was destroyed by a bomb explosion. The crew of 40 were killed and the huge shed utterly destroyed.

Peninsula Press

No. 94   Monday, December 27th. 1915   Official News.

Local News.

In accordance with the altered conditions of the general strategy in the near East the evacuation of the Suvla and Anzac areas was successfully carried out during the two nights of the 18th and 19th December by the light of a full moon, the last lot of men being taken off the shore well within the scheduled time. As a military feat the evacuation deserves to rank high in history, being conducted without loss of men, or material other than perishable stores: the guns, except two or three worn pieces which were first rendered useless, and all the animals were taken away by us. The weather conditions were perfect for the combined operations by land and sea. The enemy, notwithstanding the fact that in various places along the Anzac front our own and the enemy's trenches were actually touching one another, was still unaware at dawn on the 20th December that the evacuation had taken place.

MEDITERRANEAN - The fortification of the environs of Salonica is proceeding apace. As yet no enemy troops have crossed the Greek frontier. The Greek troops at Salonica have been moved off, the V Corps towards the valley of the Struma (Nigrita), the III Corps to the river front of the Vistritsa. Only the 2nd Division remains at Salonica. Greece evinces at present, a, strong determination not to allow Bulgarians to set foot on her territory.

According to the Bulgarian Minister at Athens, the Serbian towns of Ghevgeli and Doiran are to be surendered to Greece, but he made uo mention of Monastir.

British casualties in Macedonia up to 11th Dec. are stated by Mr. Tennant in the House of Commons, to be 30 officers, 1246 men, of whom 1 officer and 85 men were killed.

From Athens it is reported that the Russians have landed troops at Varna; also it is stated that inconclusive engagements have taken place between Russian and Bulgarian torpedo boats off Varna.

WESTERN FRONT - Conflicting reports have arrived concerning the recent fighting in the Vosges at Hartmaunsweilerkopf. Both French and Germans claim successes and considerable numbers of prisoners captured. As the position is a round topped wooded height it is possible that both accounts are substantially correct: the actual summit is not an easily defined area.

Field-Marshal Sir John French in his farewell message to the armies in France says that he is convinced that, thanks to their heroic efforts, a glorious termination of this war is not far off. In Paris huge crowds waited outside the Elysee Palace whilst the Field-Marshal bade farewell to the President of the Republic.

Lord Derby also declared in London that the end of the war would come sooner than people believed generally.

BALTIC - During the last week the Germans have lost one fighting ship in the Baltic, the "Bremen," of "Leipzig" class, and a torpedo boat accompanying her: both were sunk by our submarines. The presence of our submarines in the Baltic has already had a marked effect in curtailing trade between Germany and the Scandinavian Powers, and in strengthening the hand of Russia.

News has been received from an Italian source that Germany even if defeated, has been obliged to recall frorn Servia and Bulgaria considerable forces in order to meet the new Russian offensive.

LONDON - Under Lord Derby's scheme a proclamation was issued on 19th December warning four groups of men to hold themselves in readiness to join the colours. The announcement has been generally welcomed in all quarters.

Germany is apparently feeling the drain of men, as she has, on her own admission been obliged to send back to the front 90% of wounded.

An explosion at a German powder factory at Munster, in Westphalia, destroyed the building and killed over 400 persons, mainly women and children.

This news coming soon after the report of the destruction of a new Super-Zeppelin, and previous accounts of damage done to munition factories more of which have been set to the enemy's account in German reports affords some proof of a feeling of unrest among the German labouring classes.

Economic Position of the Two
Belligerent Groups.

Whereas on the side of the Entente Powers the financial resources of England and France, the two chief pillars of the financial structure, have been able to stand the strain of war, on the enemy's side the case is far different. Austria seems to be on the verge of bancruptcy, and Germany by aid of unsound financial measures is finding an increasing difficulty in meeting the demands on her exchequer. England in spite of extravagance in many of the spending departmeuts, and of very few signs of thrift evinced by the bulk of her population, is still able to raise money for all her needs without compeiling the country to feel the pinch of war; her command of the sea and the resuliting free exercise of her import and export trade has contributed to this result. She has had no occasion to pile up enormous sums of gold in a State Bank, as most of the other belligerents have done. In fact the gold reserve in the Bank of England comes only sixth in the list of national gold reserves and after even those of Spain and Italy. France, whose export trade is enormously curtailed by (1) the fact that some of her most important manufacturing districts are in the enemy's hands and (2) by the necessity of making the utmost use of the machinery that remains for the output of munitions of war, has still been able to prove her financial strength by raising a loan exceeding the most sanguine hopes, at a comparatively easy rate of interest. Her thrift and the intense patriotism of the peple coupled with the fact that she is in normal times almost self-supporting, has enabled her to bring about this successful result. The other side of the picture shows Germany, her import and export trade cut off, obliged to finance and arm her needy Allies, and raising the necessery money by issuing paper loans on the credit of previous paper loans, and by impounding all the gold found in private strong boxes of banks. Various rumours of the increasing difficulty that, Germany is finding to support the drain on her finances have leaked out-apart from the self-evident testimony of the fall of German credit on neutral Bourses – to quote as example:- The Secretary of the "Industrial League of Bavaria" has just been presenting to this company a pessimistic report, which contrasts in striking fashion with the recent statement in the Financial Minister's speech in the Reichstag. The Secretary of the "Industrial League of Bavaria" said that "he does not see how Germany can finish the war except at an enormous cost of money, due on account of the interest and the capital of Government Loans, on pensions, and to provide fresh armarments." He is sceptical as to how the enemy, even if defeated, can pay an indemnity, and he predicts an economic agreement between Germany and Austria, that is open to serious objections in commercial Germany.

Peninsula Press

No. 95   Monday, January 3rd. 1916   Official News.

The Evacuation of Suvla - Anzac.

Seen through German glasses.

We are indebtecl to the German wireless telegrams for a most interesting, and quite new account of our last days in the Suvla – Anzac area. Comment is unnecessary as the details speak for themselves. According to this account, which purports to be that of eyewitnesses who have arrived at Salonika, "the English made one last fight at Ari Burnu and Anafarta to break through the Turkish lines, aided throughout the day by the continuous fire of their guns, on land and on shipboard: this attack was repulsed by the brave and heroic Turkish troops, and therefore on the night of the 19th-20th Dec. the flight of the English commenced – a flight which was observed by the Turks at 3 a.m. The Turks inflicted gigantic losses on the English and took spoils that extended for kilometres, including poker cards, whisky flasks, enourmous quantities of corned beef, jam, cocoa, soda water, lemon juice – these from the officers quarters – not to mention such things as electrical installations, ambulance wagons, spare wheels, complete wireless apparatus etc." A recently captured Turkish prisoner has just informed us that the Turkish Commander has been decorated as a reward for his victury.

Local News

HELLES – The chief item of news in the Helles area is the successful operation carried out on the 29th December by the 52nd Division, which resulted in the gain of Turkish trenches and the capture of 26 prisoners, apart from a considerable number of the enemy overwhelmed by the explosion of two of our mines. We have consolidated our gains and apparently instilled such a wholesome respect for us among the enemy in that section, that though they were seen to fix bayonets they would not leave their trenches.

SALONIKA – During the last week we have extended our lines so that they now run from the river Vardar on the west, with our left flank resting on the marshes that extend as far as the sea along both banks of the river. The extreme East of our line is on the Gulf of Orfano where the stream that takes off the waters of Lake Beshik enters the sea; and the distance from the Gulf of Orfano to a point some 7 or 8 miles due

North of the town of Salonika gives a line of approximately 40 miles, running almost due east and west, to be held by the Allied troops. More than half of this front of 40 miles lies along southern shores of the two lakes of Beshik and Aivisal. Outer lines of defence have been prepared further to the North of Salonika, and the whole forms a very strong fortress. Indeed, in the opinion of the French general Castelnau, who has just paid a visit of inspection, it is an impregnable fortress. The Peninsula of Chalcidice with its three promontories jutting out like fingers is varied in character and affords complete room and excellent manoeuvre ground for a large army.

At the present all the high mountains to the North of Salonika and the Peninsula of Chalcida are snow covered, rendering military operation difficult. The easternmost finger of the Peninsula has a double interest from its past and present associatons. Xerxes, King of Persia, having under his command no mean army even reckoned by modern standards (Herodotus gives it as 2,600,000 soldiers and as many more non-combatants, e.g. camp followers and Greek and Egyptian "Labour Corps") caused a canal to be dug across the narrow neck of the isthmus to spare his fleet the dangerous passage round the promontory of Mt. Athos. In Medieval and Modern times the promontory of Mt. Athos has consisted of a semi independent religious enclave peopled with the inmates of the numerous monasteries of the eastern Church, with a subsidiary population of Greek and Bulgarian cut throats who have saught its sanctuary. No female, of the human or brute kind, may live within the enclave; so strict is the rule that the monks have to import even the eggs necessary for their ascetic mode of life.

GALICIA – A great battle is now proceeding in eastern Galicia on the Middle Strypa between the Russians and Austrians; nothing is known of the result as yet. Also in the Adriatic, off Cattaro, the Allied Fleet (possibly including British cruisers) encountered an Austrian Naval Division and put it to flight; the Austrians lost two ships.

MESOPOTAMIA – Troops are being steadily pushed up to reinforce General Townshend. The Turkish Government has become seriously anxious about their position at Baghdad and has hurried troops over to the front. Distances are great in Mesopotamia and the rate of travelling neccesarily slow. It takes under ordinary conditions, about three weeks to move a Division to Baghdad from Mossul, the next important military centre upriver. The Turks if they use river transport, have the advantage of the current which is swift, but above Baghdad the Tigris is only navigable for light craft, rafts of inflated skins being the usual method of transport.

It must always be remembered that the possession of Baghdad (with Kerbela) as the ancient capital of the Caliphs is of more importance to the prestige of the Turks than any other Moslem city, with the possible exception of Mecca and Constantinople.

CHINA – Apparently, from reports received from the Far East, the republican party is not going to watch the passing of the Republic, from which they had hoped so much, without raising forcible protest against the establishment of a new Monarchy. The Province of Yunnan has already declared its independence and other provincial Governments may follow suit. The central Government is satisfied as to the loyalty of the other provinces and will send troops against the revolutionaries. When the Mahomadans of Yunnan rebelled some years ago the province was "pacified" by the extermination of nine tenths of the whole Moslem population.

Peninsula Press

No. 96   Monday, January 10th. 1916   Official News.

The publication of the Peninsula Press will not be continued after this day's number; but it will have served its purpose to the full if it has been read with some degree of interest by those who have passed many long days in the trenches on the Peninsula.

Local News

The evacuation of Helles is more than a matter of local interest; it means the close of a chapter in the history of the great war. Soon after 4 o'clock on the morning of the 9th January the last of our chaps quitted the Peninsula of Gallipoli, eight hours after the commencement of the final phase of evacuation. Thanks to excellent arrangements by the 8th Corps the enemy were kept in complete ignorance of our movements and the evacuation was unmolested, though it was carried out in weather conditions which, but for the skill of the Navy and the devoted work of the Beach personnel, might have endangered the success of the operations. As it was, the evacuation, like that of the Suvla-Anzac area, took place without any loss of life. Two days previous to this an attack on our lines seemed imminent. The Turks, after a continuous bombardment of three hours, which at one time became intense, were seen to fix bayonets; but in spite of the efforts of their officers they only came on to the attack at two points, and were there driven back with heavy loss by the 7th Battalion of the North Staffordshire Regiment. It may therefore be fairly concluded that the strength of our resistance deceived the Turks as to the imminence of the withdrawal from the Peninsula.

The contents of the recently captured British letter bag on board a Greek steamer has served to provide the German news agencies with something amusing for their readers. Extracts from private letters have been published apart from their context with a view to embittering Anglo-Greek relations. The incidents that accompanied the loss and recovery of the bag, which was in the custody of a British officer, were themselves ludicrous and unexpected that in this instance the German Press can hardly be grudged its short triumph. The Allied Military Authorities at Salonika were not long in delivering their counter blast in the form of a publication of various items contained in the correspondence of the enemy's consuls, as the result of a search of various consular premises. Thanks to this search the Greeks now know, *inter alia* that they are, in the (written) opinion of the German Consul's wife "such swine". The Turkish Press characterises in strong terms the arrest of the foreign Consuls at Salonica as being unworthy of a great nation. Meanwhile these gentlemen of the Press quite forget that not so many years have passed since the time when the Porte seized and imprisoned as a matter of course, in the castle of the Seven Towers overlooking the Marmora, the persons of Ambassadors accredited to the Porte on, or even before, the outbtreak of hostilities between Turkey and those other Powers. The unfortunate diplomats, if they saved their lives, were kept in confinement so long as hostilities continued between the respective countries.

Some Notes on our Air Service

The flying machines of the R.N.A.S. include in addition to areoplanes and seaplanes, kite balloons and submarine scout airships. Of aeroplanes the war has thus far evolved three classes viz: - long distance reconnaissance machines, (2) big fighting machines, and (3) small very fast scouts. Of these the first is generally a two seater, often fitted with wireless apparatus and is used for spotting work: the second is almost invariably of the "Pusher" type i.e. with the propeller behind the pilot and gunner – this enables the latter to have a clear field of fire: the third consists generally of single seaters, whose great speed and ability to climb quickly make them also valuable auxiliaries for attacking and driving off hostile aircraft. The armament of aeroplanes takes the form of light machine guns and hand grenades, and nearly all machines now carry machine guns, though such guns can only only be used really effectively for aeroplanes of the "Pusher" type – in other types the tractor and various wires limit the arcs of fire. All types of aeroplanes carry bombs but for this purpose the large "Fighters" are most suitable.

The Germans possess both "Tractors" and "Pushers." They have so closely copied our types of machine that from a distance only an experienced eye can tell the difference. The only really safe guide is the markings under the wings. The markings of British and French machines are invariably concentric circels of red and white and blue, while those of the Germans and Turks are black Maltese crosses. If however the tail of the machine when seen in silhouette is shaped like a fish's tail the machine in nine cases out of ten hostile. The wings of German machines are also more swept back than those of ours. While machines of which the wings form a crescent are invariably German.

It is interesting to note that monoplanes of which there were a fair number in use at the beginning of the war, have been almost entirely supplanted by biplanes. The latter are generally speaking stronger in construction and offer better facilities for view. The only type of monoplane to win use with the Allies is the French "Parasol" Morane.

288

In this type the fuselage is slung beneath the wings and the pilot and observer thus obtain an excellent view. The enemy have not used any monoplanes in the theatre. Seaplanes have been extensively used in the course of the operations. These craft are carried in ships specially fitted up as seaplane carriers. The seaplanes are lifted in and out of the ship by the means of a crane and can rise from and land on a moderate sea. Their great value lies in their being able to accompany ships to distant localities and there operate without the necessity for a landing ground being prepared.

In conclusion it may be of interest to state briefly the work that the aeroplanes of the R.N.A.S. have been called on to perform over and around the Gallipoli Peninsula area:-

Since August last the average distance flown each month has been more than 30,000 miles. A photographic survey was made of all the Turkish positions: many thousands of photos were taken from a uniform height. These furnished material to the G.H.Q. Map and Survey Section which was essential in complilation of the detailed maps of the enemy's works. The labour involved obtaining these photographs was very considerable, as each photograph represents a piece of country about 1000 yards square. The Anzac Suvla front shown was some 12 miles in extent and this was photographed to a depth of 9,000 yards to take in gun positions.

ENGLAND – An event of the greatest importance to our own future share in the war has just taken place in England. The House of Commons by an overwhelming majority, has passed a Bill which renders liable to military service (until the conclusion of the war) all unmarried men between the ages of 18 and 41 as well as widowers who have no children dependant on them. Apparently the scope of the Bill is confined to what is called "Lord Derby's recruiting area."